IRISH MILITARY INTELLIGENCE 1918–45

MAURICE WALSH

The Collins Press

First published in 2010 by
The Collins Press
West Link Park
Doughcloyne
Wilton
Cork

British Library Cataloguing in Publication Data

Walsh, Maurice.
In defence of Ireland: Irish military intelligence 1918–45.
1. Ireland. Army. G2—History. 2. Military intelligence—Ireland—History.
I. Title
355.3'432'09417–dc22
ISBN–13: 9781848890282

Typesetting by Carrigboy Typesetting Services
Typeset in Goudy
Printed in Great Britain by J F Print Ltd

CONTENTS

Appendices

ACKNOWLEDGEMENTS

I wish to express my sincere thanks to a number of people whose guidance and assistance have been invaluable throughout my research.

Dr Andrew McCarthy, my tutor, has been courteous and enlightening in his advice, guidance and encouragement during the course of my studies, for which I am most grateful.

I appreciate the support of Professor Keogh and his secretariat in the Department of History, University College Cork.

I thank C. F. Breathnach, Dr Edel Bhreathnach, my daughter Sláine and her husband, James Hayes, for their assistance.

Commandant Peter Young, RIP, and his successor, Commandant Victor Laing, in Military Archives contributed generously to my research, for which I am grateful.

Army veterans, named and unnamed, I thank for the benefit of their reflections.

Paul Hunt and Paul Glavin assisted me during my difficulties with computer literacy, for which I am much indebted.

Finally, I tender my sincere thanks to my wife, Frances Mary, whose encouragement throughout my research proved a very worthwhile incentive.

ABBREVIATIONS

Abwehr	German Foreign Intelligence Service
ACA	Army Comrades Association
ASU	Active Service Unit
C3	Garda Security Section
CIA	Central Intelligence Agency
CID	Criminal Investigation Department
CIO	Command Intelligence Officer
COS	Chief of Staff
DD	Dublin District – Branch of Royal Irish Constabulary
DFR	Defence Force Regulation
DMP	Dublin Metropolitan Police
EEI	Essential Elements of Information
G2	Irish Army Directorate of Intelligence
GC&CS	Government Code and Cipher School (Bletchley Park)
GHQ	General Headquarters
GOC	General Officer Commanding
GOC-in-C	General Officer Commanding-in-Chief
GPO	General Post Office
IO	Intelligence Officer
IRA	Irish Republican Army
IRB	Irish Republican Brotherhood
LDF	Local Defence Force
LSF	Local Security Force

MA	Military Archives
MI5	British Intelligence (Domestic)
MI6	British Intelligence (Foreign)
NAI	National Archives of Ireland
NCO	Non-commissioned Officer
NLI	National Library of Ireland
OKW	Oberkommando der Wehrmacht, German high command
OS	Ordnance Survey
OSS	Office of Strategic Services
QMG	Quartermaster General
RIC	Royal Irish Constabulary
RUC	Royal Ulster Constabulary
SIS	Supplementary Intelligence Service (a G2 network)
SIS-UK	British Special Intelligence Service
SOE	Special Operations Executive
TPD	Temporary Plans Division
UCDA	University College Dublin Archives

INTRODUCTION

This book analyses the history of G2, its evolution from the War of Independence through the Emergency period. It also explores the role and methodology of G2, to illustrate its contribution to the evolution of the state. The Irish military intelligence system prioritised as required by changing domestic and international circumstances. Directors of intelligence had a clear appreciation of the conditions that existed in Ireland before and during the War of Independence. If one accepts the axiom that philosophical, sociological and economic factors are inextricably linked to the evolution of history, then the history of Ireland during the late eighteenth, nineteenth and early twentieth centuries provides a basis for such a view.

It is imperative for those who study military intelligence to understand the term as well as its multifaceted application in various circumstances. The internationally accepted definition of military intelligence describes it as a product resulting from the collection, evaluation, analysis, integration and interpretation of all available information on an enemy and his area of operations, of immediate or potential significance to one's own planning and operations.[1] Counter-intelligence is closely linked, with subtle differences. It includes a methodology to detect and counteract hostile intelligence, subversion, sabotage, assassination and terrorism. Both activities are relevant to peace and wartime situations, are intrinsically linked to operations, and differ only in strategic or tactical prioritisation as dictated by commanders.[2]

Throughout the centuries the Irish engaged in periodic violent struggle. With the probable exception of the Land League's virtually bloodless campaign of protest, all other attempts at insurrection were doomed to failure. This failure was rooted in the capacity of the British to infiltrate every movement, thwarting the prospects of any Irish success. During the War of Independence from 1919 to 1921, that situation changed dramatically. The IRA's awareness of the need for accurate and timely intelligence and counter-intelligence systems arose from sheer necessity during that war. Their methodology involved destroying the Royal Irish Constabulary's (RIC) capacity as a British intelligence agency. The actions of the flying columns in Cork and Collins' Squad in Dublin showed the British just how ruthless their opponents could be. On 25 May 1921, the IRA burned the Custom House in Dublin, and despite the decimation of the Dublin IRA brigade, the action proved a severe blow to British administration in Ireland. The burning and blowing up of tax offices from Easter Sunday 1920 resulted in the destruction of much of the local government records as well as most tax records for the country. Other elements of the British administration throughout the country were also targets for the IRA. The war devolved into an organised creation of what Charles Townshend describes as the 'intelligence gap' in favour of the IRA, arguably the most potent factor in the battle for the hearts and minds of the people.[3]

Michael Collins was IRA Director of Intelligence from 1919 to 1922. His modus operandi was replicated by Major Florence O'Donoghue, an outstanding intelligence officer, and ruthless guerrilla commanders such as Tom Barry, Seán O'Hegarty and Frank Busteed. They believed that elimination of one spy was better than the killing of a thousand soldiers, because of the damage one spy could inflict. Collins' tenure as Director of Intelligence was ultra-significant. His most important success was organising his 'Squad' on 'Bloody Sunday', 21 November 1920, to execute fourteen of the so-called 'Cairo Gang'. It led to retaliation. But nevertheless it destroyed the capacity of the most important sector of British intelligence operating from Dublin Castle. Collins had effectively paralysed the British government's spy ring in Dublin. He was outstanding in the field of military intelligence, counter-intelligence, assassination and arms procurement. The IRA's intelligence in Cork city and county reciprocated Collins' Dublin network.

Andrew's description of what he terms the 'Irish debacle' is a brilliant synopsis of both the British and Irish intelligence systems during the period 1916–22.[4] It complements the work of Townshend[5] and paved the way for those studies by O'Halpin,[6] Neeson,[7] Augusteijn,[8] Foy[9] and Hart.[10] Andrew accepts that in all Irish troubles the British administration in Dublin had informers in the rebel camp. By 1919, the IRA under Collins turned the tables on the Castle. IRA agents infiltrated the Castle, the headquarters of the RIC and Dublin Metropolitan Police (DMP). The Castle had great difficulty in recruiting informers. Andrew cites military intelligence as acknowledging that 'the bulk of the people were our enemies and were therefore far more incorruptible than has been the case in former movements.'[11] The IRA action against informers became increasingly brutal and was effective because of its sheer brutality. Andrew acknowledges that military intelligence accepted that Collins' Squad had temporarily paralysed their Special Branch intelligence organisation on Bloody Sunday. He also acknowledges an almost universal ignorance of all ranks among the British in Ireland as to what intelligence might be. It was generally regarded as the secret service and nothing else; some army officers scarcely bothered to read the lengthy intelligence summary circulated by the Central Raid Bureau, which was often more than 100 and sometimes over 200 foolscap pages long. Officers stated that intelligence summaries were a waste of time and labour and a source of leakage of information.[12] Lack of coordination between different branches of the intelligence community complicated British intelligence gathering in Ireland.[13]

Just as the British were not able to appreciate the intelligence situation then, historians still differ on the reasons why military activity varied throughout the country during the war. Rumpf and Hepburn believe that lesser economic ties with Britain and a strong tradition of violent agitation accounted for Munster's pre-disposition to violence.[14] However, Augusteijn's study of the socio-demographics of the war considered regional comparisons and the circumstances which motivated the process of radicalisation that became prevalent among the younger generation.[15] His study determined the causes of regional variations in mobilisations and activity in Ireland during the war. Hart went further and contended that violence seemed to thrive in more urbanised areas with better land and seemed to be hampered by poverty and physical isolation.[16] However, Augusteijn accepted Garvin's reinforcing of the Rumpf–Hepburn thesis, asserting that Cork was a classic example of a core area of resistance embracing an extremely high level of IRA activity.[17] This author accepts this point, and accordingly focuses on Cork in the course of this work.

The Civil War ended on 24 May 1923. The pro-Treaty victory resulted from four distinct advantages: a clear policy, a common purpose, a united leadership, action and public support. All such factors were relevant to the pro-Treatyites in bridging the intelligence gap. The contretemps which arose between Michael Collins and Defence Minister Cathal Brugha and their different philosophies is also considered in this book. They were men of different mindsets, even if sharing a common long-term objective of a republic. During the Civil War and the Treaty negotiations Collins held his organisation intact. He sent arms over the border to Johnny Haughey, father of the later Taoiseach Charles J. Haughey, and to a man known as 'Dangerous' Dan McKenna, later to become chief of staff of the Irish army during the Emergency. While both men died in the conflict, it is questionable whether Brugha had the ability or mindset to match Collins.

The role of intelligence in Ireland changed dramatically from the War of Independence, during the Civil War and again during the Emergency. The so-called 'army mutiny' in 1924 was quickly identified and crushed.[18] Subsequently, the military intelligence system reached its nadir when transferred from the army to an organisation based at Oriel House. Professional military standards were virtually non-existent by 1939. Three officers maintained a continuous watching brief on what would normally have been the responsibility of the intelligence structure at army headquarters and its contributory sources throughout the various commands. These officers were Colonel (later Major General) Michael J. Costello, Colonel Liam Archer and Lieutenant Colonel (later Colonel) Dan Bryan, all of whom filled the appointment of army Director of Intelligence in sequence. Bryan was without doubt highly impressive in his capacity as a strategist and his ability to run and implement the covert sections of G2 during the Emergency. Bryan's predecessor as Director of Intelligence, Colonel Liam Archer, was responsible for ensuring that G2 was a formidable intelligence organisation on the outbreak of war in 1939.

John M. Regan's graphic account of the period 1921–36 states that within the context of the early 1920s profound paranoia was the component of any new regime.[19] This was certainly true in the aftermath of Kevin O'Higgins' assassination. G2's collaborative role with government ruthlessness in the Civil War coincided briefly with the prolonged period accounted for in Regan's work. O'Halpin states that personal vendettas were behind some of the most notorious murders during and after the Civil War.[20] There seems to be no evidence that ministers were implicated either directly or indirectly in directing the terror. However, they can be fairly criticised for the public equanimity with which they greeted unequivocal and repeated evidence of murder by government agencies. O'Halpin concludes that: 'It was death sentences and executions, not murders that broke the IRA's morale.'[21] The validity of O'Halpin's contention that death sentences and executions were not equivalent to murder is questionable. The first decade of independence nevertheless saw the emergence of the institutions of the new state and of a democratic society.

Financial strictures resulted in post-Civil War decay of army professional standards. Theo Farrell has addressed the problem.[22] His reasoning is based on the fact that, politically, the Department of Defence attracted exceptionally low levels of government support and resources. The policy of the mandarins of the Department of Finance was tantamount to absolute fiscal rectitude,[23] and Farrell argues that this policy was responsible for the enfeeblement of the army. The single occasion on which Finance's suggestions were overruled by the Cabinet committee on Emergency problems occurred on 21 October 1940. The committee overruled Finance's suggestion that its department be authorised to commandeer vehicles for various purposes. The Cabinet committee insisted that such powers should be vested in the military authorities.[24]

The author of this book poses the rhetorical question: was the army mutiny of 1924 the primary causal factor for the beginning of the thread of dysfunctionalism that lingered throughout army/Department of Defence/Department of Finance interface during the 1930s and 1940s? Maryann Gialanella Valiulis contends that the army mutiny of 1924 emphasised the resultant importance of an unquestioned obedience to government by the army and its commanders. It had a direct result on the formation and development of the Irish Free State and had a significant input into both its immediate and ultimate political structure and its resounding affirmation of the supremacy of civilian authority over the army.[25] Her statement is of significance insofar as the title of commander-in-chief of the defence forces has never since been vested in a military officer. The titular head and title of commander-in-chief of the defence forces is allotted to the President of Ireland, and executed through the government via the Minister for Defence. J. J. Lee states that the army mutiny was an unedifying episode for the opportunist cynicism it exposed among the civilian politicians, as regards the military threat to civilian government.[26]

After the 'mutiny', defence policy became crisis management. The available files in the archives on this period are quite sparse. A small collection of Department of Justice files point to discreet cooperation between Garda and army intelligence, but there is never enough material to build a reconstruction.[27] General Costello and Colonels Archer and Bryan showed commendable foresight in detailed advance planning, which influenced government policy from 1939 to 1945 to the benefit of the state. Strategic censorship planning originated in 1925. On 9 March of that year, under Costello, G2 floated 'Proposals for Establishing a Censorship Bureau'.[28] It was attributable to a Captain Liam Walsh and coincided with a paper attributed to Archer and Bryan titled 'Censorship in Time of War and Peace', issued from general headquarters.[29]

While that was a key development for G2, arguably the most important intelligence document was issued in May 1936. 'Fundamental Factors Affecting Saorstát Defence Problem' was written by Dan Bryan and passed to government by the then chief of staff, General Michael Brennan.[30] It analysed the various options available to the Irish government, and strongly recommended neutrality in the foreseen conflict. This book considers that document of crucial importance, and asks whether the British chiefs of staff recommendations for government in July 1936[31] acted as a catalyst for Bryan's paper, in respect of the stance to be taken by the Irish Free State in the Second World War.

The organisation of Irish army intelligence during the Emergency embraced a format and tasking system to achieve its relevant results. G2 was responsible for the production and distribution of military intelligence and the organisation of counter-intelligence, including estimation of potential enemy capability in chemical and biological weapons. Military intelligence was distributed on a need-to-know basis by means of reports, maps and summaries, while successive Directors of Intelligence remained alert to the need for counter-intelligence measures, designed to nullify potential enemy intelligence and preserve Irish security. G2, in consultation with Signals Corps headquarters, determined policy on codes, ciphers, and the issue of codewords and stipulated measures for care and custody of codeword lists. These tasks are considered insofar as archival sources allow an insight.

Although Ireland did not term any German, British, or American agents as prisoners of war, all were detained and interrogated by G2 officers prior to imprisonment. The link between G2 and G3[32] manifested itself in field security, security investigations on native or alien military or civilian personnel, camouflage, track discipline and concealment policy and training. Military intelligence maintained a consistent link with signal personnel in communication intelligence and security. Strategic planning made an important contribution to the implementing of censorship, before and during the Emergency.[33] Because of the stringent censorship laws, relations between the state authorities and the press were, to say the least, strained throughout the Emergency.

G2, meanwhile, carried out many miscellaneous tasks, mainly in the provision and control of interpreters and countermeasures against sabotage and subversion, sometimes risking the annoyance of senior Garda personnel where boundary of responsibility was breached.[34] Despite meagre resources, G2 was responsible for air photograph supply, distribution, interpretation and coordination of air reconnaissance in conjunction with G3, development of air and artillery targets and of air and ground reconnaissance targets or areas of interest for surveillance. One should not be surprised that Dan Bryan, on becoming Director of Intelligence in 1940, chose to prioritise counter-subversion as his principal concern in G2.

From 1939 on the Garda cooperated with the army on coast-watching duty, with both services observing seagoing and aircraft movement.[35] They also cooperated in keeping an eye on subversives.[36] Although in my view G2 and de Valera must have known that the result of

Ireland's coastal watch was quickly made known to British Admiralty intelligence,[37] no admission of a breach of Irish neutrality was made by Ireland nor questioned by the British or Germans. The Garda authorities both understood and were prepared to engage in the holistic concept of war and replicated McKenna's order.[38] Cooperation between both army and Garda forces was of paramount importance during the Emergency.

It took all de Valera's guile, and both Bryan's and McKenna's wisdom and advice to de Valera, to maintain what Lee called a 'half-armed neutrality'.[39] Ireland maintained a neutral posture, but neutral on the side of the Allies. This position is extensively documented, and Lord Cranborne's 1945 admission of the extent of Irish cooperation has been well highlighted by Ronan Fanning. Viscount Cranborne, the British Dominions secretary, informed the British War Cabinet on 21 February 1945 of the remarkable extent of Irish cooperation during the war.[40] The Irish conceded the use of Lough Foyle for naval and air purposes, conceded overflights on the Lough Erne corridor, arranged for passing on reports of submarine activity, as well as Air Observation Corps reports. They supplied valuable meteorological reports, and shared transmitting equipment at Malin Head. They supplied particulars of German aircraft crashed and personnel landed and interned all German fighting personnel, but allowed all Allies to depart freely and fully assisted with recovery of Allied aircraft. They allowed free movement of persons wishing to serve in the United Kingdom forces, and exchanged information regarding all aliens.[41]

Recently, Kennedy has examined the coast-watching service in an excellent focused study that illustrates beautifully the nature of that relationship;[42] he traces Irish intelligence reports to the Admiralty and air force archives in London. Yet nowhere does one get the picture of how the Irish 'handed over', so to speak, the information. There is enormous difficulty in documenting this cooperation between the British and Irish services, just as there is difficulty reconstructing the nature and modus operandi of cooperation between agencies within Ireland, such as G2 and the Garda. This point was reinforced with my own research. While Kennedy had given an excellent account of the treatment of the captured U-260 submarine, he could not relate how the Irish intelligence reports had reached London, simply because it was not documented. It was almost by chance, when interviewing Justice Susan Denham, daughter of Douglas Gageby who initially interrogated the U-260 crew, that I learned that an American Office of Strategic Services (OSS) operative, Edward Lawler, had taken documents from the U-260 to London and returned them to Dublin – on the instructions of Dan Bryan.[43] This, of course, raises more questions than it answers, and indeed raises questions for which there may be no answers. The use of an American operative immediately implies wider cooperation; entrusting original documents denotes an established relationship; being able to retrieve them suggests a pattern. And the lack of any further evidence points to speculation, however informed the surmise may be. And that is the difficulty in documenting the intelligence sphere: the researcher cannot improvise!

O'Halpin feels that G2's Emergency performance was not the result simply of an improvisation. Many of the security problems with which it dealt during the Emergency, together with the kinds of measures necessary to address them, had been anticipated and studied professionally, even when political, financial, staff and policy constraints prevented any action.[44] The magazine fort raid on 24 December 1939 presaged an associated crisis of government confidence in the army. During the raid the IRA captured a vast portion of the army's reserve ammunition and weaponry.[45] The background to the raid is relevant. This author takes issue with General McKenna's contention during his lecture delivered to the Command and Staff course at the Military College on 12 October 1967 outlining details of the raid.[46] McKenna stated that the raid's success resulted from one dishonest storeman's treachery. However, it is clear from research that years of neglect in the pursuit of duty, traitorous activity involving trafficking in ammunition and uniforms to the IRA, and conspiracy and complicity by army personnel and one civil servant in the Department of Defence meant that the IRA were made aware of the security system of the fort, and its defects, prior to the raid.[47]

The action by the army to recover the ammunition was wholly successful.[48] Of all the officers and other ranks who were summoned before the ensuing military court of inquiry, Major General Michael Brennan and some senior officers emerged unscathed from the debacle; others were severely censored.[49] IRA men throughout the country were apprehended and tried by military courts of justice.[50]

Whether Commandant-General Tom Barry was either wrongly cashiered or covertly seconded to the Supplementary Intelligence Service is a moot question. Barry kept close personal contact with Costello during the entire course of the Emergency and was of invaluable assistance to him throughout the period. Evidence exists, as indicated in this author's interview with an ex-officer who served at the time, Commandant Richard McIntyre, to prove that Barry assisted the army during the course of the Emergency.[51] It reinforces the belief that he was seconded to the Supplementary Intelligence Service, a service that played an invaluable role in Bryan's intelligence network.[52] It was initiated by Florence O'Donoghue, an outstanding intelligence officer during the War of Independence and equally outstanding during the Emergency.

The army general staff's strategic plan of 1944 embraced the chief of staff memorandum, COS Memo 4/44, which was proscribed for research until 2002.[53] Its proscription left a void in historical research until recently. COS Memo 4/44 was submitted to the Minister for Defence, stating that the views expressed represented the considered opinion of the general officers and senior officers of the army.[54] It details a futuristic planning sequence of measures to ensure a continuous viable defence force organisation.[55] But despite its obvious importance it was never acted upon by the government. Ironically, some of its recommendations have become politically viable recently, having been shelved for sixty years.

This book outlines a systematic consideration of G2, its role and methodology; it explains its organisation at the height of the Emergency and outlines the methodology it used during that time. It gives various instances of how German parachutists, all supposedly trained in intelligence methodology, were captured within a short time, with the exception of Hermann Goertz, who evaded capture for eighteen months.[56] G2 was considered to have been totally cooperative with MI5 and MI6 and with the American OSS, which later became the Central Intelligence Agency (CIA). The book also instances the diplomatic disloyalty of Charles Bewley, senior diplomat and Nazi apologist. Éamon de Valera managed to force him out of his post as a diplomat in the Department for External Affairs in 1939. The question of aliens in the army during the Emergency, and G2's influence on the immigration of Jews to Ireland is examined. Keogh's recent work on aliens in the army during the Emergency holds a mirror to the face of Irish society, long accustomed to viewing its history as a tale of victimhood.[57] G2 showed a particular zeal in keeping an eye on them.

The outstanding work of cryptologist Dr Richard Hayes is also addressed. Hayes' papers, acquired by the National Library from his widow, deal with his wartime activities relating to code-breaking.[58] They contain copies of telegrams (nearly all in cipher), mainly between the German legations in Dublin and Washington, transcripts of telephone conversations, correspondence, burnt fragments of cipher mounted on glass plates, photographs of these, and some internal army documents (some by Hayes). The latter relate to, inter alia, Joseph Andrews, Anthony Deery, Stephen Carrol Held, Eduard Hempel, Hermann Goertz and Wilhelm Preetz.

A considerable amount of the collection consists of Hayes' own efforts at cipher-breaking. Hayes summarises much of the activity which the collection represents. New unpublished material shedding further light on Hayes' work has been made available to the author by Mr J. R. Hayes, Richard's grandson, and features in the main text. The unpublished material made available to me further enhances the cryptographer's diligence and commitment to his work, and is of significant importance.

But perhaps more important was another individual and his records – Dan Bryan. Fulsome tributes paid to Colonel Bryan on his death in 1985 by the then chief of staff, Lieutenant General Gerald O'Sullivan, and by Colonel Doyle, testify to his outstanding mastery of his brief.[59] His papers illustrate his vital contribution as chief staff officer G2 branch, his planning of defence policy, military intelligence and counter-espionage, memoranda on the general work of G2 and investigations into German nationals resident in Ireland. Perusal of the Bryan Papers illustrates the depth of intelligence material issued by G2 in the years before and during the Emergency. Records of the activities of the counter-espionage section within G2 contain details of the German nationals who were investigated, while the Bryan Papers give definitive details of the Stephen Held, Werner M. B. Unland, Wilhelm Preetz, Walter Hermann, Christian Simon and Gartner, Obed and Tributh cases. The material includes a section of a report titled 'Irish-born Groups' which discusses Irish Friends of Germany, the IRA in Germany and Irish communist groups.

The volume of work handled by G2 increased enormously during 1940. In 1939–40 the country was quite unconscious of either espionage or war problems. This was true to such an extent that it can be taken as reasonably certain that when a parachutist landed at Ballivor, County Meath, towards the end of April 1940, no attention seems to have been paid to the incident locally.[60] Developments in the European situation soon afterwards, followed almost immediately by the Held case, led to a complete change in the public attitude to suspicious or other incidents that might indicate activities of an espionage nature. A parachutist incident in Wexford and new developments in the war reawakened the public to the direct effect of the conflict in Ireland, including matters of espionage. Bryan and his agents were well capable of the counter-espionage role prioritised for G2.

Looking at Irish army intelligence in isolation is useful. But it is more enlightening to view it in comparative perspective with other western European intelligence services. In looking at intelligence generally, the literature throws up some common threads, and indeed some unique experiences. Among the more valuable work illustrating the state of historiography on intelligence in Britain is that by Christopher Andrew.[61] Not unlike the Irish situation, British intelligence (domestic, MI5), the Secret Intelligence Service (SIS) and the Government Code and Cipher School (GC&CS) were badly run down during the interwar period and filled rare vacancies with some men from a military background; few opportunities existed for university recruits. Up to 1936, British organisations had many difficulties in common with their counterparts in G2 in Ireland and with the Irish army in general. Yet again, in common with the Irish problem of recruitment, a form of crisis management sought to resolve the problems facing these organisations from 1938 onwards.[62] By way of contrast, there is no evidence of an infiltration of G2 with moles and spies. During the war, Andrew noted, Bletchley Park took little account of rank or hierarchy; everybody was left to get on with their own work in an atmosphere of real academic preoccupation. But by 1941, the staff at Bletchley had moved on from being cryptanalysts and translators and offered their own appreciation. Such flat structures were replicated elsewhere, such as in Israeli intelligence establishments since the end of the Yom Kippur War,[63] but, to the best of this author's knowledge, did not happen in G2. The cryptanalysts in G2, led by Richard Hayes, passed on the decoded material to Colonel Dan Bryan, Director of the organisation. Bryan discussed it with the chief of staff and, as necessary, with Éamon de Valera. Bryan, no doubt, did not pass on everything he knew, as both he and Hayes would be regarded as intelligence analysts second to none.

It is, in my view, much more desirable for a military intelligence organisation, whether in Ireland or any other country, to give the politicians the unvarnished truth in any intelligence summary. Whether the politicians want to hear it or not, at least the intelligence branch will have acted from a point of principle rather than expediency. Again, to the best of my knowledge, Bryan and his G2 operatives always acted on points of principle rather than expediency, and trusted in de Valera and McKenna's acceptance of their summary, even if they did not always act in accordance with the intelligence summary.

Although the Bletchley Park cryptanalysts are credited with finally cracking the Enigma code, Singh's in-depth analysis of the process of cracking the code gives overdue and well-deserved credit to the Polish Military Information Cipher Biuro, Szyfrow.[64] Richard Hayes' belief that code-breakers had to be eternal optimists and also await a stroke of luck was as applicable to his British counterparts in Bletchley Park as it was to G2.[65] Intelligence is interrelated, irrespective of its origins. It is also, as Andrew contends, related to the political, military and diplomatic conduct of policy; he deprecated successive British governments' discouragement of study of the British intelligence community and blocking of research. In more recent times, the decision to allow Professor Keith Jeffery access to hitherto proscribed MI6 files must be seen as a positive development. Against that, this author's searches and queries in archives were not as fruitful. Military Archives in Dublin were not prepared to allow access to all material, and indeed were surprised to learn that certain restricted files regarding the magazine fort raid in 1939 had previously come into my possession! The Garda Síochána relieved me of the onerous task of searching their archive, and instead informed me there were two files relevant to my queries. Despite the initiative with MI5, in my view it would be no more than a pious aspiration on the part of academics to expect the archival floodgates to open.

One can certainly agree with Andrew's contention that while studies of secret intelligence in twentieth-century Britain vary greatly in both quantity and quality, they cannot be ignored. Bryan's 1936 paper, 'Fundamental Factors',[66] bears out Andrew's contention that any analysis of government policy, particularly on foreign affairs and defence, which leaves intelligence out of account is bound to be incomplete and may also be distorted as a result.

Distortion can also occur within the channels, and it takes a supreme operator to ride above that. Nigel West assures readers that Guy Liddell, appointed director of B Division of MI5 in 1940, and deputy director-general in 1945, was the pre-eminent counter-intelligence officer of his generation. He was respected by his adversaries and admired by his subordinates and had an unrivalled reputation for discretion, an intuitive talent for handling the politically charged atmosphere caused by Whitehall officials and senior politicians. If one accepts West's tribute to Liddell, is it not in conflict with his statement that Liddell's ill-advised friendship with Guy Burgess and Anthony Blunt compromised his MI5 career and prompted concern as to his loyalty?[67] Guy Liddell's contacts with Irish army Directors of Intelligence, Archer and Bryan, are mentioned in his diaries but do not record any exchange of details of future plans; they simply reveal an interchange of current or recent events.[68] Bryan always adopted a cautionary approach in consultations with MI5, despite the unbridled respect which both Liddell and MI5 accorded him and G2.[69]

With the exception of de Valera and Frank Aiken, most other politicians were blissfully unaware of G2's operations during the Emergency, a situation that did not distress either element. The same situation did not prevail in Britain or the USA, whose intelligence organisations, vast by Irish standards, were subject to political interference. Beevor criticised Churchill and Dalton for their over-enthusiasm, in addition to opposition from other departments and services as being detrimental to Special Operations Executive (SOE) efficiency. Eisenhower expressed gratitude to Special Forces HQ at the end of the war for 'a very considerable part in our complete and final victory'.[70] He did not mention the importance of unified direction. Beevor accepts the numerous arguments in favour of such a concept. He notes the Abwehr's unified direction of intelligence operations and counter-intelligence, and likewise the American OSS.[71] Gubbins also concludes that coordination in wartime of the activities of secret surveillance, political warfare and SOE activities required all three departments under one minister.[72] The OSS, the American equivalent to the SOE, evolved from Roosevelt's view that America needed an alternative strategic service to the highly efficient Federal Bureau of Investigation (FBI) for wartime overseas missions. In June 1942 the Office of Co-ordination of Strategic Information was converted into the Office of Strategic Service.[73] In a sense, the Americans were stepping up a gear after going into the war, just as G2 had stepped up to the Emergency.

Sweets' treatise on the French resistance movement in the Second World War suggests that the Auvergne experience epitomises the resistance pattern elsewhere in France.[74] In many ways its modus operandi was comparable to Irish resistance against Britain during the War of Independence. The major resistance movements, the Mouvements Unis de la Résistance, Front National and Résistance Armée (Maquis), controlled organised resistance. Its subdivisions included specialised intelligence units, propaganda distribution and direction of military components. The Maquis carried out guerrilla attacks and open combat against Germans and Milice (French Militia). The administrative wing of the resistance established a shadow government ready to take over power at the liberation of France – all reminiscent of the revolutionary Irish movement. Unlike the Irish movement, however, the transition from the Vichy regime to the Provisional Government was smooth. Within a year of liberation the political system was virtually back to normal. Internecine conflict did not occur. Occasional disagreements did not deter the OSS, SOE and French resistance movements from the deserved Eisenhower accolade at the cessation of the Second World War. Despite occasional frustration and differences of opinion between G2 and Garda agents during the Emergency, Bryan and senior Garda officers managed to avert major animosity between the forces through astute liaison and ignoring minor faux pas on each other's part.

ONE

The Genesis and Development of the Irish Army Intelligence System

War of Independence, 1919–21

Augusteijn felt that since the home rule struggle, most Irish Catholics believed in separatism, and that the immediate events surrounding the home rule crisis of 1912 were causal factors in the formation of the Irish Volunteers in 1913.[1] The executions of the leaders of the 1916 insurrection led in turn to the emergence of the Irish Republican Army (IRA), phoenix-like, who waged guerrilla war against British forces in Ireland from 1919 to 1921. The initial guerrilla engagement occurred on 21 January 1919.[2] Cork and Dublin epitomise IRA fighting activity and its intelligence network, from inception to maximisation. Such strife increased in other counties, particularly in the southwest. Augusteijn's study investigated the radicalisation process and tried to explain regional variations. Before 1920 military activity was largely confined to Munster and particularly to County Cork. Connacht Volunteers were willing to defy the police, but violence was sporadic. In Leinster, many undercover operations were carried out, largely concentrated in Dublin city, while in Ulster, turmoil was to a large extent confined to Belfast and Derry, mainly the result of sectarian riots sparked off by the wider hostilities.[3]

Explaining the conflict escalation post-1920, Augusteijn states that, in line with the rise in the number of offences, a large increase in casualties was recorded from the end of 1919 onwards. He adds that almost one third of the 1,545 members of the Crown forces killed or seriously wounded by the IRA between January 1920 and the truce on 11 July 1921 suffered their fate in County Cork. Other violent spots were Dublin city and the other Munster counties, with the exception of Waterford. Each of those counties had between 84 and 163 casualties. Most Connacht counties followed with around forty losses each, and Ulster counties around fifteen each. Outside Dublin city, the Leinster counties recorded the lowest level of violence, with between two and fourteen losses suffered by Crown forces in each county. However, in comparing the relative level of conflict, Augusteijn contends that the number of casualties in each county, including those among the Crown forces, the IRA, and civilians, is proportionate to the number of inhabitants. He allows that this somewhat alters the picture depicted earlier, but maintains that although Cork stands out alone, its lead is less pronounced. Cork recorded twenty-six casualties per 10,000 citizens; Tipperary and Clare followed with sixteen casualties; Dublin city and Kerry with fifteen; and Limerick and Belfast with fourteen each. Particularly unaffected counties were located in Ulster and the southeast.[4]

Augusteijn noted Hart's contention that violence seemed to thrive in more urbanised areas with better land and seemed to be hampered by poverty and physical isolation.[5] IRA activity flourished where it had the backing of the population, while high-calibre local leadership resulted in the development of effective IRA units. For instance, well-known IRA leaders in Cork were never betrayed, whereas in Trim, County Meath, the IRA on one occasion were hampered by the civilian population when arranging to occupy their positions.[6]

In 1973 Lyons stated that the theories of revolution, nationality and history needed re-examination, and that the time was ripe to break the great enchantment which for too long had made myth so much more congenial than reality. Ireland's predicament stemmed from a wrong reading of history; archives could be used to propound propaganda. Lyons conceded that a patriot such as Thomas Davis knew well that history could be made an essential ingredient of nationalism, and he posed the rhetorical question: 'Whoever claimed that revolutions are made by the dull grey masses?'[7] Was it not perfectly obvious, he contended, that revolutions are made by minorities whose superior insight allows them to see to the heart of things, and open the eyes of every man to injustices he has been too blind, too stupid, too downtrodden to see for himself. He added that revolutions in the minds of some people spring not only from minorities, but from the ideas formulated within those minorities by the intellectuals.

The advent of Michael Collins and his clear-cut appreciation of establishing an intelligence system came closest to formulating those ideas. The IRA, whose hierarchy Collins had infiltrated with members of the Irish Republican Brotherhood (IRB), had by 1919 a burgeoning awareness of the need for an accurate and timely intelligence and counter-intelligence system. This arose from sheer necessity, bordering almost on desperation during the War of Independence. As a result of British forces' success in capturing, interning and, on numerous occasions, executing men caught bearing arms, field commanders were forced to take salutary countermeasures. Directed against military targets, individual and collective, as well as convicted spies and informers, whether British, Anglo-Irish or native Irish, these countermeasures had the effect of enhancing the IRA's capacity to wage war in a most efficient and pragmatic manner.[8]

G. A. Hayes McCoy maintained that it was vital that hostilities were not confined to one area or to a few places and that the cities, and particularly Dublin, were involved also. A prime example of the IRA's lack of military preparedness in west Cork, a barometer of the most active areas, even by mid 1920, is outlined by Tom Barry:

> The West Cork IRA were lacking in war experience, untrained in the use of meagre arms resources, backward in foot-drill and without tactical training, difficulties compounded by a dearth of transport, signal and engineering equipment. In mid 1920, armament comprised thirty five rifles, twenty automatics or revolvers, meagre ammunition and a small supply of explosives and shot-guns.[9]

At least one of the Dublin Volunteer units was as well equipped with captured Lee Enfields and bayonets as a regular British army formation.[10] Much of its military resources were transferred to help other poorly armed units, but the total transferred never satisfied IRA leaders such as Tom Barry, Liam Lynch, Seán O'Hegarty and others, whose appetite for continuous and ruthless engagement remained unsatiated.

At this time, according to Major General E. P. Strickland, general officer commanding (GOC) of the British 6th Division in Cork, there were 12,600 British troops on a war footing in Cork city and county, excluding naval and marine personnel.[11] Little wonder then that Hayes-McCoy concluded that it was something new in Irish history that movements of British forces were contested in the Dublin streets and that the large-scale attack on the Custom House on 25 May 1921 showed the British authorities just how ruthless their opponents could be. The end result, even allowing for the Pyrrhic factor of the decimation of the Dublin Brigade, struck a severe blow at British administration in Ireland. Many Local Government records as well as much of the tax records for the country were destroyed in the conflagration. British governance of Ireland, by any civilised means, became impossible. Hayes-McCoy stated that 'Britain was exasperated by an assault that she considered underhand merely because it was unorthodox, and felt herself increasingly forced to extremes.'[12] He adds:

> Britain was not, and could not have been, militarily defeated. There was an answer to the methods of the Volunteers – for the country ambush the armoured car and the machine gun, for the attack

> on the city streets the foot patrol. The concentration camps might have been enlarged. It should not have been difficult to deny the Volunteers ammunition. The limit of terror had not been reached. But the price of victory on those terms, in the twentieth century and between two civilised and not unfriendly peoples, would have been too great. Terror was unworthy of Britain. It was to her credit that – even though belatedly – she recognised it was. It was the British who called for the truce.[13]

Hayes-McCoy is acknowledged as a respected academic historian. This author, however, having studied military tactics and strategy throughout his forty years of military service, does not agree with Hayes-McCoy's conclusion. It exemplifies historical selectivity and is patently casuistic. Terror unworthy of Britain? He seems to have conveniently excluded historical examples of British use of terror tactics, such as:

- The crushing of the Indian mutiny (insurrection?) of 1857.[14]
- Massacre of peaceful demonstrators by General Dyer's Gurkha troops in Amritsar in 1919.[15]
- Incarceration of 110,000 Boer women, children and old men, in British concentration camps, causing the deaths of tens of thousands from inevitable rampant, untreated, contagious disease.[16]

Britain was no less able and willing than any other colonial power to institute and practise terror in crushing mutiny/insurrection of indigenous peoples of its empire. The misjudged introduction of the lawless, undisciplined Auxiliaries and Black and Tans in 1920 epitomised Britain's politically mandated terror campaign, and IRA anti-terror tactics inevitably evolved to counteract this strategy throughout the War of Independence, showing scant regard for the concept of British invincibility. Leaders of the calibre of Collins, Barry, MacEoin, Moylan and Lynch, commanding rank-and-file Volunteers, fought the British in both urban and rural areas. The fact that the British, despite their use of ruthless terror tactics, agreed to a truce and subsequent treaty is testament to their reluctance to continue the conflict. But one should not hold a naive notion either that the IRA never used terror tactics. They used them as and when they saw fit, as seen after the destruction of their flying columns at Dripsey and Clonmult. Whether any side could claim a military victory is a judgement issue. The IRA won the struggle for the hearts and minds of the people, and also organised a superior intelligence system.

Tom Barry's analysis and advice to guerrilla resistance movements states that sentiment has no place in stopping terror tactics, such as torture of suspects, burning of houses and barns and unlawful random killing of innocent civilians by foot and mobile patrols. Only a ruthless counteraction campaign by the IRA could halt such tactics, and to achieve this a superior intelligence system was required. It seems a very good military/politico tactic to use guile, and to carefully select who and when to attack. Barry acknowledged that many British people passionately loved justice, hated imperialism and championed emancipatory movements, yet could never prevail on their government to act with human decency towards the weaker peoples. He mentions Commander Kenworthy, Royal Navy, who by 1949 was Lord Strabolgi, as deserving special mention for his unceasing efforts in that connection.

Eoin Neeson views the War of Independence, supported by an overwhelming majority of the people, as a prototype for guerrilla warfare. Over its four-year period it shook the very foundations of the British empire at a time when the empires of Austria, Germany, Turkey and Russia had already been shattered.[17] It is my contention that Britain decisively lost what in modern military parlance is called the 'psyops' battle, the struggle for the hearts and minds, not only of the majority of the Irish people but also of an influential and increasing set of British politicians, media, and public. Coincidentally, Britain's standing as a civilised arbiter of its rapidly crumbling empire was losing face at an unacceptable rate on the world stage. The War of Independence had created what Charles Townshend describes as 'The Intelligence Gap' in favour of the IRA, arguably the most potent factor in the battle for hearts and minds.[18] Barry, Neeson and Townshend agree that a superior intelligence system was the *sine qua non* of the IRA's conduct of the war.

Michael Collins: Director of Intelligence, 1919–22

Michael Collins' achievement in establishing and controlling a republican intelligence effort during the

Michael Collins (courtesy of the *Irish Examiner*).

War of Independence became part of popular memory. The guile, impertinence and ruthlessness of the 'Big Fellow' in orchestrating the secret war against the Crown in Dublin made him a living legend within the IRA as well as among the wider nationalist community.[19] Eoin Neeson notes that Collins

> . . . devoted enormous interest to intelligence work, agreeing with the principle that not only is good intelligence work worth three divisions, but also to deny intelligence to the enemy was worth as many more. To that end he was ruthless and resourceful, and soon had a network of agents in what the British considered their most secure areas – the British army, the RIC, the Civil Service (of which Nathan wrote before 1916; 'for some reason which I am unable to fathom a large proportion of the people treasonable to England are to be found in the lower ranks of the government service'), even in Dublin Castle itself. His men had 'colleagues among engine drivers, ships' crews and stokers, post-office clerks, office cleaners, domestic servants – in every position where information of enemy plans might be obtained'.[20]

Collins' modus operandi was replicated particularly in more active areas such as Cork, where Florence O'Donoghue proved himself an outstanding intelligence officer (IO) and where the guerrilla commanders were equally ruthless and resourceful. Among them were Tom Barry, Seán O'Hegarty and Frank Busteed, all of whom epitomised the ruthless pragmatism of Collins' policy.

Busteed believed spies and informers should be exterminated ruthlessly, that none of the previous Irish uprisings or national movements could have succeeded, because the British knew of their plans through informers in their ranks.[21] He argued that 'the elimination of one spy was better than the killing of a thousand soldiers or Tans. Because one spy could do more damage. It was easy to replace soldiers, but the British couldn't replace local spies. They were their eyes and ears.'[22]

Collins, writing about his espionage and counter-intelligence operations in a series of articles in the *New York American* in 1922, stated that the military war commitment could be paralysed by the extermination of its spies. Spies were indispensable and could not be replaced as easily as normal military casualties. The IRA adopted this strategy, which proved most successful.[23]

The British establishment has remained reluctant to accept the hearts and minds principle outlined by General Sir Gerald Templer in 1952: 'The answer lies not in pouring more soldiers into the jungle but rests in the hearts and minds of the Malayan people.'[24] Collins, Busteed and Barry, all exponents of guerrilla warfare, recognised a similar strategy. Intelligence and the 'hearts and minds' factor are irrevocably fused in order to pursue successful guerrilla war.

Arguably the two most important figures to emerge in terms of the organisation of military intelligence on behalf of the Volunteers were Michael Collins and Florence O'Donoghue. Both successfully infiltrated the enemy at the same time as the Volunteers, particularly in Dublin and Cork, began to adopt guerrilla tactics against the regular forces. Neeson makes the point that some of the tactics employed by the IRA during the War of Independence, most notably Tom Barry's actions at Kilmichael and Crossbarry in County Cork, were later studied in military colleges in places as diverse as Sweden and Egypt.

Piaras Béaslaí outlines the beginning of Michael Collins' association with intelligence work following Britain's declaration that conscription be extended to Ireland. Éamon Duggan was IRA Director of Intelligence but, as Béaslaí states, circumstances put Collins in touch with an important source of information that was to lead to some remarkable developments, particularly in Dublin. The political section of G Division of the Dublin Metropolitan Police was the principal source of spies employed by the British government in Dublin at this time. Their job, according to Béaslaí, was to monitor the activities of all prominent members of the national movements. And although they were very effective in their work, Béaslaí outlines how some members were in secret sympathy with those upon whom they were spying. He describes how one member of G Division, Éamon (Ned) Broy, got in touch with a well-known Sinn Féiner, Micheál Ó Foghlugha, through whom he conveyed important information to Collins. Later Broy arranged a system of sending information through a relative. Tomás Gay, a librarian, got in touch with another detective of patriotic leanings, named Joe Kavanagh, and through him with yet another, James McNamara. All information was communicated via Gay to Harry Boland, then to Collins. Another Volunteer, Seán Duffy, acted as liaison officer with Kavanagh, as did Greg Murphy.[25]

Béaslaí outlines the importance of Broy and Kavanagh as intelligence agents for the Volunteers:

> On Wednesday 15 May 1918, Broy gave Collins a list of prominent Sinn Féiners liable for arrest on Friday 17 May. Friday evening, Kavanagh warned Gay that Dublin Castle agents had prepared for a series of arrests that night. Gay at once informed Boland who sent word to Collins. Collins warned a meeting of the executive of the Irish Volunteers that night, at 44 Parnell Square, to go to safe houses. De Valera, Arthur Griffith, WT Cosgrave and others refused. Between midnight and daylight, police and military raided the houses of a number of leading Sinn Féiners in Dublin, and throughout the country, and arrested over 80.[26]

This shows that the British had an intelligence service of no little merit, but some, among them Michael Collins, slipped through the net. The prisoners, including de Valera, Griffith and Cosgrave, were deported to England and interned in various prisons.

Through a number of intermediaries, Collins dealt with political detectives who were secretly in sympathy with Sinn Féin. Joe Kavanagh, James McNamara, Ned Broy and David Neligan, among others, were destined to do much important work for him. Broy was eventually exposed, however, and arrested in 1921, as was David Neligan.[27] Collins' work also involved the smuggling of men and arms into Ireland, chiefly through Liverpool, under the direction of Neil Kerr and Stephen Lanigan. Kerr, who was in the employ of the Cunard Steamship

Company, had sailors working for him on ships between Dublin and Liverpool. Béaslaí describes how Collins often made flying visits to Liverpool with a view to understanding all the machinery.

At this stage, Collins' appointments as Director of Organisation, Adjutant General and Director of Intelligence were overlapping. He gave much attention to this work, and used his intelligence system to carry it out to the absolute. Stephen Lanigan, a very able and active IRB worker, held an important position in the Liverpool Custom House and as such was invaluable to Collins; he kept in close contact and was a frequent visitor to Dublin. However, in December 1920 both he and Kerr were arrested and interned. Many other sailors on cross-channel boats also gave valuable assistance to Collins' network, notably Ned Kavanagh, Paddy McCarthy, Willie Verner, Paddy Wafer, Maurice Byrne and Harry Shaw. Collins also made important allies of some of the Atlantic seamen, including Tom O'Connor and Dick O'Neill, the latter often meeting Collins at Vaughan's Hotel in Dublin.

Collins' London friend Sam Maguire rendered valuable assistance through his influence in the British postal service, while Collins also made contact with sympathetic Dublin postal officials. This area was to assume great importance; for instance, during the Black and Tan war, Collins had workers in every important post office in Ireland, with the result that most of the government, military and police cipher messages were intercepted and decoded. Collins also developed a system of communications with Volunteer prisoners in Irish jails by means of sympathetic warders. For instance, Michael Staines kept contact with prisoners in Mountjoy Jail through a prison official named Berry, with whom he was friendly. Other Mountjoy warders who later proved very valuable to Collins included Peter Breslin, a man named Frawley, and others by the names of Daly and Murphy. Even in Belfast and other jails where Volunteers were confined, similar means of communication were tapped.[28]

In London Collins got in touch with John Chartres, then in the British civil service, who had worked for him for four years prior to the Treaty. Among other tasks, Chartres helped convey arms and ammunition to Collins on a number of occasions; he was later one of the secretaries to the Irish delegation of plenipotentiaries who negotiated the Treaty. Although republican elements were aware that Chartres had served in British intelligence during the First World War, Collins trusted him to complete tasks, mainly intelligence gathering, without argument or fuss.[29]

Brian P. Murphy enhances Coogan's account of Chartres' intelligence role and his service to the Irish delegation in 1921.[30] Seán T. O'Kelly knew Chartres empathised with the republican aspirations of Sinn Féin after the 1916 Rising, which had had a dramatic effect on him.

> It shook me from the ground up, when I met my colleagues at supper that night and heard such harsh abuse of Ireland and the treachery of the Irish, something worked inside me which had been dormant for a long time. That night I realised that I was not an Englishman but an Irishman. All my

> sympathy was with Ireland and I would have to fight for her.[31]

Collins dealt with Chartres directly, and was concerned that he was involved in a very dangerous enterprise, necessitating absolute secrecy.[32]

Those of the Sinn Féin executive who had evaded capture had little personal acquaintance with Collins, and regarded him as a wild young man. They disliked his brusque manner but after some experience of working with him in committee, they began to realise the value of his intelligent viewpoints. Nevertheless, some of Collins' proposals fell on deaf ears.[33]

The first public assembly of Dáil Éireann was fixed for 21 January 1919. Collins was made Minister for Home Affairs at the meeting, and his appointment as a minister, young as he was, caused no surprise. Those who least liked him had learned to recognise his energy and capacity. Cathal Brugha, chief of staff, not yet estranged from Collins, had thought how indispensable a man his young colleague was.[34]

The rescue of de Valera from Lincoln prison took place on 3 February 1919. It was organised by Michael Collins, ably abetted by Frank Boland and Collins' intelligence network, both in England and Ireland. The network was also responsible for the jailbreak of Piaras Béaslaí, Austin Stack and D. P. Walsh from Manchester prison. Collins showed his characteristic audacity when, under an assumed name, he visited Stack in prison. The escape was organised by Collins, and involved Rory O'Connor's initial inspection and recommendation of the plan to General Headquarters.

On becoming official Director of Intelligence in 1919, having acted in a de facto role previously, Collins set about creating a regular department. He selected Liam Tobin, intelligence officer of the Dublin Brigade, as his chief intelligence officer. Tom Cullen was later drafted in to intelligence, and Collins set up three permanent offices: Cullenwood House, Bachelor's Walk and a finance office at 6 Harcourt Street.[35] The intelligence staff was built up slowly; suitable men were not easily found. Among the earlier members were Joe Dolan, Frank Saurin, later a colonel in the Free State army, Joe Guilfoyle, Charlie Dalton, Paddy Caldwell and Frank Thornton. Later additions, about the end of 1920, were Peter McGee, Ned Kelleher, Dan McDonnell, Charlie Byrne and Paddy Kennedy. At a later date Caldwell was transferred to the Adjutant General's branch. Collins' Squad consisted of a small band of Volunteers attached to the Intelligence Department, specially selected for dangerous and difficult jobs. They were required to give their whole time to the service of the Volunteers, and be always available.

Their commanding officer was Mick McDonnell, with Paddy Daly as second in command; later Daly succeeded McDonnell as officer commanding. Among the other members were Tom Keogh, Jim Slattery, Vincent Byrne, Joe Leonard, Eddie Byrne, Ben Barrett, Paddy Griffin and Seán Doyle. As time progressed other Volunteers reinforced the Squad as necessary. These were Frank Bolster, Ben Byrne, James Conroy, J. Brennan, Pat McCrea, Paddy Drury, James Connolly and Bill Stapleton.[36]

Tim Pat Coogan infers that Seán Lemass assisted Squad operations, which is probably true in relation to the extermination of the 'Cairo gang', a group of British intelligence officers, fourteen of whom were executed on the morning of Bloody Sunday 21 November 1920.[37] John Horgan infers Lemass was possibly a member that day, but his inference is unproven.[38] The courage, loyalty, and secrecy of the members of this small body resulted in the success of many of the operations in Dublin, which inflicted severe damage on the British machinery of coercion and oppression. The 'Squad', a body of ruthless killers, played a big part in the subsequent fighting in Dublin. The Bloody Sunday murders led to retaliation in Croke Park during the course of a match that afternoon, leaving fourteen dead and about sixty wounded.[39]

At weekly meetings with detectives Broy and McNamara in Tomás Gay's house in Clontarf, Collins gained a close insight into the enemy intelligence system, including the methods, outlook and intentions of his opponents. The keys to police and official cipher documents and codes were ascertained, and gradually a system was established by which British official messages were tapped at various postal centres and decoded. Important confidential reports, and other secret documents of the British, found their way into his hands.

Collins understood that the principal organisation by which Ireland had been held in subjection was the Royal Irish Constabulary (RIC). These men, all Irish, acted not only as a British garrison but also as intelligence officers for the British government. Frustrating their work became an important branch of Volunteer activities. A party of nine Volunteers began the task on 21 January 1919, in Soloheadbeg in Tipperary, capturing gelignite, and shooting dead two armed RIC men.[40] Attacks on police barracks became common in Cork, Clare, and Tipperary. Guerrilla warfare, and social ostracism of members of the RIC, as decreed by Dáil Éireann, helped render the force unpopular.

The attitude of Divisional Commissioner Smith[41] caused resignations among Listowel RIC. He practically initiated murders, and was duly shot dead by the Cork IRA in July 1920.[42] By the end of the War of Independence, the RIC were almost out of commission. Collins kept contact with certain RIC men who were sympathetic to the national cause, and used them very effectively in counter-intelligence.

By December 1919 Collins had practically paralysed the British government's political spy system in Dublin. Half a dozen detectives kept Collins informed of every move, to such an extent that the *London Globe* remarked: 'Every step taken by the Castle is known an hour afterwards, it is almost enough to make men believe in spirits.'[43] By this time also, attacks on RIC patrols had greatly increased in frequency, with the Volunteers now waging a form of guerrilla warfare.

Collins' attempts to assassinate Lord French, Lord Lieutenant, General Headquarters, showed his careless devil-may-care bravery and impetuous lack of judgement. Coogan describes an occasion when Collins got word that Lord French would be passing through College Street at a certain time. He procured a gun and rounded up anyone (presumably IRA) who happened to be nearby to ambush French. Coogan then alludes to the extraordinary magnetism of Collins in persuading others to join in the hare-brained scheme, some of whom hardly knew how to fire a weapon, never mind being au fait with ambush techniques.[44] Coogan does not give this episode a specific date, but Béaslaí describes various failed attempts by Collins' men to carry out the assassination, including one at Ashdown on 19 December 1919 in which an attacker named Martin Savage was killed.[45]

By late 1919, Collins was Minister for Finance and held three positions in the Volunteers – Adjutant General, Director of Organisation and Director of Intelligence. He had no option but to resign as Director of Organisation and concentrate on his work as Director of Intelligence.[46] At that time, four spies arrived in Dublin, and Collins and his Squad tracked, exposed and executed all four within a month of their arrival.[47] The British recognised that their intelligence organisation in Ireland had been undermined, so William C. Forbes Redmond was brought from Belfast as second assistant commissioner to the Dublin Metropolitan Police (DMP) to reorganise the detective force. Collins, only too aware of the threat posed by Forbes Redmond, remarked: 'If we don't get that man he'll get us, and soon.'[48] Forbes Redmond emulated Collins by cycling around Dublin. He distrusted G Division and planned to strengthen the force of detectives with Belfast RIC men. However, Collins' organisation tracked him down, and assassinated him within four weeks of his arrival.

The second of the four spies was a remarkable type of agent provocateur. He had been admitted to the councils of the organisers of the British police strike, and also passed himself off as a Bolshevist. While his name was Byrne, he assumed the name of Jameson. He too was shot by the Squad. The British then planted Fergus Brian Molloy, ostensibly an army sergeant stationed in the pay office, General Headquarters (GHQ) Parkgate, in another attempt to eliminate Collins and his intelligence organisation. However, Collins exposed him and he was shot dead in Wicklow Street in broad daylight. The fourth spy, Quinlisk, an ex-corporal of the Royal Irish Rangers, had as a prisoner of war enrolled in Casement's brigade. His only reason for coming to Ireland in 1919 was to compromise Collins' security to the British and collect a £10,000 reward. Collins sent him on a false trail, suggesting that the IRA's Director of Intelligence would be in Wren's Hotel in Cork. A coded message was sent to the Cork RIC to arrest Collins, but the IRA in Cork held up police mail and discovered that Quinlisk was an agent. Quinlisk was intercepted by the 1st Cork Brigade IRA who duly executed him.[49] Collins' intelligence officers tracked down District Inspector Swanzy of Cork, leader of the murder gang who executed Lord Mayor Tomás MacCurtain in cold blood. Swanzy was quickly transferred to Lisburn where he was shot dead by Cork IRA men.

Arguably the deadliest blows to the British administrative system in Ireland were carried out on Easter Saturday 1920 – when the IRA raided the income tax offices in Dublin, Cork and other cities – and 25 May 1921, they raided and burned the Dublin Custom House. On the night before Easter Saturday 1920, Collins planned the countrywide coup, despite tight security. The offices were set on fire, and all records relating to income tax were destroyed. In effect, the collection of income tax in Ireland was paralysed. On the same night, in a secondary operation, no fewer than 315 evacuated RIC barracks were destroyed by fire.

The burning of the Custom House also had a devastating effect. Planned by Collins, it was executed by the 2nd Battalion of the Dublin Volunteers, augmented by members of the Squad and active service unit (ASU). It was one of the biggest operations of the War of Independence. Over 100 Volunteers were involved, approximately the same size force commanded by Tom Barry in Crossbarry.[50] Six Volunteers were killed, twelve wounded and about seventy captured during the operation. Collins was greatly concerned at the losses and deemed it a Pyrrhic victory. However, the burning of the Custom House meant that most of the documents and records connected with Local Government, Inland Revenue, Customs, company registration, the Stamp Office, the Assay Office and Stationery Office were destroyed.

British Intelligence System, 1920

The British army's intelligence system, or lack of, was outlined in a report to General Macready on 23 July 1920 in which General Jeudwine highlighted two main problem areas: communications and intelligence. There was a scarcity of wireless equipment, landing grounds and personnel, and an omission of intelligence expertise.[51] This admission led to an important development of their intelligence system until the curtailment of British army raids in April/May. The only consolation for British intelligence was that the reinforcements of May/July made it possible to reduce the size of local intelligence areas. Their divisional staffs were also expanded and their brigade intelligence officers were graded as general staff officers. Imbalances marred the Crown intelligence system, which appeared when Dublin district was given an intelligence chief who outranked the intelligence officer at GHQ. The latter was reduced to providing 'only a small bureau for the Commander in Chief rather than the directing and controlling force for military intelligence throughout Ireland'.[52]

Only in Dublin District (DD), where a Special Branch had been built up unofficially in mid-1919, was there any consistent success in penetrating republican organisations. Lieutenant Colonel Wilson, who took over Dublin intelligence in May 1920, was a brilliant secret service chief. Yet DD Special Branch suffered a large number of casualties, and other intelligence groups suffered still more and achieved less. Typically, the British decided in 1919 to place Irish secret service, with the exception of any agents already employed by the intelligence branch at GHQ, under the control of the head of the Criminal Investigation Department (CID) in London, Sir Basil Thompson.

The difficulty of coordination minimised the contribution of the London-based organisation. The fusion of the Crown intelligence system under Colonel Ormonde Winter made very slow progress, lacking the essential local coordination between the army and the police. In April 1921, General Macready opined that Winter 'is, I fancy, a born sleuth but I doubt his organising power, and that is what is holding up the machine'.[53] Townshend states that after the formation of IRA flying columns, security became more stringent due to increased vulnerability, and the execution of 'spies and informers' – whose corpses were left suitably placarded in public view – helped inspire a belief in the IRA's omniscience. The main military objection to the police intelligence system had been its reliance on personal knowledge and intuition, rather than formal organisation. Added to this was its shunning of the distinction between intelligence functions, which were categorised as: service of information; security or counter-intelligence; and organisation and administration. Personal friction abounded within the Dublin District Special Branch, who preferred to associate with Dublin military authorities than serve under Winter's direct control in 1921. Winter was accused by the army of trying to build incrementally an intelligence system to fit given circumstances rather than adapting a sound system and adjusting it to suit circumstances. The result was an extraordinarily complex and involved organisation.[54]

Hart's editing of *British Intelligence in Ireland, 1920–1921* fails to accord a more favourable perspective on Ormonde Winter's intelligence organisation than the standard portrayal he imputes as generally agreed by historians. His work is basically an apologia for the British army's intelligence system and an attempt to minimise his acceptance of Collins' genius:

> Collins was brilliant – although not quite the soldier and strategist of the standard portrayal – but

> we need to scrape away the layers of mythology and idolisation that have encrusted his reputation and we must be aware of the limits of his reach. His secret service may well have bested its vaunted rivals, but theirs was one battle, not the whole war.[55]

He bases his army intelligence apologia on Volume II of the British Irish Command staff history, *Record of the Rebellion in Ireland 1920–22*.[56] Its conclusions outline a litany of failure caused by 'vacillating negligent government, a hostile population and an intelligence system lacking unity, direction or leadership'.[57] Despite the oxymoronic thrust of his argument, Hart still concludes that Collins' organisation's intelligence success depended on information from G men and spies, producing essential negative and partial intelligence results. Collins was a daring, organisational genius and one of the heroes of the resistance. Colonel Ormonde de l'Épee Winter is described by his peers as 'having had no experience in intelligence or police work', 'a wicked little white snake' whom Hart would have us believe made a vast improvement to close the intelligence gap between the IRA and the British.[58]

Collins' Characteristics and Lifestyle

Augusteijn contradicts Neligan's account of Collins' lifestyle.[59] Neligan states that Collins never drank anything other than sherry when he was in his company.[60] Augusteijn comments that the less serious attitude of some of the Volunteers irritated the more ardent officers. Some of these accused Collins of abusing drink and of using funds to buy people's loyalty, an accusation which got them into serious trouble; in turn Collins made fun of the overzealous attitude of these men.[61]

O'Halpin attributes four main characteristics that marked Michael Collins out as a remarkably successful Director of Intelligence. First is his appreciation of the importance of the collection and assessment of information. Second, the efficacy and ruthlessness of Collins and his Squad ensured the success of most actions, based on good intelligence. Third, his success in preserving the security and efficiency of his own organisation, both in Dublin and in Britain prevailed, despite the constant threat of raids, arrests and the capture of documents.[62] Fourth, his commanding personality was of more significance than his formal intelligence responsibilities in shaping his relations with officers in the field.[63]

Intelligence during the War of Independence can be categorised under the following headings: military intelligence; counter-intelligence; assassinations; arms procurement. All four were necessarily clandestine, and depended on disciplined and trustworthy people capable of following orders discreetly. Arms procurement was a separate operation involving purchasing and smuggling networks abroad and in Irish ports. The difference between intelligence proper and assassination was marked at an organisational level in 1919 with the creation of the Squad, a unit of gunmen under Collins' direct control and independent of IRA headquarters.

Operational intelligence on police strength or on troop movements was the responsibility of the local units who would use it. The quality of local units' information, where success or failure depended largely on the vision and energy of the responsible local officers, was a reliable litmus test of its general efficiency. Florence O'Donoghue contended that Collins would have been 'largely powerless outside Dublin were it not for the work done by the local brigades'.[64] He maintains that the regular and reasonably speedy exchange of information between the three Cork brigades, and between each of them and the Director of Intelligence, for which O'Donoghue was mainly responsible, was not matched in other parts of the country. These areas remained largely inert, despite the best efforts of Collins and Mulcahy to galvanise them into some form of action through the despatch of men such as Ernie O'Malley to help local units into some sort of shape.[65] Analysis and verification of Florence O'Donoghue's view is worth consideration.

IRA Intelligence Network Structure: Cork City and County

Pat Lynch states that the brigade IO had the task of obtaining all available information on enemy movements, dispositions, posts, weapons, vehicles, identities, etc. He was responsible for building an information network on which he could rely. When the number of British troops in garrisons or posts in the IRA brigade area was increased, or when a new regiment or detachment was posted to the area, the local intelligence agent forwarded his information through what Lynch describes as the grapevine to let the brigade IO know what was happening, in the shortest possible time. The IRA excelled at this work.[66]

The methodology corresponds to the textbook definition of military intelligence; the system is analogous to the Collins-inspired structure and organisation in both Dublin and England. Agents were found among telephonists, clerks, waiters, porters and other posts, where an alert man or woman could learn much. Lynch adds that the communications system set up by the brigades played a vital part in the speedy transmission of information to the officers.[67] Engine drivers, train guards, porters and others employed at railway stations were among those who made a noteworthy contribution to the communications system, often at great personal risk. It was not uncommon for the driver of a train conveying enemy troops to be the bearer of an IRA despatch, which he secreted in his engine.

O'Callaghan gives a clear insight into the organisation and methodology of the 1st Cork Brigade.[68] Collins depended on information from brigade and battalion intelligence officers in the rest of Ireland. As O'Callaghan explains, the network was not served by highly trained spies but by ordinary people going about their work. Internal and external systems of espionage were established in every British military area. The internal system was manned by those employed in barracks, shore installations and in the Post Office. These agents, in particular the Post Office employees, did magnificent work. Mail for British officers and soldiers was steamed open, read, and any important information copied. Although they had radio equipment at their disposal, the RIC and the auxiliaries continued to send messages by cipher. These were deciphered with the key regularly supplied by Collins. O'Callaghan claims that the British forces never really appreciated the scope and efficiency of the IRA's intelligence network, particularly in the closing phase of the war. The IRA's use of post offices staffed by sympathisers constantly baffled the British.

The 1st Cork Brigade developed a courier system whereby interrogation of an arrested agent could compromise no more than one other. O/C Seán O'Hegarty was well served by intelligence officer Florence O'Donoghue and his assistant, Seán Culhane. They developed a network capable of deciphering codes, improved lines of communication, and trained battalion intelligence officers, who in turn trained key company intelligence officers.

Josephine Marchmount Brown proved an effective stenographer-cum-spy against British 6th Division headquarters. Recruited by Florence O'Donoghue, whom she later married, she provided a constant stream of intelligence for the IRA, who in return kidnapped her son from her family in England and brought him to join his mother in Cork.[69]

But the Cork IRA were also susceptible to British counter-intelligence, as instanced in autumn 1920 when Frank Busteed was assigned to execute a spy within the IRA. During interrogation the informer stated that another double agent recruited him with 'easy money'; the spy and double agent were executed without delay.[70] The Cork IRA identified and eliminated two civilian spy rings, both of which were run by Mr Nicholson, manager of Woodford Bournes, wine and spirit merchants. With the help of Marchmount Brown, correspondence between Nicholson and the military allowed the IRA to identify members of the inner ring. Subsequently Nicholson was shot in Bishopstown, another member, Alfred Reilly, was shot in Douglas, while a third, Harrison Beale, was also shot dead.[71] Other ring members panicked, and some fled to England; one such, George Tilson, was found with his throat cut in a lavatory on the Fishguard–London Express.[72]

General Strickland, O/C British 6th Division, had no illusion about the strength and efficiency of the IRA, believing it was almost as well organised as the British army. Given his insistence that martial law of the severest type be imposed in Cork, he became a prime target for the IRA. Several attempts were made on his life; he escaped all, including a gun battle ambush arising from information leaked by Marchmount Brown. General Macready contemplated reprisals in response, and on 9 December 1920 the British Cabinet declared martial law in Cork, Tipperary, Kerry and Limerick. On 24 December General Strickland signed the proclamation in Cork which, among other penalties, made reprisals official.

Churchill wrote: '. . . by early summer 1921 the British forces were using the ruthlessness which the Russian communists adopted towards their fellow countrymen in an odious and shameful form of warfare'. His wife had advised him by letter on 18 February 1921 '. . . to use your influence *now* for some sort of moderation or at least justice in Ireland. Put yourself in the place of the Irish – if you were their leader, you would not be cowed by severity & certainly not by reprisals which fall like the rain from Heaven upon the Just and the Unjust . . .[73]

Churchill described the subsequent government policy volte-face as the most 'complete and sudden . . . reversal of policy in the history of British government'. Jenkins outlines how 'In May the whole power of the State and all the influence of the Coalition were used to hunt down the murder gang: in June the goal was a lasting reconciliation with the Irish people.'[74]

Counter-intelligence Operations

O'Halpin contends that counter-intelligence was unequivocally the realm of intelligence activity in which Collins' organisation excelled.[75] Counter-intelligence was the decisive element in the War of Independence, compensating for the IRA's numerical weakness and lack of material. It usually protected the leaders of the independence movement from capture and enabled key elements of the underground Dáil administration, most importantly the Department of Local Government, to function to surprising effect.[76]

The killing of suspected British agents on Bloody Sunday 1920 is acknowledged as a severe body blow to British intelligence.[77] O'Halpin felt it slowed, rather than halted, British intelligence gathering, which had improved under the Restoration of Order in Ireland Act. The upward spiral of violence had a domino effect, proportionate to the growing numbers of combat-hardened IRA men radicalised by the fighting. These were responsible for killing many government agents and alleged spies.[78]

IRA ASU Columns Annihilated because of Security Lapses

In Clonmult, east Cork, the flying column of the East Cork Brigade was virtually eliminated because of a total lack of security and a vainglorious attitude. An analysis of the column's demise reveals the security defects. First, the members of the column were too long billeted at a farm – six weeks – and, not surprisingly, their presence was noted by British intelligence. In addition, they espoused a cavalier attitude of invincibility despite such lapses of security. They had not planned escape or withdrawal routes, and no protective scout screen existed, all of which was the responsibility of the local (non-column) Volunteers. In comparison, Tom Barry's tactics in west Cork were an example of how things should be done.[79]

Ballycannon was similar in ways to the Clonmult debacle. No security precautions were taken by what the British army called the Blarney Street Murder Gang.[80] The British saw the annihilation of the IRA in this episode as, in the words of General Strickland, a methodology of saving the trouble of court martial. In his discussion of Ballycannon, Hart is economical with the truth, omitting to state that the IRA were butchered and tortured to death in the course of the British operation. What could be termed the 'abattoir syndrome' – where animals become agitated on entering a slaughter-house – deterred any form of livestock from grazing in areas mentioned by *Examiner* reports.[81]

Following Ballycannon, the IRA failed initially to flush out a spy nicknamed 'Cruxy Connors', an ex-British soldier who had received the Croix de Guerre in the First World War. But after fleeing to America, he was eventually traced. Seán O'Hegarty, O/C 1st Cork Brigade, despatched two gunmen to execute Connors; they did so, and returned home unscathed. Further attempts to trace British personnel involved in the massacre met with little success, with the exception of a report on a constable mechanic William Phogdale, by then stationed in Gormanstown depot. The report gives details of his height, build, eyes, accent, and ascertained that he had driven the party of police to Clogheen and participated in the massacre.[82] No account exists as to any retribution exacted.

The *Cork Examiner*, considered to be of constitutional Redmondite nationalist ethos, gave full coverage to the incidents in Clonmult and Ballycannon.[83] The paper recognised that feelings ran so high in the Ballycannon area that it despatched its own special correspondent to investigate the incident at first hand.

Details of the Clogheen/Ballycannon Massacre

The *Cork Examiner* was somewhat cautious in detailing the exact nature of the IRA men's injuries, which included: eyelids torn and hacked off; fingernails tortuously removed; tongues cut out; multiple bayonet and bullet wounds.

Hart refers to Clonmult and the killing of the IRA East Cork active service unit (ASU) by the Hampshire Regiment on 20 February 1921. Like the Macroom auxiliaries three months before, the men of the 4th

Battalion in east Cork had become overconfident and had fallen into a traceable routine. The column was attacked and besieged by a combined force of soldiers and police, and both sides suffered losses.

According to the official British communiqué, several guerrillas came running out with their hands up but others continued to fire. A number of Black and Tans were shot as they went to accept this false surrender. Out of twenty Volunteers, twelve were dead and four were wounded before army officers got the enraged policemen under control. The Irish survivors testified convincingly that there was no treachery on their part; the Volunteers surrendered in good faith and were gunned down as they emerged, or else placed against a wall and executed. The IRA's reaction was that every suspected informer after Clonmult, and every man in uniform, including coastguard and marines, became a legitimate target, to be shot on sight.

The emerging intelligence gap in favour of the IRA hampered police activity, particularly in west Cork[84] and Galway.[85] According to Townshend, the Galway RIC reported that on the whole the police were receiving no information from the people. This was due to the IRA's fomenting of a popular boycott of the RIC, who were by now widely regarded as traitors to their own nation. Apart from a minority who believed they could physically eject the British, the IRA mostly appreciated the political and psychological benefit of guerrilla warfare applied in conjunction with modern publicity techniques.[86]

The British army introduced new measures, including the mass arrest of all known IRA leaders and a deportation of those who could not be legally convicted by 7 January 1920. Destroyers were placed on standby at Kingstown, Arklow, Greenore and Waterford to take deportees to Britain. Military commanders prepared lists of wanted men and arrested substitutes for those who could not be found. Despite martial law, introduced in January 1920, the British experienced problems in the area of intelligence. Ireland drifted into armed rebellion as the British failed to identify, arrest and deport leaders. The police intelligence system was paralysed, with officers reluctant to convey any information to the military.[87] This, combined with a lack of trained intelligence officers, forced the army to construct a system of its own from scratch.[88]

Despite attempts in January 1920 to arrest all the leaders of the IRA, Lieutenant General Shaw, general officer commanding-in-chief (GOC-in-C) Ireland, in a report dated 25 March, stated: 'The first real result of this policy has been the capture of most valuable documents, from which the organisation of the Irish Volunteer Army has been deduced . . . They have a very powerful organization, which can only be crippled through its leaders.'[89]

Townshend interprets Shaw's memo as an admission that the attempted arrests in January were premature, and again he points to an effective intelligence service as the first priority. He contends that later events suggest Shaw's analysis of the dependence of the republican movement on its leaders was flawed, and that the new movement had more internal drive and resilience than former political organisations. However, he does argue that it was not poor intelligence or false analysis that wrecked the British military policy in Ireland so much as the oscillation of the government.[90] Liddle Hart contends that it is vital for guerrillas that their enemies be kept in the dark while they themselves operate with superior local knowledge combined with reliable information about the enemy's activities.[91]

Most Irish nationalists were aware that to betray IRA personnel to the government was very different from disapproving of their methods. The likes of Barry, Busteed, Collins, Breen, O'Hegarty and others knew that the execution of spies and informers would act as a deterrent to the public at large.

The 'hearts and minds' of the Irish people were at last finding a true allegiance to replace their uneasy subjection to the British Crown. IRA operations depended upon the cooperation of the public, which, whether through loyalty, respect or fear, ensured protection from the forces of the Crown. In Dublin, notable daylight assassinations included those of Assistant Commissioner Redmond of the DMP on 21 January and ex-senior police official Alan Bell, who was brought out of retirement to investigate the republic's secret bank accounts. Collins ordered his Squad to abduct Bell from the tram on which he travelled to work and shoot him, as his security escorts remained at his departure and arrival points. The order was duly carried out on 26 March 1920. No such fate awaited de Valera on his return from America, where he had managed to withhold approximately half of the $5 million bond certificate loan with which he founded his family newspaper empire, the Irish Press Group.[92]

The psychological element of the conflict was fundamentally important. The ambitious attacks on the RIC barracks which began in January 1920 became so widespread as to ensure their evacuation. As scorched shells, the evacuated barracks became a chilling advertisement of the government's retreat.[93]

Hart's description of the British and IRA intelligence systems differs essentially from all others. He focuses on the IRA use of the word 'informer', and states: 'To understand where these suspicions led, we must turn first to the term informer itself. Calling someone an informer was in fact a standard rhetorical weapon in all manner of disputes – factional, agrarian, labour, domestic, or political – regardless of revolution.'[94] Against this, he says: 'By far the best intelligence [for the British] however came from inside the IRA itself. The killings on Broad Street and the massacre at Clogheen, the ambushes at Nadd, Mourne Abbey, the roundup at Crossbarry, and many seizures of arms, were caused by Volunteers who fell out with their comrades, or were in turn intimidated by British intelligence.'[95]

In Hart's final lines on spies and informers, which purports to be his description of the intelligence system, he concludes:

> Like the events of April 1922, the war on informers must be seen as a part of the tit for tat dynamics of violence, driven by fear and a desire for revenge. It was now, however, merely (or even mainly) a matter of espionage, or spies, and spy hunters. It was a civil war between communities, with the battle lines drawn by a whole range of social bonds

> and boundaries . . . Beneath the welter of pretext and suspicions, beneath its official rhetoric of court martial and convictions, the IRA were tapping a deep vein of communal prejudices and gossip: about grabbers, black Protestants and Masonic conspiracies, dirty tinkers and corner boys, fly boys and fast women, the Jews at number four and the disorderly house at number thirty . . . Revolution had turned these people and their families into strangers, and their neighbours into enemies.[96]

THE CIVIL WAR, 1922–23

Failure to preserve unity over the Treaty was to some extent a resurfacing of the differences between constitutional and revolutionary nationalists of the nineteenth century.[97] The decrease in support for the use of violence that had set in during the final phase of the War of Independence was maintained after 1923. Revolutionary republicans continued to form a visible section of Irish society. The anti-Treaty forces lost the hearts and minds of the people during the Civil War, even though they did not lose total empathy with them. The pragmatism of the pro-Treaty politicians won the support of those who wanted peace, which assisted their victory in the Civil War.[98]

Griffith and O'Grady laud Tom Barry's account of his success in the struggle, which Barry attributed to the IRA intelligence network.[99] With the exception of west Cork and Kerry, however, the hearts and minds of the people remained with the Provisional Government.

Commander of the pro-Treaty forces in the southeast, General Prout, had the worst possible reputation. His leadership lacked professional capacity. Rampant indiscipline, treachery and traitorous behaviour within his command gave rise to adverse publicity during the Civil War, and extremely strained relations with GHQ ensued. The Free State army had remained at its professional nadir from the start of the Civil War until 1923, when organisation, discipline and leadership improved.[100]

GHQ chastised Prout accordingly: 'Your officers and men are letting us down at a critical moment and throwing away the fruits of months of work', while on 13 October 1922 it alleged that 'indiscipline is reported to be common among our troops especially in the Clonmel district . . . a deputation consisting of the mayor and town clerk recently interviewed Major General McGrath. They reported a very poor condition of affairs in this area, charging our men with drunkenness etc.' A Callan priest told Cosgrave, leader of the Free State government, that Prout 'is too weak as well as too guileless to handle traitorous or semi-mutinous incompetents'.[101]

The worst feature of this was the treachery of officers, and in some cases commanding officers, and absolute indiscipline of the troops under their control. For instance Callan, Thomastown and Mullinavat, as well as Carrick, were quickly surrendered and handed over to the anti-Treaty troops led by Tom Barry. Hopkinson states:

> Phelan, the Free State Army's Intelligence Officer, put Callan's capture down to the lack of discipline of the pro-Treaty troops and the failings of the local

> O/C Captain Barrett . . . the pro-treaty O/Cs at Callan and Thomastown, Somers and Kerwick, agreed to hand over their posts when their commissions expired on the 6 December. Information on the activity of pro-Treaty flying columns had previously been given to the other side by Somers, Kerwick and Captain Kelly, the O/C of Mooncoin barracks. The Command Intelligence Officer [CIO] reported on the 16 December: the procedure for betrayal was the same in all cases, he (Somers) entertained the three Garrisons, shaking hands with the Officer in Charge, having a party of Irregulars with him in full National Army uniform.[102]

Extreme lassitude, treachery, misbehaviour, a lack of faith in the military capacity of junior officers' leadership and a belief that the anti-Treaty army possessed superior intelligence sources caused constant worry to Free State commanders. While this situation prevailed mostly in Cork and Kerry, the vast majority of the people wanted peace.

The distribution of the British army's Irish command, as in spring 1920, justifies academic comment in connection with both the Anglo-Irish War and the Civil War. It is clear from the distribution state that most of the British brigades were stationed between Dublin and Cork.[103] The Anglo-Irish War was essentially a Munster and Dublin city affair. After Seán MacEoin's arrest and the consequent decline in military activity in his isolated stronghold in County Longford, Collins wrote: 'Cork will be fighting alone now.' Patrick Hogan, later the Free State Minister for Agriculture, claimed that 'no shots were fired in the war in twenty of the twenty six counties.'[104] A large proportion of the west saw very little fighting, while the midlands, the area north of Dublin and the prosperous farming counties of Kildare, Carlow and Wicklow were virtually inactive. Kilkenny, Waterford and Wexford were much the same, while Kerry was ready to fight only when the truce came.[105]

Dan Bryan's capacity to use intelligence proved devastating to the anti-Treaty forces in Dublin during the Civil War, as Hopkinson explains:

> The outlook for the republican IRA in the capital was to remain a bleak one. Arrests were frequent, partly because old colleagues knew where they were to be found. John Cullenan recalled: 'It was difficult to stop at home, for Dan Bryan our former I/O knew us all, and he also knew all our haunts. I didn't stay at home. Battalion and company organisation in the city had been broken up, and it took several weeks before a flying column could be set up in South Dublin.'[106]

In a report to Liam Lynch dated 6 August Ernie O'Malley stated: 'One has to be patient here, but certainly the circumstances are most peculiar and it is very difficult to counteract enemy espionage. Dublin is very severely tried.' Similarly, Hopkinson outlines how quickly after the start of the Civil War Oscar Traynor and a number of other senior officers in Dublin were arrested, on 27 July. O'Malley admitted: 'Petty jealousy, insubordination and organised opposition have prevented columns which he instructed to operate from doing anything active.' Todd Andrews summed up the situation in a characteristic and blunt manner: 'Things were hopeless in Dublin. Only a few young fellows active', while *An t-Óglach* stated in January 1923: 'It had not entered the wildest . . . dreams of the Irregulars that they could capture or hold any position in Dublin city at any time since July.'[107]

Military Intelligence: Its Collaborative Role with Government Ruthlessness in the Civil War

The 1922 election, in which both factions in the impending Civil War attempted to fix an acceptable outcome by means of an electoral pact, resulted in an anti-Treatyite vote of 21.3 per cent as against 38.5 per cent for pro-Treatyites and 39.7 per cent for Labour, Farmers' Party and Independents. The latter three were effectively pro-Treaty. De Valera acknowledged that an election immediately prior to the Civil War would see the defeat of the anti-Treaty side, as did his election pact with Collins. Yet perversely, the anti-Treaty side fought and lost a war, and sacrificed the support of many more of its followers. The war was scarcely over when, in the face of incredible odds, the anti-Treatyites returned a remarkably high poll at a general election in 1923, with Sinn Féin achieving 27.4 per cent of the vote. It was a remarkable result for a party that had just been involved in a rebellion against the established government, whose president and 1,200 activists were in jail, and which maintained an abstentionist policy. The result indicated a solid base on which to build successful future challenges to the pro-Treaty parties, particularly its main rival, Cumann na nGaedheal, which polled 39 per cent.[108] Lee quantifies corresponding seat figures as follows: Cumann na nGaedheal, sixty-three seats; Sinn Féin, forty-four; Labour, fifteen; Others, thirty-one.[109] Neeson believes the vote showed that, whatever about the effect of the Treaty and the Civil War, a strong minority of the people still supported the anti-Treaty side.[110]

After the initial stages of the Civil War the guerrilla tactics employed by the anti-Treaty troops were the only viable ones. The pro-Treaty forces controlled all the major centres of population, transport and communications system, the bureaucracy and the national treasury, but the June election of 1923 showed they enjoyed a much reduced majority support. Sabotage, arson and assassination made the country hard to govern.

O'Halpin explains the flawed intelligence system that still existed up to spring 1923 in the pro-Treaty army. It remained largely the preserve of the commands, where progress depended on the initiative of individual IOs and the interest of local commanders. Contact with army intelligence, at headquarters level, was a matter of chance. Dublin-centricity did not work satisfactorily, even though the army intelligence system at headquarters and the initiative of local commanders should have made it easier in the capital. Operations were complicated due to differing priorities. O'Halpin conveys Bryan's concerns:

> Bryan complained many years later that, for most of the Civil War, intelligence headquarters

> completely failed in its proper function of co-ordination, analysis and distribution. This he attributed to a pervasive raiding mentality, with armed officers hanging around the office, hoping the next tip off would give them premises to search or a suspect to arrest, instead of leaving such action to the CID. Bryan maintained that local sources, such as the discovery of the IRA's plan to destroy railway bridges around Dublin, were not properly exploited, and that the thousands of IRA documents seized in raids were never adequately appraised. He believed that the inevitable consequence was a lost chance to crush the anti-treatyite military campaign in the autumn of 1922.[111]

O'Halpin also argues that the indifferent performance of the army intelligence organisation gave cause for concern. In February 1923 the Army Council called for a scheme for military, secret service, foreign intelligence to be submitted at the earliest possible moment. A week later it directed that all captured documents should be forwarded to headquarters, a significant step towards the development of a central intelligence bureau, yet again Dublin-centric. He makes the telling point that these orders presaged a major reorganisation at the end of April 1923, just days after the republicans formally abandoned the fight.

Despite the army's alleged military and other failings, to the world the government presented a united and uncompromising face. After the sudden deaths in quick succession, in August 1922, of Griffith and Collins, the government pursued its aims with unwavering and ruthless will; possession of arms was made a capital offence. Its aim was to defeat the IRA and crush social disorder. But government unwillingness to curb the murder of prisoners, detention of republicans and summary execution of four unconvicted republican leaders in December 1922 transgressed its legal powers. Military courts dispensed justice in a cursory fashion between November 1922 and May 1923; in one instance evidence recorded on a single sheet of foolscap resulted in seventy-seven republican executions.[112]

The government claimed outrage at its pro-Treaty army killings, but was not unduly critical of those perpetrated by Oriel House, the CID satellite, a plain-clothes unit responsible for a number of murders during and immediately after the Civil War. The motives for many killings were also obscure, with personal vendettas behind some of the most notorious actions. There seems to be no evidence, according to O'Halpin, that any ministers were implicated, either directly or indirectly, in sanctioning this terror. They can, however, be fairly criticised for the public equanimity with which they greeted unequivocal and repeated evidence of murder by government agencies.

The government might well have won without recourse to the measures used, and without the various atrocities for which its forces were responsible.[113] But at some point or other it had to meet force with greater force. Death sentences and executions broke the IRA's morale. People accepted the use of such draconian laws as necessary for the suppression of disorder caused by the lawless and undisciplined ruthlessness of the IRA's own campaign.[114] The end of the Civil War saw the anti-Treaty forces dumping its arms, as ordered by IRA chief of staff Frank Aiken. The government strategy set a grim precedent which some future government would have to confront in the event of disorder.[115]

The unrest caused to the government concerning various overtures by the anti-Treaty forces, since January 1923, to the Bolshevik organisations throughout Europe and in Russia in the quest for both money and arms provoked Cosgrave to speak publicly. Soviet denial was almost certainly true given their lack of interest in Ireland.

O'Halpin cites documents captured which suggest that during the Civil War the government had three main classes of information on republican activities in Europe and America. The first was the intelligence obtained by its own forces in Ireland through interrogation of prisoners, interception of correspondence, and analysis of captured documents; the second came directly from a handful of Irish officials abroad; while the third was that provided by the British government, which came from British intelligence agencies, British diplomats and consuls, and from material passed to the British by friendly governments. O'Halpin believes the British continued to be Dublin's principal external source of intelligence on republicanism abroad. In addition, as the new state consolidated its standing internationally, a certain amount of information came directly from foreign governments, police and security agencies.[116]

The defensive mindset of the anti-Treaty leadership and strategy presaged inevitable defeat. The morale of the troops inevitably suffered, and the initiative passed to the opposite side, which saw an increase of 50 per cent in their forces in the field and a consequent boost for morale.[117] Tom Barry, one of the outstanding anti-Treaty military leaders, felt that other leaders on the anti-Treaty side were a joke in a revolutionary movement.[118] Neeson cites an unidentified officer of the East Cork Brigade as having said that at no time did he see a plan of attack. He says they never took over proper control of communications and that there was a complete absence of organised military efficiency.[119] Victory for the pro-Treatyites was due to distinct advantages they held: a clear policy, a common purpose, a united leadership and action, and the winning of the 'hearts and minds' that ensured them a superior intelligence quota.

The latter was made easier by the persistent condemnation of the anti-Treaty side by the Catholic Church. There was nothing extraordinary about the Church taking sides, as it had done many times throughout Irish history. But it resulted in many anti-Treatyites returning to their homes, with the remainder, to a greater or lesser extent, suffering serious moral doubt.[120]

All over the country harried anti-Treaty troops hid their arms, and control of the pro-Treatyites became absolute. The anti-Treaty side had attempted under de Valera to negotiate equitable conditions in respect of their peace agreement, but those conditions were not conceded. The anti-Treaty Cabinet and Army Council met on 13–14 May and admitted that the situation from a military point of view was beyond hope and agreed to end the war. They never formally surrendered; they dumped arms. Executions without trial of seventy-seven anti-Treaty prisoners forced their comrades to take the action they did. Pragmatic anti-Treaty leaders such as Barry, Breen and de Valera would have brought this pointless campaign to an end sooner, but the irredentist influence of Liam Lynch as commander in chief was a stumbling block, until his death in an operation mounted by the pro-Treaty troops in the Knockmealdown Mountains. The ceasefire solved none of the problems that the Treaty brought; indeed it aggravated them instead. The pro-Treaty party emerged the stronger, with an uncompromising devotion to the Agreement. The anti-Treaty side, meanwhile, emerged with their ideals intact, but still without a civic political campaign or common leadership.[121]

MICHAEL COLLINS/CATHAL BRUGHA CONTRETEMPS

Collins was ever the pragmatic arch-conspirator who believed that his goals could be attained by intrigue, secrecy and violence. His methodology was one of using absolute force to inflict the most rather than suffer the most. He literally renounced Terence MacSwiney's self-proclaimed epitaph that those who could endure the most rather than inflict it would in the end win out. Brugha adopted MacSwiney's philosophy, which inevitably led to his death in the early days of the Civil War.[122]

Cathal Brugha was an implacable irrational irredentist in respect of the Easter insurrection in 1916, throughout the War of Independence, and for the initial week in which he was instrumental in starting and fighting the Civil War. He was intractable, even megalomaniac to the point of believing at the commencement of the Civil War that his willing death, disdaining any form of self-defence at the very end, would be the blood sacrifice that would also end the Civil War *quam celerrime*. He was wrong in that belief. Collins was as irredentist as he was, possessing the same ultimate objective: de Valera's concept of an independent, undivided island nation state. Collins was, however, devoid of the same purist ideas as Brugha, but rather the supreme pragmatist who did not disdain from using covert means in extremis to gain his ultimate objective. His capacity for intrigue and secrecy alienated de Valera, Griffith and Liam Lynch and deteriorated to hatred on Brugha's part. Such alienation impeded his judgemental capacity. At the heart of their difference lay the IRB. Cathal Brugha shared de Valera's view that the nascent state should not embrace the IRB, and neither had any respect for secret organisations. Serious differences arose with Collins in regard to the acceptance of the Treaty.

Collins had very little option but to attack the Four Courts on 22 June 1922. Within a day of the subsequent bombardment, the fissure arising from the vote taken in favour of the Treaty split not alone the IRA but also the IRB. Collins retained literally full field control of the pro-Treaty forces, while Brugha, de Valera and Austin Stack joined the Dublin Brigade and were soon elected members of the general staff of the anti-Treaty forces. The bombarding of the Four Courts continued throughout Wednesday and Thursday 28 and 29 June until midday on Friday. The garrison surrendered at 3.30 p.m., and thereafter pro-Treaty forces captured all anti-Treaty outposts in Dublin. Cathal Brugha was killed, having ordered his garrison to escape, arguably deliberately fulfilling a death wish consistent with his quintessentially fundamentalist republicanism and irredentism.[123]

Ó Dochartaigh's eulogy of Cathal Brugha's life and death, his general characteristics as a man, a soldier, a government administrator, his half-hearted membership of the IRB, and his refusal to reconstitute the IRB after the release of the prisoners of the insurrection in 1917 may indicate to what extent Brugha's wounds had hardened his intransigent anti-British stance.[124] Collins modified IRB doctrine to ensure the survival of the organisation; Tom Barry's doctrine on guerrilla warfare was based on a similar principle.

Despite Ó Dochartaigh's lionising eulogy of his uncle, throughout the book he accepts that Béaslaí recognised basic errors in Brugha's traits of character. Cathal Brugha lacked judgement in regard to policy matters; he was headstrong to a point of often accepting unreasonable formulae and misplaced opinions as matters of principle. Tom Barry and Ernie O'Malley did not easily interface with him. Brugha was of the opinion that nothing could happen unless it was proclaimed to be allowable by the headquarters of the IRA. But nothing could be further from the truth, as Collins so well knew. The commanders on the ground were virtually bishops within their own dioceses and did not always look for permission to commence or finish operations within their own areas of operation and sometimes outside it.

Ó Dochartaigh describes Brugha's interviews with Tom Barry and Ernie O'Malley. Barry was openly castigative, stating that Brugha asked almost monosyllabic questions, while Barry was given virtually monosyllabic answers to any of his own queries. Barry felt that Brugha was tight-lipped and simply did not believe in having any interviews with people. He gained the impression that Brugha was more interested in his ministry than in the policies or operations of the IRA or of defensive measures. Ernie O'Malley had much the same idea, but excuses Brugha by stating that, in his opinion, Cathal Brugha was simply not a man given to advice or conferences, and was most certainly not a committee monger.

These men simply reflected a microcosm of different mentalities during those turbulent times. Mulcahy admitted that he also had the same difficulty with Brugha even though he was his Assistant Minister for Defence. He had the full advantage of intercommunication with Collins, and Collins would give the information on anything he needed to know.[125] Ó Dochartaigh felt that Brugha thought he appointed all members to the various posts within the defence ministry. Collins not alone appointed such members, but ensured they were members of the IRB.

Ronan Fanning considers Collins to have been the most accomplished and successful revolutionary in modern Irish history.[126] Henry Kissinger, writing of the American debacle in Vietnam, has best made the point: 'The guerilla wins if he does not lose. The conventional army loses if it does not win.'[127] One might compare the hindsight war psychology of Kissinger with that of both Michael Collins and Tom Barry, but not so that of Brugha! His was quite the reverse of Collins in his identification of what the rhetoric of republicanism meant. In Collins' words it was the freedom to achieve freedom of the entire country.

Hopkinson and Neeson throw further light on the differences that existed between Brugha and Collins. With the probable exception of Collins, Hopkinson states that the character of the conflict exacerbated divisions between the attitudes of GHQ in Dublin and the fighting men in the provinces. He adds that Cork column leaders like Tom Barry and Seán Moylan were quick to label their divisional OCs, Liam Lynch and Mulcahy, as pen pushers rather than fighters, a somewhat harsh observation, especially in the person of Lynch.

Tensions were heightened by personal animosities that had a much greater effect than in a conventional army. Mulcahy also had abrasive relations with the South Tipperary Brigade leadership, and with Seán O'Hegarty in Cork No. 1 Brigade. Despite his good personal relations with Collins and Mulcahy, Liam Lynch declared that in the Anglo-Irish War GHQ 'showed all-round inefficiency and gave very little help to the country'. Mick Leahy of Cork No. 1 Brigade told Ernie O'Malley that 95 per cent of the GHQ staff were a crowd of fossils.[128]

Hopkinson throws further light on the mental dichotomy between Brugha and Collins. Brugha and de Valera held that the new government could only impose its authority over the military if IRB influence was ended. Following the Anglo-Irish War the IRB changed its constitution to accommodate recognition of the Dáil government. General Mulcahy, who was by then a member of the Supreme Council, recollected that after

March 1918 the IRB issued no orders on military matters; such orders were essentially a matter for the local commanders.

Florence O'Donoghue affirmed that the IRB's significance was less in its numerical strength than in 'the character, integrity and loyalty of its personnel, in its water tight organisation, and its genius for working inside other organisations'. IRB men dominated the IRA's GHQ staff, but such control was much less easily achieved in the provinces.[129] Hopkinson states that the majority of Cork Brigade officers were members. Tipperary and the west, however, were badly served in this sense. In Munster there was a deliberate policy of recruiting key officers, and Liam Deasy recalled that 'we put any men of importance in West Cork into the IRB.' Therefore the movement was meant to act as a revolutionary elite.[130]

Brugha and de Valera's disagreement with the very nature of the IRB's modus operandi was given expression, especially during the period of the truce. They referred particularly to Collins and the IRB role within the IRA. Before the truce Brugha had persistently complained about the methods by which the IRB had purchased arms from Scotland, hinting at corruption. He also had a singular disagreement with Mulcahy at the time and had demonstrated his personal bitterness by reproving Mulcahy and Collins for inefficiency and possible negligence. Their alleged inefficiency allowed a deputy chief of staff's appointment to be made, of Mulcahy's choosing. Brugha disagreed with not being informed of the killing of Mrs Lindsay and her butler by the IRA in Cork, shot as spies. One must take into account, however, that Mulcahy and Collins were as unaware of it as Brugha, who was somewhat begrudging of some members of the delegation who went to negotiate the Treaty in England. Brugha is quoted by Hopkinson as using Liam Mellows as Director of Purchases to challenge Collins' control of arms sources. During the Treaty negotiations Brugha was thought to be encouraging arms purchases in Britain, which caused considerable embarrassment to the Irish negotiators and was against the terms of the truce.[131] Intrigue abounded. The Machiavellian intelligence capacity of Collins was to emerge victorious during the Civil War; however, the high priest of Machiavellism, de Valera, lay in waiting.

Mulcahy and M. J. Costello (who was to play a very important role in both military intelligence and its intrinsic relationship with operations throughout the history of the Free State army, up to and including the end of the Emergency) both thought that Brugha was in touch with certain disaffected sections of the army which had poor relations with GHQ.[132] The Treaty, and control of the IRB by Collins, as against the adamant reservations of Brugha in respect of the IRB, led to their disagreement by the time the Civil War started.

Neeson notes that the IRB was again infiltrating the army as it had the Irish Volunteer movement before the 1916 Rising. He accepts that while political differences could have been expected to arise anyway in the normal course of political events, these were deeper and darker shadows. He states that Collins made the IRB, of which he would soon become head centre, his power base. Collins held the view that the president of the Supreme Council of the IRB remained the president of the

Republic, despite the inevitable rivalry between himself and de Valera, president of both Sinn Féin and the Volunteers. Collins opposed the idea of the army being brought under the political control of the Dáil, which in fact occurred following a proposal from Brugha. Collins was not, of course, opposed to its being under the control of the IRB, and many army officers were – and remained – IRB men. The most interesting fact that emerged was that the IRB did not relinquish its claim that its president was president of the Republic. Neeson cites General Seán MacEoin's contribution in *With the IRA in the Fight for Freedom*, stressing its importance.

> From the date of the Proclamation of the Republic in 1916, until the assembly of the first Dáil in January 1919, the Government of the Republic was in the hands of the Supreme Council of the IRB, to whose President all members had sworn obedience and allegiance as the Titular Head of the Republic . . . as the struggle continued there was a danger that the elected government and Dáil might at any moment find themselves exterminated by enemy action. Should this occur, the Supreme Council held itself in readiness to carry on the fight as a caretaker government.[133]

Neeson maintains that MacEoin's important statements do not appear to have received due attention from historians. They also demonstrate the extent of Collins' power base in the IRB and the extent to which the IRB is likely to have influenced events up to 1924. While de Valera was in the United States in 1919 and 1920,

Collins strengthened his IRB power base within the IRA enormously. He became Director of Organisation of the army, and other IRB officers acquired prominent positions as Director of Communications and General Secretary.[134]

The IRB, according to Ó Muirthile, was essentially Collins' elite headquarter circle, and was Dublin-centric, with little to indicate that Collins or his fellow brothers knew much about the organisation beyond the Pale.[135] Yet the IRB was of crucial importance at national level. Their control of GHQ, and Collins' ascendancy within the movement, gave them a privileged position within the power structures of the revolution. This privileged elite gathered around Collins and became an important subculture within the movement.[136] Theoretically they controlled the army, and also ministerial and sub-ministerial appointments through the influence of Collins. The IRB, as tentacles of power brokers, ruled supreme, particularly at GHQ. They enjoyed the mystique of power that all secret organisations inculcate in the uninitiated and possessed the potential to realise real power within the revolutionary movement. They were central players in a centralising regime and were guided by the risen star, Michael Collins.

On balance Collins' policy, embracing the pragmatic, efficient work ethic, was undoubtedly more desirable than Cathal Brugha's brand of sacrifice typified by failure.[137] The decisive battle of the Civil War was fought between two opposing elites in Dublin, to capture the hearts and minds of the people. The pro-Treatyites were determined that opposition to the civilian government in the Free State would be defeated in such a way as to ensure that there was no reconciliation between the militarists, and no second revolution.[138] Both Collins and Brugha were of one mind in relation to the achievement of a Republic. The difference was that Brugha was both a doctrinaire and an irrational irredentist.

Winston Churchill's observation on Collins is of significance. 'Successor to a sinister inheritance, reared among fierce conditions and moving through ferocious times, he supplied those qualities of action and personality without which the foundation of Irish nationhood would not have been re-established.'[139]

The Intelligence Network during the Civil War

The intelligence networks in place on either side in the Civil War could not compare with those set up by Michael Collins and Florence O'Donoghue. After all, those on opposite sides were former comrades during the War of Independence, and as such had ample intelligence on one another. Dan Bryan made Dublin an impossible place for the anti-Treaty troops to find safe houses, such was his knowledge within his area of operations during the War of Independence.[140] Equally so, in west Cork and Kerry the pro-Treaty side found that the people favoured the other side, making intelligence a difficult task. Collins' loss as Director of Intelligence when he became commander in chief was of monumental proportions to the pro-Treaty side. The Squad, whom he trusted so much, were essentially gunmen, not men of Collins' intelligence or experience or capacity for organisation of intelligence. David Neligan, however, was qualified. Collins trusted him implicitly to infiltrate Dublin Castle, and convince A. W. Cope, in the extant British secret service, of Collins' determination to pursue and win the Civil War. Neligan states that: 'Mick Collins sent me into Oriel House, a kind of intelligence bureau for the new government, after the treaty.'[141]

Hopkinson sheds light on why the intelligence capacity of the pro-Treatyites deteriorated.[142] He cites Cathal O'Shannon on the difficulties of establishing a responsible intelligence system in the new regular army: 'You cannot always make a good officer in anything like a regular army out of a good guerilla fighter.'[143] Realising that O'Shannon's inference was true, Collins employed former British army officers to staff and special services. He posted his former colleagues to the intelligence department in Oriel House, and thereafter to various appointments throughout the South, in all of which they had difficulty in adjusting to regular soldiering.[144]

Northern Pogroms

Collins was anguished by the draconian laws and vicious pogroms against Northern nationalists, where floggings and death sentences were normal and discriminatory. His angst resulted in ambivalent actions with regard to the strict procedure of the law. Vehement protests to Craig and the British Cabinet coincided with an arrangement with Liam Lynch, commander in chief of the anti-Treaty forces, for the transfer of arms to Northern IRA units to defend the Catholic population. Collins' emissary to Sweeney in Donegal arranged for 400 rifles to be taken to the Northern Volunteers by Dan McKenna and Johnny Haughey.[145]

An affidavit of Thomas A. Kelly, San Giovanni, Cornageeha, Sligo, gives further credence to Kenneth Griffith and Timothy O'Grady's comments on Collins' pre-Treaty ambivalence in respect of the transfer of arms to the Northern command of the IRA.[146] The Northern command comprised the 1st Northern Division under General Officer Commanding Joe Sweeney, later a major general in the army;[147] the 2nd Northern Division under Officer Commanding Eoin O'Duffy (Second Officer Commanding Charlie Daly from Kerry was later executed during the Civil War by a firing squad organised by one of his best friends, Major General Sweeney); the 3rd Northern Division under Tom Morris, a former major in the British army; and the 4th Northern Division under Officer Commanding Joe McKelvey, later executed in Mountjoy prison.

By 1921 Thomas A. Kelly was attached to the 2nd Northern Division as divisional engineer. He outlines that Dan McKenna, who was later chief of staff of the Irish army from 1940 to 1949, was deputy officer commanding the division and claims that considerable activity took place later in 1920 and up to the truce the following year.[148] Kelly instances a bank robbery at Maghera, and a sum of about £1,700 purloined to pay the debts incurred by the divisions. The money was later settled by GHQ and all outstanding accounts were paid, and the money, being no longer required, was returned to the Maghera bank by General Eoin O'Duffy, liaison officer for Ulster. It became clear, according to Kelly, that officers within the divisions feared that the six counties would be excluded from any settlement made within the Treaty. He also states that the troops operated in those six counties up until the terms of the truce took effect.

At Christmas 1921 the RIC and the special constabulary raided IRA training camps at Grenagh in the Sperrin Mountains, and from then until August 1922, Kelly claims that the struggle in the six counties was intense, and quite successful from the IRA point of view.[149] The vast majority of the Northern IRA supported Collins, with the exception of Charlie Daly, a divisional O/C who failed to carry his division with him. Kelly's affidavit continues that he cannot recall any officer or members giving serious consideration to the merits of the Treaty or the alternatives proposed, and his definite recollection is that, faced with failure at that point, they sought the source they felt would offer the best hope in the future – they placed their faith in the hands of Collins.

Kelly states that supplies of equipment, ammunition and explosives arrived from GHQ at Beggar's Bush Barracks after the signing of the Treaty and that regular payments were made to staff officers. Kelly reported to Dublin in March 1922 to meet General O'Duffy, then chief of staff, and secured 200 Enfield rifles and 100 rounds of ammunition per rifle. All these decisions were made with the knowledge and approval of Collins. The rifles and ammunition were brought by army transport to Donegal and later moved into County Tyrone in a compartment of an oil tanker. Only one member of the

IRA escorted the consignment through the special constabulary barricade at Strabane/Lifford bridge. He was Johnny Haughey, father of Charles Haughey, who was minister for finance at the time the affidavit was made.[150] Kelly believed that Collins and O'Duffy took a huge risk in supplying these weapons and ammunition, all of which were part of the arms handed over by the British forces to the Provisional Government. Kelly also recognised the valuable assistance given by the South to the intensive struggle waged by the IRA in the six counties throughout the greater part of 1922, with operations carried out along the border in an effort to relieve the pressure on those operating inside the six counties.

Kelly attended a special meeting as ordered, in the officers' mess in Portobello Barracks, Dublin, in August 1922, at which the government and the army were represented by Collins, then commander in chief, who presided, Richard Mulcahy who had resumed the office of chief of staff, Gearóid O'Sullivan, Adjutant General, and (he thinks) Seán McMahon, the Quartermaster General (QMG). The situation in the six counties was examined fully and carefully, with many views expressed, often quite heatedly. In Kelly's view the only statement of importance was the final summation of Collins, which, over the years, remained clear in Kelly's mind:

> With this Civil War on my hands I cannot give you the help I wish to give and mean to give. I now propose to call off hostilities in the North and to use the political arm against Craig so long as it is of use. If that fails the treaty can go to hell and we will all start again.

Collins realised that many members of the IRA who could not remain in the organisation in the North would be accommodated in the South. After Collins' death, General Mulcahy honoured the promises made by Collins; many Northern IRA joined the army in Hare Park in the Curragh, others the Garda Síochána. Some joined the anti-Treaty forces, while the remainder emigrated, mainly to the US. Kelly states that by 1923 the Northern group had ceased to exist and he concludes that Collins did not let Northern nationalists fend for themselves but provided help to what extent he could.

TWO

Post-Civil War Strategic Military Planning, 1924–36

Political Maelstrom: Intelligence and Intrigue

The *idée fixe* of the pro-Treaty elite after September 1922 had been to constitutionalise and centralise power in the Free State. Richard Mulcahy, chief of staff of the army, planned various measures, other than constitutional, to redeem the defeated IRA. The feasibility of Mulcahy's plan was questionable. He proposed a reconstituted IRB, never considering the fact that it was a secret society, potentially dangerous to the stability of the nascent state. Mulcahy showed a profound lack of political acumen, which indicated an incomplete understanding of the political culture within which he was operating.

The fear that democracy could be overturned by dedicated minorities was central to the whole defence of the new state. Profound paranoia was a component of new regimes in post-war Europe, beset by subversive minorities, an all-pervasive fear of secret societies, and the havoc they continued to cause. Bolshevism, the murder of the Polish prime minister during winter 1922/3 and revolutions in Bulgaria and Albania contributed to government paranoia, complicated by the anti-Masonic attitudes and Catholic Church worry about every organisation outside its own ultramontanist strictures.[1]

The Directorate of Intelligence continued to monitor the activity of the anti-Treaty IRA, both free and as released from internment. Reports of such activity were circulated under confidential cover to members of the Army Council, and included the chief of staff, Adjutant General and Quartermaster General. Such reports illustrate the concern among army intelligence of the importance of continued monitoring of the anti-Treaty IRA. These reports are attached as Appendix V.

Arguably the most dangerous post-Civil War threat to the stability of the state was the old IRA. The senior officer, Liam Tobin, led the army mutiny in 1924. Intrigue followed intrigue in the immediate aftermath of the mutiny, and Kevin O'Higgins used the powers he had taken unto himself, having persuaded President Cosgrave to remain in bed, ostensibly sick, to force the Army Council to resign. These had been scapegoated as having been the source of the discontent.[2]

O'Halpin notes that the Director of Intelligence achieved a significant coup concerning the detection and rapid crushing of disaffection within the army in November 1924.[3] It took the form of a half-baked plot among some army officers to issue an ultimatum to the government, but army intelligence officers had little difficulty in uncovering the plan.[4] Its leading lights were hopelessly indiscreet – Bryan remarked that their scheme was launched 'in a haze of whiskey – and they were promiscuous talkers on the telephone'. The Irish saying '*scéitheann an fhíon an fhírinne*' (wine gives away the truth) seems appropriate. The conspiracy/ mutiny was a fiasco. It could have been disastrous for the country, according to O'Halpin, and it and other less dramatic episodes of indiscipline convinced the government that the military was not under proper control.[5] The army accepted the restrictions, however, and made the transition from a politically involved guerrilla force to a professional disciplined national army. O'Halpin argues that army intelligence, having uncovered the mutiny plot, later discovered plans to murder the Minister for Home Affairs, Kevin O'Higgins. O'Halpin's view corroborates that of Terence de Vere White that O'Higgins' murder was no chance happening. O'Higgins did not exempt the army from reform. In 1925–26 army intelligence was ordered to concentrate strictly on military intelligence and on internal army security. Political crime, subversion and protection of politicians became the exclusive responsibility of the police, to whom army intelligence transferred some 30,000 personal and subject files.[6] Army intelligence also relinquished control of its informants to the police.

While the Director of Intelligence always had direct access to the chief of staff and the Minister for Defence, the intelligence section (G2) became something of a backwater until 1938. Bryan's 1936 strategic paper, 'Fundamental Factors', forced the politicians to deal with reality. G2, emasculated as it was, did not completely stick to its brief of conventional work on foreign armies. Army intelligence still maintained a watching brief on aspects of life overseas, especially military life and organisations, carefully debriefing army showjumping teams and keeping a stern intelligence brief on internal army security. This pertained particularly to the Blueshirt movement, originally founded as an ex-serviceman's organisation.

When responsibility for domestic security was transferred to the police, Dan Bryan, from the end of the Civil War, was considered to have comprised the secret service virtually on his own. Although moved out of military intelligence, he maintained unofficial contact with some of his old cohorts and kept an eye on affairs generally. In 1929 he sought the re-employment of a source formerly found trustworthy by the military intelligence section who had approached him with information on communist activities. The source maintained that the police did not take sufficient precautions to ensure his safety in his dealings with them. O'Halpin believes Bryan's view was the correct one but, as had become the norm, the proposal was ignored. Bryan is also credited by O'Halpin with defusing the incipient plot, two years later, among a minority of officers who talked of refusing to take orders from a Fianna Fáil government if such came to power following the 1932 election.

When that party did come to power in 1932 Bryan was ordered back to intelligence to destroy certain records, principally material on Civil War informants.[7] This led, despite his formidable record in intelligence against the republican movement up to 1925, to the Fianna Fáil government allowing him to return to the Intelligence Directorate in 1935.[8]

The mutiny demonstrated the maturity and stability of the army and civil–military relations, defining their parameters rather than establishing them. The general staff did not necessarily have to resign. It is not unlikely that most of the army would have followed Mulcahy and the general staff had they decided not to abide by O'Higgins' deviousness and have resignations forced upon them. It was, however, far from the last chapter in the saga of civil versus military authority in the Free State, as has sometimes been suggested: 'In 1927, 1931 and 1932 military officers contemplated coup d'état. However, the removal of the loose cannons in the old IRA organisation undoubtedly added to its stability.'[9] The army now obeyed politicians, even those arguably in the wrong. Mulcahy and the other generals deserve the plaudits that have been given to them as essentially good democrats.

O'Higgins lived in a culture of doubt, whispering accusations, tale-telling, and denigration of the warrior myth. He capitalised on every scintilla of evidence that cast aspersions, increased anxiety and damaged the army. This stemmed from his frustration at being unable to secure accurate information about the IRB, and so he began his morality campaign against the army. Given to fits of pique, he told an army enquiry that what likely happened at Kenmare – the physical and probably sexual attacks on the local doctor's two daughters – and the blatant revenge murders of anti-Treatyites, blown up at Ballyseedy Wood, could be blamed on General Paddy Daly, Captain Flood and a Captain Clarke.[10] Whether David Neligan's name can be added is a moot point. However, O'Higgins believed that they were guilty without any trial other than such enquiry as has been held. He also alluded to the incidence of venereal disease in the army, and in particular sexual crime, tabulated or insinuated, which could be defended by no member of the Cabinet or the regime. And, deprived of any other weapons with which to beat the army, O'Higgins used every covert method at his disposal with a vengeance. Such was his belief in the correctness of dismissing the army general staff, he declared that neither he nor the institutions of state would ever again take their stride from a soldier's boot.[11]

The Assassination of Kevin O'Higgins

Kevin O'Higgins was assassinated on Sunday 10 July 1927, on his way to Mass, by three IRA men, Archie Doyle, Tim Murphy and Bill Gannon. Kevin O'Higgins has been represented both as 'everything that evilly disposed people find inconvenient' and 'one of the most blood-guilty Irishmen of our generation'.[12] A civil war breeds unnatural hatreds and O'Higgins attracted the principal share. He was absolutely ruthless, as demonstrated in sanctioning the execution without trial of seventy-seven captured anti-Treaty fighters. These included Erskine Childers, Rory O'Connor (his best man just one month previously), Liam Mellows, Joe McKelvey and Richard Barrett.[13] When casting judgement on the character of O'Higgins, one must take cognisance of his belief that the anti-Treatyites planned to exterminate everyone of responsibility in the Provisional Government.[14]

O'Higgins/Archie Doyle: An Unresolved Enigma

Úna O'Higgins O'Malley infers in her autobiographical narrative that Archie Doyle, one of her father's killers, said that he had danced on her father's grave.[15] Doyle, a builder in Rathgar, was the leader of the group. His career and escapades with the IRA are documented by Uinseann MacEoin in his biography of Harry White,[16] in which White is mentioned on a total of eleven different pages.[17] White states that Doyle 'was one of the main movers in what was going on'.[18] By February 1942, Archie Doyle had been appointed to the post of IRA quarter-master general. He seemed to move between Dublin and the north of Ireland, impervious to any danger. The virtual demise of the IRA between 1943 and 1946 was the result of most of its important people being incarcerated.

White says of Doyle: 'Archie lasted for some time after that. I am not sure how he was run to earth, or if he was run to earth at all. He was such a seemingly colourless transparent person, he could merge into any group and cease to be noticed.'

The Assassination of Detective Sergeant O'Brien

The career of Detective Sergeant Dinny O'Brien constitutes a continuous linkage, from the insurrection in 1916 to his anti-Treaty Civil War role, unbroken IRA membership until 1933, his volte-face conversion to the Broy Harriers and ending with his assassination in 1942.

O'Brien, according to White, together with his brothers Larry and Paddy, saw action during the insurrection of 1916. He became as rapacious as the most dyed-in-the-wool Free State agent, and by 1942 had turned into a vicious and determined hunter. Archie Doyle decided he should be assassinated. According to White, Doyle had his own sources of information, one of them in Dublin Castle. O'Brien was duly killed outside his house on 29 September 1942. An interesting point is that O'Brien's bodyguard had been removed at his own request, and Doyle decided that it was an opportune time to strike.[19]

Doyle also seemed to know that Kevin O'Higgins had not been using an armed escort the day he was assassinated, and it was more than coincidence that his sources made him quite sure that O'Brien had also dispensed with his bodyguard. It is notable that Doyle is described as a seemingly colourless person who could merge into any group and cease to be noticed, not unlike Collins during the War of Independence. Doyle was also on the list for minor works contracts, as administered by the Board of Works, with whom he was employed. The board operated from Dublin Castle during the period in question. Dangerous times breed strange liaisons![20]

There is an uncanny resemblance between Doyle's capacity to gather such information from sources in Dublin Castle and Collins' access to the same types of sources some time previously. Doyle was never captured or interned during the Emergency years; the IRA were literally put out of commission by the combined intelligence systems of the Garda Special Branch and Bryan's G2.

The only reference to Kevin O'Higgins in Uinseann MacEoin's work refutes the allegation that Doyle danced on O'Higgins' grave.[21] On Sunday 10 July 1927 at Cross Avenue, Blackrock, Archie Doyle, accompanied by Billy Gannon, one of Collins' Squad, and Tim Murphy of Rathmines (later shot dead by undercover man Seán Harling at Woodpark Lodge, Dartry Road), shot Kevin O'Higgins, Minister for Justice of the Free State. Terence de Vere White does not believe it was a chance encounter. The men who killed O'Higgins, who was unarmed and alone, had carefully planned the execution.[22] Harry White stated to MacEoin that it was an operation said to have been considered but disregarded by George Gilmore, the brains of the movement. The unobtrusive and slight Doyle, meanwhile, although briefly held by the police at a hold-up at Kenny's builders in Donnycarney in the mid-1920s, remained in IRA headquarters staff as one of its senior officers until 1944.

Liam Burke can recall one afternoon in 1942 walking in Glasnevin Cemetery. Doyle pointed at O'Higgins' grave, remarking: 'There he is, six feet down.' It was his only reference to the episode. Years later, Doyle gave Harry White a short Webley revolver as a memento, and informed him that it was the one that shot O'Higgins. Conspiracy theories as to why Archie Doyle was never interned, having lived until 1980, remain unproven.

De Valera forthrightly condemned the O'Higgins killing.[23] The IRA should have heeded de Valera's words, a portent of his future plan to accept political democracy. He nevertheless cynically used the IRA to secure support for Fianna Fáil candidates in the 1932 and 1933 elections; he subsequently formed a government and virtually obliterated the IRA during his prolonged period in power.

David Neligan joined Collins' pro-Treaty army when the Four Courts fight triggered the beginning of the Civil War.[24] Hopkinson describes Neligan's continued existence as an intelligence officer, first for the army and then for the police, until he became a victim of the great political reshuffle in 1932. De Valera unceremoniously placed him in one of the safest sinecures of all, the Land Commission.[25] De Valera fully realised that, on taking power after the 1932 election, the IRA, which had helped him secure victory, would not accept Neligan, O'Duffy and others as comrades in arms. Neligan served in the Civil War as a Free State intelligence officer in Kerry,[26] and in its aftermath became one of the principal architects of the new state police force.[27] The army intelligence department, run by Professor Hogan out of Oriel House in Dublin, had lost its direction after the Civil War, which cannot have surprised Neligan. Professor Hogan asked Neligan, by then colonel, to report on what might be done with it. Neligan suggested that it should be entirely disbanded, but that those of its officers who were willing should be transferred to the police as detectives. Kevin O'Higgins was anxious that army control be transferred from Oriel House to the government. Neligan's suggestions were accepted and he was appointed to take charge of Dublin's detective branch. The DMP and assimilated former CID men were amalgamated into one force in 1925 to form the nucleus of the Garda Síochána. Neligan became head of its Special Branch for the entire Free State, a sensitive unnerving job, its principal brief being to hunt down what remained of the IRA. Neligan states that many of his prime targets were comrades from the pre-Treaty days, though old loyalties did nothing to decrease the enmity between the Free State and the republican position, which grew more bitter in the fifteen years following Aiken's orders to dump arms.[28]

Neligan wanted nothing to do with O'Duffy's plot to refuse to recognise the government in 1932. The latter drafted a document that was in effect a call to arms to unseat de Valera. He circulated it for supporting signatures among his comrades in the army and the police, but Neligan said he would have nothing to do with it.[29] Cosgrave, who believed parliamentary democracy was the only salvation for the fragile state, heard about O'Duffy's seditious document and anxiously summoned Neligan to report, but by then the brief life of that particular plot had come to an end, and Neligan reassured Cosgrave that there was nothing to worry about.[30]

De Valera underwent a metamorphosis, having consolidated his position with a snap election in 1933, commencing with a few key dismissals. He sacked Neligan first and then O'Duffy after the 1932 election. It is ironic that he appointed Colonel Éamon Broy, who, like Neligan, had spied for Collins within the ranks of G Division during the War of Independence. Broy had remained loyal to de Valera, and was now appointed to replace O'Duffy. He recruited from the IRA. The division he created, known as the Broy Harriers, eventually hounded republicans with remorseless tenacity, just as Neligan had. O'Duffy passed through the permutations of home-grown fascism until his return from Spain, where he had led an Irish pro-fascist brigade in a brief operational capacity during the Spanish Civil War. He died in 1944 and was accorded a state funeral by de Valera.[31] David Neligan served out his time in the Land Commission, until his retirement in 1964.[32]

After 1925, army intelligence no longer had any part to play in seeking or maintaining external sources of intelligence. An extract from the formal 'Request for Direction on Defence Policy, Defence Council of Executive, 22 July 1925' identifies the possible options for government in relation to defence policy, and some fundamental principles and facts in war and defence.[33]

- The development of our individuality as a nation; the gradual assumption of responsibility for defence and the development and organisation of our resources into a complete defensive machine.
- The organisation and maintenance of Defence Forces which would be an integral part of the British Imperial Forces, and would, in the event of war be controlled by the Imperial General Staff.
- The abandonment to England of responsibility against external enemies and the formation of a force to deal with internal disorders.[34]

The Council for Defence identified its concept of a modern war as follows:

> Modern war is not a war of armies; it is a war of peoples. The Nation as a whole, our industrial, administrative and agricultural activities, and our

> unarmed citizens are as much subject to attack as our Defence Forces, if such attack suits the ends of our opponents, and our defence must be the defence of our entire population and our vital activities. If the occasion demands we must be prepared to employ all our resources in our defence. Defence as thus visualised is more than actual combat; it is the struggle for the continuance of our national life, the preservation of our population, our resources, our institutions and our international position.[35]

The Executive Council's reply emphasised the size of the army being consistent with an army training directive capable of effecting both tactical and strategic roles. The reply lacked any mention of necessary economic measures to give practical effectiveness to its evasive policy directive. It stressed the primacy of the Executive Council, and cunningly referred to the Minister for Defence's secondary function to that of the Minister for External Affairs in international matters. The policy statement coincided with a similar directive to the Minister for Defence which included a rider as follows:

> In so far as the international aspect of the matter is concerned, the Minister for Defence in his capacity as a member of the Executive Council will be kept in touch with situations as they arise by the Minister for External Affairs, and the policy in each particular emergency will be decided by the Council as a whole.[36]

The period 1923 to 1932, the first decade of independence, saw the consolidation of the institutions of the new state and the development of a law-bound, democratic policy. This was achieved by the unashamed bypassing of constitutional safeguards in the name of public security. The army was deployed to dispense justice, using such expedience as internment without trial and intrusive domestic political surveillance in order to meet the continuing challenge from militant republicanism and the associated evil of communism.[37]

Theo Farrell describes the army in post-revolutionary Ireland, from 1922 onwards, as being in a feeble state in at least two senses. 'Politically . . . it attracted exceptionally low levels of government support and resources. Strategically . . . it sought to defend the State in a manner that even its own planners advised against.'[38] Farrell's assumption that the army's general staff would have taken an illogical stance in respect of their planners' estimate is questionable. Military commanders, as a norm, issue guidance to planning staff, in order to allow the staff to study and produce plans, tactical and strategic, to react to current and future events. Farrell gives no clarification of what exactly he means by his opaque expression.

While accepting his argument in respect of the low levels of government support and resources, his second thesis is questionable. Farrell also rejected contentions that Ireland did not really need a standing army. A holistic war strategy rather than guerrilla tactics was favoured by military planners. The state's legitimate international credibility depended on its capacity for organised resistance to invasion.[39] The army and other departments of state were under-resourced because the state could barely afford to maintain an army. Cutbacks in army expenditure were excessive and had serious implications for army intelligence. The Department of Finance refused to finance plans to establish a national radio station.

The policy of the Department of Finance was one of fiscal rectitude,[40] which, according to Farrell, was the primary reason behind the enfeeblement of the army. He quotes Ronan Fanning,[41] who argues that the massive expansion of the army during the Civil War in 1922–23 placed a huge burden on public finances, and one could not but acknowledge the logic of Fanning's statement.

Maryann Gialanella Valiulis contends that the army mutiny of 1924 emphasised the importance of unquestioned obedience to government by the army and its commanders. Out of the crisis of mutiny came the affirmation that Ireland was to be governed by the will of the people, and not by the dictates of her generals.[42] The quelling of the mutiny did not rest easy with the Executive Council, whose members considered the military action in suppressing mutiny to be in defiance of the council's appeasement policy. The council's lack of political moral courage and consequent deviousness was patently evident.

The ministers demanded the resignation of the Army Council and the dismissal of General Mulcahy from his ministerial position. Mulcahy resigned in protest, not knowing that his colleagues had already demanded his head. The Adjutant General and Quartermaster General also resigned. The chief of staff, Seán McMahon, asked the government to give their grounds for demanding his resignation, and was promptly dismissed.[43]

Valiulis also states that the formation and development of the Irish Free State was directly influenced by the mutiny, having a significant impact on both its political structure and its resounding affirmation of the supremacy of civilian authority over the army. Her statement is of dual significance insofar as the title of commander-in-chief of the defence forces has never since been vested in a military officer; indeed, the chief of staff is virtually what is implied in the title.[44] Separate powers are vested in all members of the general staff. Officers of the general staff and general officers commanding commands or brigade groups have retained rights of access to the Minister for Defence since 1925. This denies the concentration of power in any one individual, an astute move by the early political leaders of the state.

Kevin O'Higgins seized the opportunity to emasculate the military intelligence establishment, which was not re-established until 1932 – in a minimalised format. Valiulis continues:

> The enduring success of the Free State maintaining liberal democratic values is due, in part, to the fact that the revolutionary leaders understood and were part of both traditions. Thus, the legacy which the future political leaders in Ireland inherited is a synthesis of the Irish Parliamentary Party and the Irish Republican Brotherhood, a fact which helps to explain the impressive degree of stability which the Irish Free State was able to achieve.[45]

Lee contends that the Cabinet's motives in 1925 provide a telling insight to its political philosophy.

> A cabinet that had failed to crush the real mutiny, and then postured in public as defenders of democracy by dismissing those who did take decisive action against the mutineers, and who posed no threat to democracy, showed that it had little to learn about the art of political manoeuvring at this level. The army mutiny was an unedifying episode as much for the opportunist cynicism it exposed among the civilian politicians as for the military threat to civilian government.[46]

Such a resounding political success, for which the Executive Council had so much to thank the army chiefs and the existing military intelligence section, has contributed to a continuous dysfunctional interface between army, Department of Defence and Department of Finance. The portfolio of Defence in terms of Cabinet seniority has never indicated that successive governments since 1925 feared the emergence in Ireland of a third world military-style dictatorship. The insidious insertion of the phrase mentioning the minister's secondary function to that of the Minister for External Affairs in international relations poses the question as to whether defence planning had even at this early stage of statehood been given other than tacit credibility. Did policy become mere crisis management? The military/finance departments' lack of mutual trust gave rise to a failure in resolution of problem areas affecting military planning. But this dysfunctionalism was rooted in the government's ambivalent reaction to the July 1925 submission by the general staff for a direction on defence policy.[47]

In common with other branches of the army, G2 became virtually non-existent during the period 1925 to 1928. One might seriously question Theo Farrell's two propositions to answer the puzzle of Irish military enfeeblement. The first states that the political and strategic enfeeblement of the Irish army was the unintentional product of choices made by the army leadership. He argues that the Irish army could have been stronger politically and strategically had it stood up for itself more effectively in the face of unreasonable demands by civilian policy makers, and had it developed a more appropriate structure and strategy as recommended by its own planners. He adds: 'The second proposition is that this self-defeating behaviour was caused by the organisational culture of the Irish army, which led it to imitate the British army.' Farrell maintains that the Irish army developed an inappropriate military structure and strategy and placed itself at the mercy of civilian policy makers, and that the British model of civilian military relations worked against the army's financial self-interests.

Farrell's thesis contradicts everything for which the Free State was set up. The hope was that it would emerge as a democratic state wherein the primacy of the civil power was sacrosanct and where the army would be the main buttress of support for the democratic institutions of state and of its leaders. There was nothing unusual in the government's treatment of its army, to whom it was politically so indebted, in the aftermath of the civil war when it rationalised mobilisation strength to peacetime levels.

However, nobody in the army expected that the Sword of Damocles would be used rather than hung over the head of the military, or that by 1932 the situation within the army would become so critical that army planners were to conclude that: 'In the usual European sense the Irish State can hardly be said to have a defence force at all.'[48] All public expenditure was placed firmly under state control by the Free State government. Departments were instructed in May 1922 to seek permission from the Department of Finance before spending any money or making any appointments.[49]

Farrell cites Ronan Fanning's conclusion: 'The general acceptance of the need for drastic economy as a major aim of government . . . represents a major triumph for the finance philosophy at a particularly crucial moment in the history of the young State.'[50] The statutory authority for revenue and expenditure of Saorstát Éireann in accordance with Article 61 of the constitution were the Central Funds Acts and the Annual Appropriations Act for voted monies by the Oireachtas. The annual estimates for expenditure compiled by departments for the financial years 1922–23 and 1923–24 were very conjectural, as departments were being organised in the middle of a Civil War situation. In one of these early years, estimates of £46 million were submitted but only £34 million was expended and £12 million surrendered to the exchequer when the appropriations accounts for the year were completed.[51]

Farrell credits army intelligence with continuing to issue reports, warning that members of the Old IRA were plotting violent action. On 19 March 1924, acting on intelligence reports, General Mulcahy ordered a raid on a meeting of the Old IRA that was taking place in a public house on Parnell Street. Eleven members were arrested and some weapons seized. The Executive Council, whose members had in effect capitulated to the mutineers' demands on 12 March, reacted harshly to Mulcahy's directive, consequent to receipt of the army intelligence reports. They considered it a grave breach of government policy, and in the absence of Cosgrave, who was ill, and subject to his approval, they ordered the immediate resignation of the Irish Army Council. The chief of staff, the Adjutant General and the Quartermaster General resigned.

The democratic mandate of the Irish people elected a civilian government, to whom the army was morally and constitutionally bound to give its absolute allegiance and to act as its buttress in respecting the democratic view of the Irish people. Farrell's comments on Irish army planners, that plans vacillated from one of guerrilla tactics and strategy in 1934 to a static defence strategy in 1940, are fatuous in that he fails to recognise that military planning must retain an element of flexibility, commensurate with fluid situations.

Colonel M. J. Costello's strategic plan in 1925, in respect of censorship, and its implementation in time of war, and lieutenant Colonel Bryan's 1936 submission to the government had more influence on government policy for the duration of the Second World War. A more detailed consideration of Costello's, Bryan's and the 1934 and 1940 planning lends credence to the author's contention.

Michael J. Costello (courtesy of *An Cosantóir*).

Strategic Planning, 1925–36

In considering the decision to take army intelligence, then the second bureau, out of domestic political surveillance in 1926, O'Halpin states: 'That was an understandable, indeed overdue part of the process of taking the army out of politics.'[52] Despite the implementation of the decision, previous planning on control of communications in wartime, censorship, counter-espionage, signals intelligence, and consideration of Ireland's stance in the event of future war proved invaluable to G2 during the Emergency.

In March 1925, Colonel M. J. Costello was Director of Intelligence. A strategic thinker and always somewhat ahead of his contemporaries, Costello believed that the fundamental flaw in Ireland's censorship and propaganda policies 'was that we were dishonest and that our pronouncements were treated with suspicion'.[53] On 9 March 1925 a memorandum on censorship, issued from Costello's office and attributed to a captain Liam D. Walsh, was produced, coinciding with a paper, attributed to Colonel Liam Archer and Captain Dan Bryan, titled 'Proposals for Establishing a Censorship Bureau'. Both the memorandum, entitled 'Censorship in Time of War', and paper were issued from GHQ, Park Gate, Dublin.[54] The memorandum heading is followed by a note: 'In this memorandum the word censorship is to be read as connoting publicity.' One finds it difficult to believe that anybody in government, Dáil Éireann, the army or any part of the security forces would be gullible enough to believe such an understatement. The paper, sixty-four pages in total, was broken down into several headings which embraced the general situation and the legislative framework of censorship of communications and media and defence priorities legislation. The general thrust of the paper recommended the establishment of a censorship bureau, with a director of censorship and publicity in time of war who would have responsibility for personnel and for coordinating all censors. Close liaison with the Department of Post and Telegraphs would ensure censorship within all branches there. The director would report to the Defence Minister.[55]

The censorship plan enacted during the Emergency was based on the criteria outlined in the 1925 document. The end product was the most stringent censorship system used by virtually any nation involved or neutral in the Second World War. The objective of the plan was to save lives in battle and eventually gain victory.[56]

The 1925 paper considered the British system and concluded that their censorship was coordinated nationally as an intercommunication agency, to include both military forces and civilian population. It included a world network control as well as a centralised authority that implemented a policy of operations and duties by both military and civilian personnel. The objective was to influence both neutral and enemy opinions against Germany. The British divided censorship into four fields: press and publicity, post, radio and cable. The planners recommended stringent control of all public and private (1,000) wireless transmitters, and wireless personnel would be vetted. All licences would be issued under government supervision.[57]

The 1925 Irish plan identified censorship as a system embracing the protection of the country and its military forces. It unequivocally agreed with censorship of all news media, and its entire objective was to prevent such leakages as would affect the life of the nation.[58] The rationale was based on the proximity of the theatre of operations. Irish planners believed that the nation should receive priority, and recommended two categories of censorship in time of war.[59] The first should guard all information dealing with enemy supply systems, information and activities, while the second would prevent leaks of damaging political information concerning industrial resources. The dual approach would be co-ordinated by government.[60]

Disloyal Post Office personnel were exploited by subversives, with the IRA having agents in various offices around the country. Censorship in peacetime included two to three officers secretly examining mail considered prejudicial to the safety of the state, of which photographed copies were sent to the Ministers for Justice and Defence. During neutrality or war, all mail, domestic and foreign, should be liable to censorship by military personnel authorised by the Minister for Defence.

The censorship department should include personnel in the Post Office and the Department of Post and Telegraphs, under the direction of the Minister for Defence, and listening-in stations in all main exchanges.[61] Pre-war planning acted as a template for the censorship system imposed in Ireland from 1939 to 1946. Used to its optimum benefit by G2, it was more stringent than that imposed by actual belligerents in the Second World War.

Military Training Courses in the USA, 1926–27

The army was allowed to send a group of officers to American military institutions for a year-long training course in 1926–27. Prior to that a limited number of officers attended military courses abroad, mostly in Britain, on specialised courses in artillery, chemical warfare, aircraft maintenance and related military subjects. The decision to send officers to the USA was an effort to broaden the horizon of the army and attach less to British military doctrine. The mission comprised six officers, led by Major General Hugo MacNeill and Colonel M. J. Costello. Both attended the Command and Staff School at Fort Leavenworth. Three attended the Infantry School at Fort Benning and one the Artillery School at Fort Sill. On their return the Military College was founded in the Curragh Camp, in the aftermath of the establishment of a Temporary Plans Division (TPD). The TPD was tasked with developing the following, all testament to the army planners' intentions and capacity to formulate a modern fighting force:

- A Theory of War on which the defence of An Saorstát be based
- Formulation of tactics, covering deployment of all arms and branches
- Necessary amendments to existing organisation, in peace and war situations
- Tables of equipment and supply
- Recommendations regarding command, staff, administration and supply

- Mobilisation schemes
- Military education

Two of its most meaningful officer instructor appointments were allotted to Costello (Command Studies) and Dan Bryan (Intelligence).

This was to have a most profound impact on the army's development, and represents the one positive initiative taken by a government otherwise determined to run down the army as quickly as possible.[62]

A testament to the moral courage exhibited by army officers was a stinging criticism from Minister Desmond Fitzgerald in editorials of *An t-Óglach*, the defence forces magazine, which led to the eventual formal warning of Colonel M. J. Costello and the banning of serving officers from the magazine's executive.[63] Yet such was the conviction of an increasingly educated officer corps that despite such vicissitudes, they possessed the ability and firm belief to state that the military general staff should be given more credence in their planning capacity by the government rather than the mandarins of the civil service. The army had become painfully aware that combat efficiency was encumbered by the allocation of just 5 per cent of total defence expenditure for weapons, ammunition, armoured transport and aircraft from 1929 to 1939. The civil servant secretariat did not react favourably to the army's analysis of its urgent military requirements.

The thrust of the 1934 plan illustrates the planners' suspicions that the Treaty did not guarantee Ireland's security. There was always the risk that Britain would re-invade if the Irish government denied it wartime access to military facilities. Britain still occupied the major harbour ports, while other military facilities such as airports, landing grounds, river lines, hill features and ancillary defensible berthing ports were of significance to both British and Irish planners. The Irish recognised what would have been the inevitable outcome and focused on the military threat posed by Britain; they were pragmatic enough to know that they lacked the resources to repel an invading British force. The 1934 war plan painted a grim picture – an invasion force from the North would comprise at least 71,000 highly trained, well-equipped and properly organised troops. The Irish force of 25,000–36,000, completely outnumbered by the invaders, would be half trained, badly armed and poorly organised. Indeed the planners concluded: 'We could not hope to successfully resist an orthodox alliance of British forces of even equal size.'[64]

The 1934 war planners settled on an inventive combination of a static and guerrilla war strategy, geared to maximise enemy casualties, each aspect of the strategy to be implemented as the opportunity arose. By prolonging such a war of attrition, Ireland would be regarded as an organised state which had not ignominiously collapsed, and would rally international support.[65] Both the 1934 plan and 1936 analysis agreed that Ireland's defence should not depend on guerrilla warfare alone, and that a guerrilla campaign would last longer than a conventional war. But at no stage did they envisage a continuous static defence against British attack, instead favouring a series of delaying actions.

Bryan's groundbreaking 1936 paper, 'Fundamental Factors Affecting Saorstát Defence Problem',[66] forecast accurately what the state's military stance should be in the event of war. He outlined the paucity of defence manpower, the army's perennial problems relating to all defence resources, and advocated the courses of action available to the government of the time, stressing the factors that emphasised neutrality. Lee's pungent comment that Ireland pursued 'a policy of half armed neutrality'[67] is testament to de Valera's acceptance of the strategic planning of 1925 and 1936 as a basis for Ireland's policy throughout the Emergency.

Bryan contended that the British military chiefs required 150–200,000 troops to reconquer Ireland – approximately the strength of the British Expeditionary Force. Against them the Irish army could field 20,000 troops.[68] Irish intelligence officers quite reasonably concluded that it would be military suicide for the defence forces to make more than a show of organised resistance. They would, as dictated by strategic or tactical necessity, revert to guerrilla warfare at light brigade strength, as soon as possible. Both plans took cognisance of a *sine qua non* of operational planning, that of flexibility, which empathised with the fundamental military principle of maintenance of the aim.[69]

Bryan assessed the threat of military action by Britain as high in his 1936 report, and in the event it was accentuated after Britain returned the 'Treaty ports' in 1938.[70] When war broke out and the British realised de Valera intended to keep the ports neutral also, they were incensed – particularly Churchill, who developed a fixation with the idea that strong-arm tactics should be used against the Irish. This was precisely what Bryan predicted in the 1936 report.[71] British military chiefs'

Plan W formed the basis for a British response to an Irish call for assistance, or alternatively an embryo plan for the British invasion of Ireland. The Irish army staff, trusting their intelligence branch, were aware of Britain's ambivalent military intentions.

Farrell thought it strange that the Irish general staff aimed to model itself on the British army.[72] There is nothing wrong with the army of a fledgling state modelling itself primarily on some other army that has for long been run on specific establishments and training modules. The army and the government realised that their weaponry, among other military resources, during any emergency or intermediary war would depend on the largesse of Britain, and on its goodwill to supply such. The matter was not given a high priority by the British. The combination of static defences followed by dispersal into brigade or battalion groups that had adequate mobility was not a flawed plan, subject to the utilising of time and space and the optimum use of terrain, akin to Tito's conduct of the war in Yugoslavia.

In the immediate aftermath of the Civil War, Kevin O'Higgins had no doubt as to how public disorder and its attendant problems should be solved. The decision to use the army to assist a mainly unarmed police force was understandable, but the military task was complicated by the government's determination to reduce the army by two-thirds.

Army intelligence became the government's chief source of information. In January 1924 the Director of Intelligence reported that a high percentage of crimes committed during the second half of 1923 were traced to members or ex-members of the army, and this view was echoed in a Royal Ulster Constabulary (RUC) report obtained by army intelligence. In addition, republicans and freelance criminals were very active in the south and west, while agrarian and labour disputes led to more crime.[73]

Army intelligence officers were critical of the propensity among policemen to 'close their eyes to a lot of things when they could pass a lot of important information on to us', while in some areas the police were hesitant to call on the military for assistance for fear of arousing local hostility.[74] During this period of chaos, the atmosphere of intrigue was heightened by the establishment of an informal caucus of ex-British officers to protect their interests and by associated rumours of Masonic influence.[75] The Director of Intelligence informed the intelligence officer in Athlone that his concept of future service did not envisage retention of indolent, indisciplined men in the army.[76]

A gradual rapprochement took place between the Tobinites (followers of Liam Tobin) and republicans who had fought each other in the Civil War. Those responsible for some of the worst excesses of that conflict became Fianna Fáil supporters. The most prominent – Joseph McGrath and Liam Tobin – had been closely linked with Oriel House. McGrath developed excellent personal relations with leading Fianna Fáil politicians, including Seán Lemass, while Tobin was made superintendent of the Oireachtas in 1940, responsible for the security of the national parliament.[77]

Kevin O'Higgins espoused a policy that envisaged an ordered, tranquil society, protected by an unarmed police force reliant on public support, and firmly under the thumb of central government. A multiplicity of viewpoints existed as to who should be responsible for internal security, external intelligence, monitoring subversion and combating armed crime. Joe McGrath put in a strong bid for such control. In addition to his ministerial responsibility for industry and commerce, he was also the political head of the CID/Oriel House. On 9 May 1923 he circulated a memorandum that gave details of a plan for a secret service. McGrath's idea included a means of collecting detailed information on the activities of the enemies of the state. Its records should include intelligence on republican clubs, the Ancient Order of Hibernians, Orange lodges, Freemasons, land and labour organisations, and communist cells. McGrath also felt that it should subsume the army's foreign intelligence activities as well as those in the six-county area.[78] He envisaged undercover agents throughout the country in a position to gain all kinds of information about local clubs and meetings, and to report on the feelings and views of different classes.[79]

Mulcahy, meanwhile, had plans to improve and expand army intelligence, while O'Higgins was determined that the conventional police forces should eventually assume responsibility for all crime and security work. But despite their disagreements, both reviled the perpetuation of Oriel House; its existence, short as it was, came to an end in November 1923.[80]

The Director of Intelligence had direct access both to the chief of staff and Minister for Defence. In autumn 1923 army intelligence acquired the bulk of the files created in Oriel House, together with the Adjutant General's files on internees. A direction that agents in

Britain and the six counties should be withdrawn was ignored, and army intelligence remained covertly autonomous.

The effectiveness of G2 activity was burdened by work thrust upon intelligence in the aftermath of the Civil War. Demobilisation virtually ended intelligence organisation and agents in various commands, while the army crisis of 1924 illustrated the successful counter-espionage measures taken by army intelligence officers loyal to the government. This had an important bearing on the failure of the mutiny in March 1924.[81]

Army intelligence was renamed the Second Bureau in spring 1924. It worked under two headings, military and political. Foreign armies, political developments abroad, warfare and weapons, their implications for Ireland, and the planning of appropriate security measures to reinforce Irish neutrality in any future war involving Britain were issues of importance to Irish military intelligence. The efforts of Northern Irish security forces to intercept and decrypt wireless communications were met by a policy of increased signal security and of reading Northern government traffic insofar as possible.

Experimental work commenced on breaking codes and ciphers, signals interception, and detecting secret ink. When such work was restarted for security purposes in 1938, it was carried out under army auspices. The plan prepared by General Costello's staff in 1925 in relation to the forming of a censorship bureau correctly anticipated both the extent of communications censorship and the pre-eminence of army intelligence in censorship policy after 1939. The army's intelligence activities, which had a definite structure, showed that military intelligence had the expertise to deal with external issues and the capacity to extend its sphere of responsibility to any internal threat. The intelligence branch at a later stage did not flinch from subjecting Commandant Brennan Whitmore, who contributed to writing the 1925 proposals on censorship, to covert postal interception because of alleged pro-German sympathies.[82] Whether this procedure applied to General Hugo McNeill is a matter for conjecture. But despite the commitment of army intelligence, Kevin O'Higgins did not exempt it from swingeing reform and – with exceptions such as Dan Bryan, who continued without permission to operate covertly as an intelligence agent – it was consigned to a backwater role until 1932.[83]

Military intelligence from army headquarters, through command and battalion IOs throughout the country, postal and telephone interception was used to penetrate suspect organisations, while outside the state it maintained an extensive network of agents working against the republican movement. Agents in Northern Ireland – with a certain, if limited, amount of success – supplied information and documents on the security forces, republican, nationalist and unionist organisations and economic affairs.

Successive Directors of Intelligence had been raising the problem of cooperation with the gardaí since the autumn of 1923, with the aim of ensuring an adequate interchange of information. In September 1924 the Director of Intelligence complained that the police were withholding reports made on organisations in industrial and communist circles whose activities might someday call for intervention by the military, and that the army was thrown back on its own resources to obtain the relevant information.[84] Bryan complained in 1925 as follows:

> Detective Division are hitting out blindly against any irregular activities that come under their notice, just as they would do in ordinary criminal cases, and apparently not dealing with the irregulars as an extensive military organisation, with ramifications not alone in An Saorstát but in the six counties, Great Britain, United States, and to a limited although very important degree, on the Continent.[85]

The struggle continued, illustrating a fundamental difference between policing and security, the one concerned with law enforcement, the other with the long-term security of the state. The police had the backing of government and the full support of Kevin O'Higgins, while the army depended on the political support of its minister, Peter Hughes, who had been appointed as a stopgap measure after the 1924 mutiny. The balance of power and influence within government clearly favoured O'Higgins; the outcome of debate was never in doubt. In the last months of 1925 Hughes gave disastrous verbal instruction to the army to transfer all Second Bureau files on individuals and relinquish control of all agents and informers in the state to the police.

The doctrine of civil supremacy espoused by O'Higgins since 1922 forced the army to leave all political intelligence and security work entirely to the gardaí. Bryan, however, took care to remain discreetly in touch with some of his republican and labour contacts.[86]

The Second Bureau turned its attention to training and the development of purely military intelligence. Bryan's contribution to the training, which took place in the Curragh, was one lecture on special intelligence agents, a subject on which he was an expert.[87] Despite O'Higgins' efforts, G2 survived the virtual emasculation of the army, largely due to the continuous efforts of Bryan's pre-emptive covert planning relating to security and intelligence. G2 retained a basis to operate and expand from the commencement of the Emergency. Strategic defence issues had been the subject of professional military studies since the mid-1920s, and the establishment of the Military College had enhanced the professional capacity of the officer body to undertake such tasks.

British Chiefs of Staff Report 491 to the Cabinet, 53, 59, 23 July 1936

Bryan retained a copy of the above report in his papers, without specifying how or, more importantly, on what date it came into his possession. 'Fundamental Factors', Bryan's strategic study of Ireland's options in the imminent world war, was written in 1936. If one assumes that Bryan obtained the British report prior to the completion of 'Fundamental Factors', by deliberate leakage or otherwise, then it must also be assumed that it was a catalyst for Bryan's study. The British report resulted from Malcolm MacDonald's letter to Inskip dated 29 June 1936 requesting that the chiefs of staff consider recommendations on Britain's position if the Irish Free State were to become a foreign country. The report, compiled and signed by the Joint Planning Sub-Committee, TSV Phillips, R. F. Adam and H. M. Fraser, was issued on 23 July 1936. It also considered relations with the Irish Free State on defence matters, and terms and conditions of an offensive–defensive alliance.[88] Its consideration and recommendations were, to say the least, ominous. If its contents were known to Bryan at the time, they must have had a major influence on his recommendation for a neutral stance in the Second World War.

The British report initially addressed the strategic importance of the Irish Free State. It stipulated the need for use of ports and aerodromes, and the requirement of unrestricted use of all ports and anchorages in wartime. It quantified British principal requirements in terms of a German–French war as follows: Lough Swilly for convoy protection vessels and as a base for auxiliary vessels; Queenstown, Kingstown and Berehaven as bases for auxiliary vessels. Their requirements in the latter stipulate Lough Swilly as a convoy assembly port, Queenstown and Berehaven as bases for main fleet and Kingstown as a base for auxiliary vessels. The distinction may be confusing, but can be interpreted as possible phases of a war.[89]

The planners did not define exactly where they required aerodromes or landing grounds in the Irish Free State but assumed that aircraft would be needed for trade protection, coast defence, and minor naval operations.

They felt it essential that in war Britain should have the right of unrestricted flying over Ireland and the use of such aerodromes as they required. Typical of a colonialist mindset, they presumed that any agreement with the Irish Free State should not only guarantee that no hostile power should ever be allowed a footing in the country but also that ports, anchorages and aerodromes should be available for use by British forces. They added that responsibility for the upkeep and modernisation of these defences should be clearly defined in any agreement and the retention of the hinterland in safe hands be ensured.

The subcommittee focused its economic examination on Irish imports into the UK and concluded that alternative supplies were abundantly available for all the commodities obtained from the Irish Free State. Using a form of mildly ironic rhetoric, it added: 'Providing these other sources of supply remain open it can be said that trade with the I.F.S. [Irish Free State] is not essential from the food point of view. On the other hand, in war, with maximum production, and taking into consideration the short sea passage, supplies from the I.F.S. to the U.K. would certainly be of value.'[90]

The report mentions the 750 Irishmen who joined the British army per annum in peacetime and stipulated that these were necessary for extra battalions in the Royal Ulster Rifles and Royal Irish Fusiliers. If Ireland were to become a foreign country, the position of those already serving would have to be carefully considered. It also stated that any agreement negotiated would have to include a clause allowing Irish nationals to serve in the British army.

The thrust of the chiefs of staff report on an assumed Anglo-Irish agreement indicated the following: They considered Ireland 'a friendly foreign power' whose strategic and economic interests would bind her extremely closely to Britain as it engaged in war with another major power; peacetime would ensure joint operations in defence of Ireland's coast in the event of war; Britain should have a free hand in peace to make all preparations necessary for war, unhampered by any considerations other than its own financial limitations; Britain wanted aerodromes as well as naval bases, but recognised that this move might be a cause of dispute between Britain and Ireland. The chiefs of staff assumed that a comprehensive offensive–defensive alliance would be 'palatable to the Irish', judging by de Valera's statements in the Dáil, an invalid assumption by people ill-equipped to interpret de Valera-speak. They further assumed that the Irish would be forced to train garrisons necessary to man the coastal defences and bases in peacetime. The chiefs of staff concluded that an Anglo-Irish alliance would ensure mutual trust leading to British use of virtually the entire strategic assets of Ireland in time of war.[91]

These recommendations portray a mindset of outdated imperialism, and are redolent of jingoistic assumptions that the Irish Free State would automatically accept a virtual takeover by Britain of key strategic facilities without demur. Nevertheless, the ongoing calculations of the chiefs of staff, exhibiting a volte-face, played a decisive role in the eventual decision to hand over the ports in 1938, 'a very reluctant concession, according to MacDonald'.[92] In 1936 such a concession would not have been contemplated. Yet again, Duggan's concept of 'the greatest threat to Irish neutrality' rings true.[93]

'Fundamental Factors Affecting Saorstát Defence Problem', 1936

Bryan's 'Fundamental Factors' had a three-fold purpose. First, to consider from a military viewpoint the effect a war in western Europe or the North Atlantic involving Great Britain would have on the Saorstát; second, to consider the military courses of action open to the Saorstát in such a war; and third, to outline the military results likely to ensue from the adoption of any of the courses mentioned.[94] The study analysed factors affecting the defence of Ireland, evaluated the forces required in the event of war, and outlined specific Irish policies to be adopted in such a case. On the subject of defence it makes a somewhat startling claim that 'The Saorstát people are, further, not prepared or educated to the stage at which they are prepared in practice to provide sufficient forces to guarantee even a relative freedom from outside interference.'[95] Suggested alternatives were neutrality, default or non-recognition, cooperation or resistance. The report was submitted to government for consideration.[96]

Bryan outlined Ireland's geographic position relating to defensive measures, its strategic position, its almost total lack of defensive capacity in trained manpower and economic resources, and its relative position to the general defensive status of other small states. He considered the abysmal lack of knowledge (presumably among other government departments and politicians) as to Ireland's strategic position, its defensive problem, and the existing political and military relations between Ireland and other countries. Without underestimating the latter factor, he postulated the caveat as to non-recognition of an Irish neutral status by any or all of the belligerent states.

The paper postulated the probable altered situation during the war, as well as likely British policy. It considered the intrinsic Irish–British relationship in defensive terms during the First World War, essentially holistic in concept, a unitary geographic island combination. The paper examined the military, political and economic difficulties facing Ireland in the event of altering that stance unilaterally, the probable British attitude and reaction, and the absolute necessity for vastly increased Irish defence forces and military resources in such a scenario.

Military preparedness affecting Irish political attitudes in the event of war, adoption of a policy of neutrality, declaring void Articles 6 and 7 of the Anglo-Irish Treaty, cooperation with Britain, and absolute armed resistance to any invasion were all analysed. Scenarios involving neutrality, non-declaration of neutrality, non-recognition of neutrality by belligerents, and resistance were also discussed. Bryan recommended a neutral stance, but noted the implications of British involvement in war. He cautioned that the Covenant of the League of Nations and abstract theories of justice were not consistent with international relations, and suggested that any conclusions of other government departments which did not take account of 'Fundamental Factors' would be misleading, and dangerous.[97] Heady inferences indeed from a lieutenant colonel in G2!

The document was circulated in its entirety to key ministers, and it served as the only considered overview of defence issues emanating from the army in the years leading up to 1939.[98] It was not until the Germans had invaded several European countries that a typical crisis management response came from the Department of Finance. Despite de Valera's predisposition of a sovereign state mindset – his '*idée fixe*'[99] – the Department of Finance's intransigent policy was conducive to a policy of half-armed neutrality,[100] and arguably a major factor in Bryan's prioritisation of counter-intelligence.

Bryan's study assessed the army as a virtual non-entity in 1936; by 1939 it plunged towards its nadir in terms of efficiency. The report's conclusions formed the basis for the only realistic policy – as adopted by the government during the Second World War. Bryan's masterly conduct of a most difficult counter-intelligence brief acted as an invaluable foil to de Valera's consummate politico-diplomatic genius. De Valera always maximised whatever opportunity became available within his double portfolio of Taoiseach and Minister for External Affairs to maintain Irish neutrality. Both ensured that Irish neutrality was studiously implemented on a more than benevolent pro-Allied basis, despite the diplomatically insensitive, ham-fisted David Gray, the US minister in Dublin.[101] Gray was 'a gauche and assertive personality' who 'lacked the finesse associated with professional diplomats'.[102]

The 1936 analysis of Ireland's defence status and military options would give more credibility to William Joyce's (Lord Haw Haw) slur that the Irish army could not have beaten the tinkers out of Galway than to de Valera's naive assertion that 'Neutrality is not a cowardly policy if you really mean to defend yourself if attacked.'[103] The assertion begs the question: defend yourself with what?

Bryan stressed the island nature of Ireland and the accepted fact that it possessed the most suitable harbours as bases for naval operations in the North Atlantic approaches to the English Channel and the Irish Sea. The US authorities had selected Berehaven as a base from which to protect troops en route to France in the First World War. He outlined the capacity of Lough Swilly, the Shannon Estuary and Galway and Killary Harbours to provide safe anchorage for fleets, presumably of either Allied or Axis forces. They could be easily protected against submarine or aircraft attack, being wide enough, without incurring major expenditure. He noted that 75 per cent of sea communications on the North Atlantic trade route passed through the English Channel, or St George's gateways to British, French, Belgian, Dutch, German, Scandinavian, and Baltic ports. The Irish Sea barrier of 300 miles with Great Britain allowing a flank approach further complicated Britain's particular problem with submarine attack. Bryan also commented on the dangers of silent economic blockade, such as affected Napoleon's defences and trade routes, and of a similar tactic employed by the Union to stifle the Confederate trade routes in the American Civil War.[104]

Anglo-Irish defence cooperation prior to the outbreak of the Second World War was essentially a misnomer. Apart from Churchill's unambiguous condemnation of the return of the ports to Irish military control, the British chiefs of staff had concluded by 1937 that the ports should be available in wartime, their view tempered by an admission of being unable to defend them against a hostile Ireland.[105] By January 1938, this view was quantified by the following conclusion: while the non-availability of the Irish ports might imperil Britain in the course of a war, the cost of retaining them would be preclusive. The British chiefs of staff estimated that it would take one British division, together with anti-aircraft defence at each port, to defend them against attack by the Irish army.[106] Anglo-Irish cooperation manifested itself in the reluctant handover of the Treaty ports by the British government and offering the Irish government access to the British War Book during summer 1938.[107]

One must assume that such anti-aircraft weaponry would be used in the event of attack by German aircraft. The ill-equipped Irish Air Corps posed no threat to the speculative British defences, irrespective of the bravery of its pilots. In autumn 1939 the Air Corps possessed four Gloster Gladiators, its only reckonable fighter aircraft, and an assortment of obsolete non-reckonable aircraft.[108]

The Irish forces' numerical strength was equally pathetic. On the outbreak of war the army's mobilised strength was 19,136 all ranks: 7,600 Regulars, 4,300 A and B Reservists and 7,236 Volunteers, totalling just 50 per cent of the war establishment. The army was neither trained nor equipped for war (nor to defend neutrality).[109] One finds it difficult to reconcile the British chiefs of staff estimate of defensive measures for the ports, considering the paltry opposition that the Irish army could offer. Nevertheless, after protracted negotiations, Irish and British delegations signed an agreement in settlement of the economic war, which allowed Ireland unconditional possession of the ports.[110] Ireland's sovereignty and benevolent pro-Allied neutrality policy were assured.

It is, however, surprising to note that what could have been considered a political coup for de Valera and a morale boost for the army was of little significance to the secretary of the Department of Finance, J. J. McElligott. In February 1938 he subjected the estimate for the Department of Defence to rigorous scrutiny and advised the Cabinet against additional provision for rearmament and defence. It set the combative tone for the Department of Finance approach to probable conflict and copperfastened Finance's influence on policy in the run-up to war and during the Emergency.[111]

Bryan's analysis of the strategic maritime importance of Ireland in 1936 is accorded a stark perspective by Captain T. McKenna's description of the dearth of its naval defence in 1939. The situation almost beggars belief, and it is difficult not to empathise with Vivian Mercer putting 'The Irish navy joke' at number three in '*Dublin Opinion*'s six jokes' in 1944:[112]

> Oh don't go out tonight, Daddy!
> The captain's Boy he cried,
> Oh don't go out tonight, Daddy,
> There's a ripple on the tide!

Captain T. McKenna, of the Naval Service, which did not exist as such in 1939, stated:

> The third of September 1939 will always stand out in maritime history not as the day the Second World War was declared . . . but as the day realisation dawned in Ireland that the country was surrounded by water and that the sea was of vital importance to her. Neutrality was declared with just nothing whatever to defend it within the internationally vital area of the territorial sea . . .[113]

The doubtful asset of the 1908 vintage *Muirchú*, originally *Helga*,[114] a British coastal defence vessel that shelled Liberty Hall and Ringsend during the 1916 Easter Rising, and the equally suspect *Fort Rannoch* constituted the entire strength of the naval forces on 3 September 1939. The Naval Service, even more so than the army, was virtually powerless, so scant was its resources to patrol 5,127 square miles of the then territorial sea on a perimeter of 783 miles and a coastline of 1,970 miles.[115]

Bryan's study quantified Ireland's isolationist position, its economic non-viability and its comparative paucity of manpower. He inferred that the significance of this situation was ignored, or simply not understood by many politicians or government departments. Fisk points out that a number of government and opposition politicians, and thousands of Irish soldiers, had fought in one or all of the Easter Rising, the War of Independence and the Civil War. He also comments that 'de Valera's praise for his hedge fighters was no mere rhetoric.'[116] With the exception of Cosgrave, Mulcahy and the army officers, many politicians still nursed befuddled romanticised notions of outmoded guerrilla warfare as a viable deterrent to prolonged occupation, as a form of panacea for all conflict resolution. Such pious aspirations, while true in respect of typical Irish will to resist, were casuistic, given the murderous ferocity of either British or German reprisal philosophy throughout previous conflicts.

Bryan recognised Ireland's lack of resources as preclusive barriers to waging a war except for a short period (meaning days rather than weeks).[117] Shortages of manpower and island status suggested cooperation with one or more friendly outside powers to obtain imports. He argued for small power cooperation or fitting in with the overall strategic aims of powerful neighbours. This author feels that such a policy might simply ensure survival, as a strategic buffer zone, dependent of course on the measure and nature of the cooperation provided. My assumption is based on Bryan's examples of violations by Germany of Belgian, Greek and Persian neutrality during the First World War. Bryan outlined how Holland's improved fortifications, mobilisation and sizeable naval force changed German invasion plans.[118] Swiss mobilisation, and the tripartite alliance of Denmark, Norway and Sweden were also effective.[119] However, Bryan also noted Ireland's isolation from powers other than Britain, and that Ireland was the only European state without compulsory military service and little or no defence force.[120] His analysis led inexorably to one conclusion: the adoption of a covert pro-Allied neutrality, while outwardly simulating an overt neutrality in respect of the Axis powers – an Irish solution to an Irish problem!

It was Machiavellian in concept, but then which belligerent could honestly cry foul? Little wonder that Ireland's survival as a sovereign state during the war was trumpeted as 'the greatest euphemism of the twentieth century'.[121] The implementation of the policy would be the most difficult task yet to face the state, one that required a political leader and statesman, complemented by a highly accomplished Director of Intelligence. Both de Valera and Bryan proved to be the men ideally suited to the onerous tasks, *sans peur et sans reproche*.

'Fundamental Factors' assessed the difficulties created by both British and Irish attitudes in advance of the impending war; these would require serious consideration. Of paramount importance was the divergence of opinion that would almost certainly arise in respect of Articles 6 and 7 of the Anglo-Irish Treaty.[122] Bryan suspected that Britain would do what was needed to implement these measures. He had difficulty predicting British attitudes in the absence of a stated Irish policy, but stressed the proximity problem, Treaty provisions, and Britain's interpretation of the British Isles as a single entity for defensive purposes. Britain, Bryan conceded, was fully aware of Ireland's lack of equipment and technical knowledge to man the harbour defences, and in 1927 had refused to even discuss their handover. Yet she envisaged Irish responsibility for local defence of the coastal forts, minesweeping and coastal patrols, aspects of naval intelligence, coast-watching, and censorship in coordination with British plans for such.

Although a neutrality stance would create difficulties, it was, as Bryan carefully argued, the best option.[123] This was an astute move on his part, defusing lingering distrust of any army initiative over the government decision-making process. The paper nevertheless continued its strategic emphasis. Articles 6 and 7 created enormous difficulties as no belligerent could take seriously any Irish assertion of neutrality while Britain controlled the reserved naval and military installations. Those bases could not be forcibly retaken without risking war and reoccupation. Also, Bryan argued, overt cooperation with Britain would imply probable political and internal security problems. Nevertheless, Bryan proposed a military treaty or convention to cater for an emergency as imperative, and the raising and training of a viable military force to be prepared for such emergency. He counselled an open, honest *démarche* to Britain as being the most likely to gain the best results. The concept of an island entity as a basis for a coordinated defence plan was acceptable to Bryan, with a caveat that should the government repudiate Articles 6 and 7 of the Treaty, it should adopt measures to meet the inevitably dire consequences.

If that course were followed, Bryan anticipated a British reaction with a force of 400,000 to retake Ireland within two months.[124] His 1936 strength estimate contrasts sharply with those of J. P. Duggan's of three to five German divisions, Charles Townshend's listing of Britain's occupation force of roughly three divisions in 1920,[125] and J. J. Lee's view that the British estimated one German division plus IRA collaboration to invade Ireland successfully.[126] This author contends that either belligerent would maintain a flexible approach to troop strength post successful invasion, dependent on Irish resistance and future operational planning. Bryan estimated that Ireland could muster a maximum of 20,000 in the same period, approximately 50 per cent of whom would be substandard. The Irish army had ten days' supply of rifle ammunition, five days' supply of light automatic ammunition, and thirty-six artillery guns with a few days' ammunition. It had a total of six operational aircraft, was short 1,300 officers and even more of the NCO complement.[127] Bryan concluded that the Irish army's position was hopeless under the prevailing circumstances, at best capable of token resistance of a nuisance value only.

Bryan's 1936 analysis, by any criteria, was the most important strategic forecast to issue from the army since the submission of the 'Request for Direction on Defence Policy, Defence Council of Executive, 22 July 1925'.[128] It was, as O'Halpin contended, an impressive performance.[129]

Bryan recommended neutrality as the only option, and Keogh states that 'de Valera had no other policy choice than to declare the country's neutrality when the Dáil met on 2 September 1939'.[130] Keogh's assessment of the inevitable demolition of Ireland's armed forces is reasonable given the vast superiority of the German army in terms of manpower, training and resources. One might comment that the British forces would have been wiped out in Dunkirk had Hitler and Field Marshal Gerd Von Runstedt not ordered the Panzers to halt their advance at Gravelines, southwest of Dunkirk, on 24 May 1940.[131] Such comment would be similarly valid in relation to a failure of the Normandy D-Day landings (6 June 1944) had Colonel Generaloberst Alfred Jodl, OKW chief of operations, agreed immediately to the release of the Panzer reserves – the Panzer Lehr and 12th SS Divisions – (ironically) to Field Marshal Von Runstedt's operational control at the latter's request.[132] Tangential speculation is revisionist, often casuistic.

Bryan and Colonel Liam Archer prioritised counter-espionage as G2's main role during the Emergency. G2's success in effecting a covert military cooperation with Britain, and the US at a later stage, was complemented by de Valera's adroit political skill in achieving the handover of the ports in 1938 and their retention. De Valera's adoption of an 'unneutral neutral' policy, as it is described by Keogh, was a crucial masterpiece of political manoeuvre.[133] Bryan's assistance to de Valera was invaluable, as conceded by Keogh.[134]

Bryan had little if any field experience, either during the Civil War or thereafter. During his military career he focused on the prioritisation of anti-subversion and counter-espionage/counter-intelligence planning at both tactical and strategic level, at which he excelled. The principal concerns of intelligence organisations are defined as: field or combat intelligence; foreign armies; air and marine movements; censorship and control of communications; signal detection and control; publicity and press relations; and military and security problems with other countries. The one discernible criticism of Bryan's stewardship lies in his shared responsibility for field or combat intelligence. O'Halpin comments that Bryan's concentration on security and counter-intelligence activities was motivated by circumstances, at the expense of combat intelligence, which could have proved a costly error. The matter was noted in the chief of staff's report for 1942–3.[135]

Essential Elements of Information (EEIs)

In all military/airforce/naval operation orders EEIs exist to allow a commander and his staff demand information from subordinate commanders and staff during an ongoing, often fluid, operation, the object being to assist the commander in postulating future operational dynamics. Undoubtedly Bryan made a pre-emptive, unsolicited and brilliant contribution to kick start government consideration of the imminent war, and to change their ambivalent concept of war, from an archaic mindset of guerrilla hedge fighting tactics to the reality of neutrality. In the 1936 paper, Bryan gave a very cogent, logical argument for his favoured course of action, indicating the political and military emphasis for a pro-Allied policy to be adopted at a later date. To that extent his contribution to Ireland's political and military survival during the war was significant. His paper focused the minds of senior ministers, in terms of preserving neutrality and respecting British interests, irrespective of the fact that their leader's neutrality was based on political expediency rather than principle. De Valera's policy was to show 'a certain consideration for Britain'. The emphasis – not generally made – was on the word 'certain'.[136]

Bryan did not deny his own preference for the 'unneutral neutrality' posture. Robert Fisk illustrates the concept in recording the views of Count Balinski, who visited Ireland in 1941 on behalf of the Polish Research Centre, a branch of the exiled Polish government. He met senior Irish officers, including General Brennan, former chief of staff, and Major General Hugo MacNeill.

Balinski recorded: 'I had a very clear impression that they have a deep admiration for the behaviour of the British nation in this war. The name of General O'Connor, one of the chiefs of the army in Africa, was mentioned to me with pride as that of an Irishman. My strong impression is that the army people I met were very pro-British.' Fisk concluded: 'This emotion was, of course, sometimes translated into real assistance for the British military authorities. Colonel Bryan of G2, whose work was in theory far too sensitive to allow him any political sympathies, admitted long after the war "that people say that I was pro-British and so in a way I suppose I was".'[137]

Whether Balinski's judgement was correct in the case of MacNeill is open to question. Fisk describes MacNeill's *démarche* to the German legation's Henning Thompson in December 1940 as an obscure relationship, in which he discussed both Irish and British military plans with the Germans. Co-founder of the Irish Military College and former director of defence plans, MacNeill is depicted by Fisk as 'a heavy drinker, as was obvious to all who knew him, very anti-British'; he possessed a tendency, in the eyes of G2, to go 'rooting around on his own', and was regarded as a 'buccaneer' by his young officers.[138]

THREE

The Army: From Nadir to Proficiency, 1936–39

This chapter illustrates the extent of the army's unpreparedness for combat at the commencement of the Second World War, due in no small part to the IRA, taking advantage of basic security lapses, stealing the bulk of the state's reserve ammunition from the magazine fort in the Phoenix Park in December 1939. The general staff, to say the least, were ashamed of the debacle, which precipitated a government loss of confidence in the army. The reasons for such, and the reaction of the newly appointed chief of staff, are debated. A Military Court of Inquiry into the raid reported on breaches of duty by army personnel; the court was ruthless in dispensing punishment. The government reaction to the IRA's outrageous deed was swift and draconian. Imprisonment, internment and executions of IRA members rendered the organisation virtually impotent during the Emergency years. Censorship of the media, strictly enforced by Minister Aiken, meant defensive measures became the norm. Censorship in Ireland was more severe than that applied in any of the Allied countries in the Second World War. De Valera's distrust of British motives for not supplying arms to Irish forces is given consideration, as is his somewhat ill-judged belief in his so-called 'hedge fighters' such as Tom Barry. De Valera was an outstanding politician and statesman. He was not a military genius.

THE MAGAZINE FORT RAID, DECEMBER 1939: A CRISIS OF GOVERNMENT CONFIDENCE IN THE ARMY

In his lecture on the magazine fort raid at the Military College on 12 October 1967, General Dan McKenna, chief of staff during the Emergency, stressed the vital importance to the army of maintaining the confidence of government and people at all times. The raid was of such proportions as to cause an almost catastrophic breach of trust between de Valera and the army.[1] McKenna described the raid as follows:

> One major calamity was responsible for this. On Christmas Eve 1939 a raid involving a considerable quantity of arms, ammunition, explosives etc. was carried out on the magazine fort. This raid, the success of which was due to the actions of one traitor, a storeman in the fort, was an embarrassment to the Government, to big sections of the people and to the army; it gave all of them a severe jolt and the Government in particular felt it keenly.[2]

McKenna was deputy QMG at the time and accompanied the chief of staff, QMG and a few other officers to the fort to meet the Taoiseach and accompanying ministers who reviewed defence arrangements. On inspection, de Valera scarcely uttered a word beyond saying 'yes, yes, yes' to everything he was told. When he came outside he looked back at the fort and said: 'It's the devil that such a thing should have been allowed to happen', and without another word walked off to his car. The other ministers left too without even saying good evening to the officers who had accompanied them on their inspection.[3]

McKenna conveyed the sense of shame felt by the senior army officers present and the residual problem of restoring government confidence in the army. The officers resolved to apply hard work and devotion to duty in an effort to increase efficiency in the army. They would also avail of every opportunity to bring the government and the army into closer contact. A few months later, when the Germans overran the French, Belgian and British armies and when invasion of both Britain and Ireland seemed imminent, that resolved increased considerably on all sides, particularly after the establishment of a Dáil all-party defence committee. While this committee had neither power nor responsibility, it did make recommendations, many of which were accepted by government.[4]

One must assume that in 1967 the Official Secrets Act restricted McKenna's authority to reveal the entire truth of what happened in the Phoenix Park. The apportioning of blame to 'one traitor, a storeman at the fort,' is a gross understatement.

The Military Court of Inquiry commenced on 29 December 1939 and issued findings exactly one month later.[5] It found that the raid resulted from a combination of factors: years of neglect in the pursuit of duty on the part of army personnel, including officers, NCOs (non-commissioned officers) and privates; downright treachery and traitorous activity involving trafficking in ammunition and uniforms to the IRA by army NCOs and privates; conspiracy and complicity by army NCOs with the IRA, whereby the latter were made fully aware of the security system for the fort and its defects prior to the raid; and a security system unchanged for years, lacking all but a semblance of inspection procedure, riven with a laissez-faire attitude, deceit, laziness, and a general malaise rampant throughout all the rank structure charged with overall and particular responsibility for the system.[6]

The chief of staff, Major General Michael Brennan, emerged unscathed from the enquiry and exercised his authority and planning capacity with a calm sagacity in the unsavoury political/military climate that followed. Brennan was the fifty-third and final witness, and outlined measures taken to recover the stolen ammunition. He liaised with Chief Superintendent Macken of the Garda Síochána to prevent the lorries transporting the ammunition to Northern Ireland. He ordered the entire guard and the military policeman on duty to be placed under arrest, an action surprisingly not undertaken by McKenna or any other officer present. He arranged for an immediate 'on call status' for all army troops, sending an immediate cryptic message to all commands: 'Take the greatest precautions at once to protect all barracks and ammunition. Give every assistance to police in search for lorries.'[7]

Ironically, a special meeting of the Defence Council on 24 December was informed by Chief Superintendent

Carroll that the IRA intended to invade the six counties, boosted immeasurably by the huge ammunition gain. Brennan did not react until he was able to identify a definite objective.[8] Archer, who had already reported that some of the ammunition was in the Straffan/Celbridge area, reiterated this at a meeting on 26 December.[9] The bulk of the ammunition was recovered in that area, proving Archer correct and vindicating Brennan's decision to trust G2. Further planning by Minister for Justice Gerry Boland, Minister for Defence Oscar Traynor, Brennan and Archer, and liaison with Colonel Murphy (general staff) resulted in a military cordon of Dublin city and a police search focused on the Kildare/Wicklow area that yielded results.[10] From 8 a.m. on 28 December searches by troops continued until nine-tenths of the missing ammunition was recovered.[11]

Brennan's successful crisis management of the situation depended on G2's accurate intelligence. Archer and Bryan had sufficient reason, intellect and experience to kick-start a semi-dormant intelligence system of an almost fossilised army into meaningful active service, and all three officers maintained the fullest measure of army/Garda cooperation throughout the recovery operation. This ability is often taken for granted by those unaware of the sensitivity that can exist in both forces in respect of overlapping of dedicated areas of responsibility. Diplomacy, tact and a maintained focus on the overall objective becomes a *sine qua non* in such operations.

The court determined that the military police corporal on entrance gate duty abjectly failed to offer any resistance or make any attempt to alarm the guard.

The sentries on two other posts were castigated for not firing on the raiders in defence of their posts, for allowing themselves to be disarmed, and for not alarming the guard. The guard commander was roundly condemned for a dismal performance of duty, arguably tantamount to cowardice, indifference and possibly complicity.[12] The court spared no soldier, irrespective of rank. It found that those on duty were of low standard and lacking morale, reflecting the dismal level of professionalism in the army at the time.

The fiasco, however, eased the way for a firmer government hand against the IRA. Internment was introduced on 4 January 1940, and by the end of the war more than 500 IRA suspects were interned, six were executed and three died on hunger strike.[13] Gerry Boland, Minister for Justice, felt that drastic measures were needed because the very existence of the state was threatened.[14]

The report on the raid went before Cabinet on 23 February. Minister for Defence Oscar Traynor reported to the Dáil that one captain was dismissed and two colonels placed on half pay for a year. A commandant and a second lieutenant were given the option to retire or face enforced retirement for misconduct or inefficiency. Ironically, the dismissed second lieutenant served on as an NCO, was recommissioned as a permanent officer in 1948 and served until the mandatory retirement age as a captain.[15] Four senior officers were censured, paraded and admonished, while two corporals and a private faced courts martial. The minister also outlined the stock of ammunition recovered and that still missing as of that date.[16]

Minister Traynor made a feeble attempt to distance the army's attendant ineptitude and corruption from the reality of the situation:

> I am satisfied that these causes of the raid cannot be attributed to defects in the general administration of the Defence Forces or any of its branches, or in the general organisation, efficiency or discipline thereof . . . the responsibility for this position lies with individual officers and reflects no discredit on the general behaviour of the Defence Forces whether Regular or Reserve.[17]

The minister's generalisation cannot be sustained, given successive governments' penurious fiscal policy, directly responsible for a virtual cessation of training, dearth of morale, and a fossilisation ethos endemic in the post-1925 skeletal military organisation. He rebutted the vitriolic rhetoric propounded by opposition spokesman O'Higgins in the debate on the Emergency Powers (Amendment) Bill on 3 January 1940 and in the debate on the Supplementary Estimate for the army on 5 March 1940. During the first debate, O'Higgins was scathing in his criticism: 'I suppose in the whole history of armies since the world began, there was never such a disaster as the picture of an army losing all its ammunition without as much as a blackthorn being used.'[18] He added that 'there was more ammunition lost in a couple of hours . . . than could be bought by all the revenue which will be obtained from the Revenue Tax and the Sugar Tax put together.'[19]

In the Supplementary Estimate debate O'Higgins stated: ' . . . all the reserve of ammunition, 28 tons in weight, was loaded deliberately, slowly and carefully in more than a dozen lorries and scattered throughout the country.'[20] Traynor replied that the army did not lose all or nearly all its reserve stock, the quantity removed being not much over 5 per cent, and if stocks stored in magazines and barracks throughout the country were taken into account then the total taken was less than 3 per cent.

This exercise in political semantics did little to illustrate the appalling vista that the raid presaged for political stability in Ireland, although de Valera certainly did realise the attendant danger to democratic rule.[21] Bryan understood the connotations for the army and particularly for G2, describing the event as 'our Pearl Harbour'. He could scarcely have used a more telling analogy. The time had come for the government to commit the security resources of the state to prevent the demise of democracy, a civil war, and the spectre of British reconquest of the Free State. The magazine fort raid was the catalyst required to take the necessary measures.

It is ludicrous to accept that one traitorous storeman was responsible. The standard military judicial process, arguably ultra humane compared to that of the Axis powers, duly punished the military personnel found in dereliction of duty. The entire saga reflects in microcosm the piteous state of the army in 1939. It was an emasculated force, devoid of morale and lacking discipline, with hardly a vestige of pride in the national ethos. This was the inevitable result of shameful political neglect and strangulation of the defence budget since 1925. The following table illustrates the accuracy of my contention.

Table 1: Defence Expenditure as a Percentage of Total Government Expenditure, Select Years in the Period 1922–45

Year	Total Government Expenditure	Defence Expenditure	Defence as % of Total
1922–3	26,580,784	7,459,104	28.1
1923–4	35,003,462	10,461,401	29.9
1924–5	24,671,570	3,003,164	12.2
1925–6	23,469,561	2,804,595	11.9
1929–30	20,769,824	1,259,500	6.1
1933–4	26,039,980	1,160,847	4.5
1937–8	28,111,919	1,511,501	5.4
1938–9	28,248,822	1,771,721	6.3
1939–40	29,464,841	2,925,610	9.9
1940–1	32,806,089	6,800,430	20.7
1941–2	35,433,211	8,015,771	22.6
1942–3	37,942,700	8,343,269	22.0
1943–4	40,034,530	8,309,583	20.8
1944–5	43,421,572	8,066,991	18.6
1945–6	47,679,814	8,844,280	18.5

Source: Estimates for Public Service 1922–3 to 1945–6 (Stationery Office, Dublin).

Both Bonar and Lee's scholarly analyses substantiate this contention. Bonar argues that as a percentage of GNP the spend on defence was 0.97 per cent in 1926–7 and 2.06 per cent in 1939–40, reaching a height of 4.15 per cent in 1942–3 followed by a continuous decrease to 3.35 per cent by 1945–6.[22] Lee maintains that Ireland came through the war relatively comfortably because 'she economised on defence'. She failed to match the expenditures of the other neutrals, Sweden and Switzerland, countries that Lee contends pursued a policy of armed neutrality as against Ireland's half-armed neutrality.[23]

The IRA: From Success to Impotence, 1939–45

Lee[24] and Bowyer-Bell agree on the relative extent of the ammunition captured in the raid, the latter contending that 'The IRA was free and clear with thirteen lorries of ammunition, 1,084,000 rounds, the bulk of the Irish army's reserve supply.'[25] Any raid on an Irish military installation was going to cause a major scandal, and Bowyer-Bell believes the IRA failed to consider the impact the raid would have on the organisation's very potential to exist.[26]

Robert Kee is of a similar view. He argues that sentimental ambivalence towards the IRA lingered in Fianna Fáil minds for a long time, but that the raid proved a turning point, hardening the government's attitude to the illegal organisation. This new climate saw four IRA men, one a veteran of 1916, executed in Dublin for killings in which they were involved.[27]

The combined security forces' action proved devastating to the IRA, with army/Garda cordon and search operations paying massive dividends in terms of ammunition recovery. Bowyer-Bell comments that the combined operations 'would eventually net more than was lost' as many old dumps around the country had come to light.[28] His account, initially critical of military planning, is thereafter complimentary, justifying the trust placed in the ability and clarity of mind of Major General Brennan in a crisis leadership role.

The chief of staff prioritised the intelligence estimates of Archer and Bryan of G2 in his operational planning, modifying plans according to updated intelligence summaries. All three officers were keenly aware of the importance of army/Garda cooperation. The fact that Colonel W. R. E. Murphy, Garda commissioner, and the army senior staff had been veterans of the pro-Treaty forces during the Civil War can only have helped.

Bowyer-Bell describes the intensity of the search:

> All police, military garrisons, and reserve units were notified. By dawn the greatest search operation in the history of the Irish army had begun. Nothing could move on the roads without attracting attention. Spotter planes were used. Roadblocks cluttered eastern Ireland. Traffic crawled from one spot to another. Everyone who might have seen or heard something was contacted. Houses of known Republicans were raided. The hills were patrolled, turf piles overturned, barns combed out, and back rooms ransacked. For days all of Ireland watched fascinated as the great December cartridge hunt continued.[29]

He outlined the almost frenetic attempts of local IRA units to hide the booty. Unwitting victims of a flawed follow-up planning process by their GHQ, they were overwhelmed by the sheer magnitude of ammunition they were expected to hide. Even 100,000 rounds was vastly beyond their storage capacity. Cellars, sheds, cars, even pianos, were pressed into use. Many half-loaded lorries were left in laneways. The mind-boggling scenario was to lead to immediate and progressive failure and eventual disaster for the IRA membership and organisational structure. By 1 January 1940, 850,000 rounds were recovered. By 29 January 1940, old dumps were exposed; many IRA members including a leading figure, Jack McNeela, was captured and an American radio transmitter was confiscated.[30] Government reaction, initially severe, escalated to the draconian. On 3 January, Boland demanded additional powers to crush the IRA.[31]

The Emergency Powers Bill, despite a plethora of legal challenges, was rapidly legislated. The Emergency Powers Order had been promulgated on 3 September 1939, and from early 1940 amendments and ministerial orders increasingly strengthened government power, including the use of military courts to try charges of exceptional gravity. Such courts could sentence to death those found guilty, while Minister Boland was empowered to intern on suspicion, a power he invoked unequivocally. An example of Boland's stance was his warning to the Seanad that even more stringent measures would be used: 'For some time past there has been no shooting or blowing up of public buildings, but if a state of war should come there will be a more drastic order . . . nothing short of drumhead courts-martial.'[32]

The gardaí rounded up hundreds of listed suspects for internment, while the military courts inexorably pursued the sentencing of those already arrested. While such summary justice was dispensed, one case in particular, that of Tomás MacCurtain, son of Lord Mayor MacCurtain of Cork, murdered by Crown forces in 1920, led to criticism of de Valera and his government. The young MacCurtain, an IRA man, shot and killed a Detective Roche while resisting arrest in Cork in 1940, and was duly condemned to death. However, his punishment was commuted to life imprisonment shortly before the execution date in July 1940. Maffey wrote that de Valera 'followed the weak course, as usual. Nevertheless he will not escape bitter criticism – Mr Cosgrave has already voiced it to me.' MacCurtain was released in 1948, and later took part in the IRA's border campaign of 1956–62. Others were not so fortunate. In April 1940 two prisoners detained since September 1939, Tony D'Arcy and Jack McNeela, were allowed starve themselves to death. The hunger strike of which they were part was subsequently abandoned without securing concessions.[33]

The magazine fort raid had a fourfold effect on military/political life in Ireland during the Emergency. First, it galvanised the government response to any internal subversive threat to its existence;[34] secondly, it reduced to some extent the political ambivalence that had prevailed since the Civil War. De Valera and his Emergency government used repressive measures of internment, military courts and the death sentence to render the IRA virtually impotent, and it proved so effective that by 25 April 1941 the Admiralty weekly intelligence report number 59 stated that 'the general impression is that . . . the Government have the IRA well in hand', an observation supported by RUC reports.[35] By January 1943 E. R. 'Spike' Marlin, the highly respected Office of Strategic Services (OSS) operative in Ireland, with whom G2 cooperated, reported to his Washington organisation that 'the IRA completely lacks anything resembling cohesion or discipline'.[36] Thirdly, Garda/army cooperation was strengthened in dealing with 'the enemy within'; and fourthly, G2 maintained more than a peripheral interest in the IRA, essentially a Garda responsibility.

Following the magazine fort raid, according to Bryan, the army – which had until then not been involved in matters relating to the IRA – started receiving reports about the organisation's activities, and from then on quite an amount of information came to intelligence from army sources. Prior to this, a reserve officer in the Eastern Command Intelligence, Captain Nicholas Leonard, had brought some unusual IRA activity to the attention of the relevant authorities, but the Garda superintendent accused him of causing alarm and Leonard was directed to cease his enquiries. Bryan does not mention who directed him but one would imagine that Hugo MacNeill, as general officer commanding, would have been involved.[37]

THE EMERGENCY: CENSORSHIP IMPLEMENTATION, 1939–45

The First World War had established propaganda as a powerful political weapon, and its power in the 1920s and 1930s was increased by the development of mass media.[38] Censorship became an important mechanism of control in the Emergency, designed in its various manifestations to maintain the security of the state. Correspondence between the assistant controller of censorship and the private secretary to the Minister for Co-ordination for Defensive Measures in 1940 clarified what the existing legislation allowed the minister to censor: complete censorship of postal and non-postal communications; complete censorship of telegrams and cablegrams and for total suspension of the telegraph service; restriction or total suspension of the telephone service; censorship of newspapers and periodicals; and the seizure of documents of any description whatsoever.[39] Further legislation to countermand any loophole that newspaper editors or correspondents might detect was envisaged.[40]

Ó Drisceoil lists the further legislation enacted,[41] which, combined with the existing law, allowed the minister, Frank Aiken, to impose draconian censorship during the Second World War. Prior to the passage of the Emergency Powers Act the censorship of letters undertaken by G2 under warrant for the Minister for Justice was operated under the 1908 Post Office Act.

The comprehensive nature of the censorship was anathema to the press, particularly *The Irish Times* editor, Bertie Smyllie. He castigated the controller of censorship, Tommy Coyne; the chief postal censor, J. J. Purcell; the chief press censor, Michael Knightley; and indeed the minister himself.

A memorandum for government issued by Aiken on 23 January 1940 epitomised government policy in relation to neutrality, censorship and democracy for the remainder of the Emergency.[42] The minister was determined to introduce censorship to suppress any published matter that might endanger the neutrality of the state. These included statements, suggestions or epithets casting doubt on the reality of neutrality or the wisdom and practicability of maintaining neutrality. Aiken included terms of a nature likely to cause offence to governments of friendly states and expressions likely to cause offence to the peoples of friendly states, whether applied to individuals, the system of government or the culture of the people of such states. He reminded the government that it was its policy both to remain neutral in the event of war and to prevent any power using this country as a base for an attack against Britain. He counselled caution against any denunciation of assertive government action intended to secure public safety and the preservation of the state.

One of the extraordinary powers the government obtained was that, whenever the government believed it was 'necessary or expedient for securing the public safety or the preservation of the State, or for the maintenance of public order' in 'time of war' (as amended), it should have the power to make an order 'for prohibiting the publication or spreading of subversive statements and propaganda and authorise and provide for the control and censorship of newspapers and periodicals'.

Aiken's memo was a scathing reminder to 'self-styled democrats who would hold on to the peacetime liberalistic trimmings of democracy while the fundamental basis of democracy was being swept from under their feet by the foreign or domestic enemies of their democratic State'. The memo concluded: 'If newspapers or ordinary citizens feel aggrieved they can make representation to their elected representatives. Whoever says he is not satisfied with such a system of democracy in 'time of war' is either a very foolish democrat or an agent provocateur for those who want to overthrow democracy or to embroil us in civil or foreign war.'[43]

Aiken attached a short report to his memorandum outlining what other neutral countries such as Denmark, Norway, Sweden, Belgium, Holland, Spain, Italy and Switzerland were doing regarding censorship.[44]

Aiken's critics did not consider him a man of high intelligence. Commenting on the minister's unyielding stance on censorship, Frederick Boland stated that, 'unfortunately, good judgement was not Frank's long suit.'[45] Gray cites James Dillon, who despised the minister, as stating that Aiken had a 'mind half way between an ape and a child'.[46] Keogh, however, believes Aiken was a worthy choice for the job of presiding over wartime censorship. 'He was rigid and unyielding, as Roosevelt had come to realise, and he was determined not to let anything past his gimlet eye.'[47]

Post, private and public telegrams, telephone communications, the conveyance of informative articles by travellers, cable and wireless communications, signalling, and even carrier pigeons were all subjected to an authorised form of control. Implementation orders were made by Aiken to give full effect to the provisions of the law.

The increasing use by G2 of the Post Office as the Emergency proceeded signalled the evolving power given to intelligence gathering. Between 1940 and the end of the Emergency the supervision of telephone conversations was overseen by the Post Office for G2. The question of the legal position was raised by G2 at the time, but no statutory telephone censorship was imposed.[48] One could not imagine G2 having any great objection to such a decision, at that or any other time.

Joseph T. Carroll suggests that the country at large had little idea of any diplomatic success de Valera might be achieving, and that the war itself seemed remote and even unreal.[49] The first censorship directives issued to the press forbade even the slightest discussion of the neutrality policy, weather reports, movements by defence forces, or any reports that could prejudice economic or financial security. The censors interpreted the directives strictly. The Catholic weekly, the anti-British *Standard*, caused the government some embarrassment by implicitly questioning whether Irish neutrality was really impartial.[50] MI5's agent in London on Irish operations was Cecil Liddle, a brother of Captain Guy Liddle, who had Irish connections by marriage, and was also in MI5. Both agents visited Dublin frequently during the Emergency and were on very friendly terms with the Irish army staff.[51] British intelligence agents who were acting without proper authorisation were arrested in 1939–40, but without any publicity, and were eventually handed back to their superiors.[52] Carroll claims that 'Stalin and atheistic communism aroused far more dread and revulsion in Ireland than did Hitler and the racist Nazis'.[53] He adds that a group including scientists, academics and administrators in various positions in Irish life and the German foreign office sailed for Germany on 11 September 1940 when in all probability the Wehrmacht could have benefited more by using them in Ireland.[54]

According to Carroll, the British government assumed that clerical opinion was similar to Irish opinion in general, given the influence of the Church;[55] consequently, British political and intelligence networks adopted certain courses of action. The *Standard* was reflective of clerical and laity opinion. Sir Shane Leslie empathised with Cardinal MacRory, a fiery Northern nationalist, who complained that he felt cut off from information, and lacked contact with government authorities. Leslie suggested that the Ministry of Information in London keep the cardinal informed.

Carroll contends that Frank Pakenham[56] had, by October 1939, become aware of Churchill's pressure on the Admiralty and the War Cabinet to take action over the Irish ports. Pakenham wrote a memorandum, passed to the foreign office, which urged that such action would have a disastrous effect on Irish pro-Allied neutrality. Despite Churchill's bellicose pressure, Pakenham advised that the Irish government be given six fast anti-submarine craft to permit them to exclude German U-boats from their waters; the boats were soon supplied by London. Pakenham's unease influenced the British not to take rash action concerning the Irish ports. Churchill, in character, was wisely restrained by Chamberlain and Eden.[57]

Keogh feels that, after de Valera received support in the Dáil for the emergency legislation in September 1939, the most important Cabinet change was Frank Aiken's appointment as Minister for Co-ordination of Defensive Measures, effectively minister for censorship. The strict censorship regime in Ireland meant that much of the public remained ignorant about what was happening in continental Europe.[58] Key censorship personnel were identified before the outbreak of war, as stipulated in Costello's 1926 military plan. Commenting on G2's strong interest in the operations of the censorship system, Keogh states that designated individuals who were of interest to Bryan as Director of Intelligence for one reason or another, had their mail intercepted and opened. Francis Stuart, Charles Bewley[59] and others known to have Axis connections were on a priority list.

Keogh's comments on G2's thorough cooperation with both Irish and British censors illustrate Bryan's implicit intelligence methodology. His interception of Leopold Kerney's[60] mail, giving information on illicit use of Kerney's diplomatic privilege by Charles Bewley's relatives, mail destined for Frank Ryan, and phone tapping of foreign legations was considered a norm rather than unusual intelligence procedure.[61]

In September 1938 de Valera regarded food supplies and external trade, followed in decreasing priority by censorship, counter-espionage and coast-watching, as matters needing immediate attention. He gave these issues higher priority than military measures and air raid precautions.[62] De Valera had a number of political priorities at that time, including a definitive authentic policy of neutrality; the desire to maintain the country's commercial life; and the safeguarding of its political integrity from external pressures. He made only minimal defence preparations, on the grounds that neutrality – if strictly adhered to – would obviate the need for enormous military expenditure. The country's economic dependence on Britain was de Valera's main concern, which he emphasised to the Dáil in February 1939: 'It is possible that . . . if we desired and tried to carry on the trade which is essential to our economic lifeline here, we would be regarded as a combatant, and our neutrality would not be respected.'[63] This was in keeping with the continuing policy of de Valera's government, and of all governments since the foundation of the state. De Valera had little alternative but to explain to the Germans how much this country's economic survival depended on Britain. He did not hesitate in showing his concern that the country's neutrality be respected by all combatants.[64]

Hempel, the German minister in Dublin, understood the message, and de Valera naturally hoped that Germany would thus accept that 'this consideration' did not impugn Irish neutrality. It was a pragmatic appeal from a head of government who knew the limitations of his untried policy. It was also an admission of Éire's vulnerable diplomatic status. In summer 1939 de Valera still appeared confident that neutrality was the only coherent policy for Éire to adopt.

For their part, the British could be under no illusion concerning the attitude of Éire.[65] De Valera's suspicions of the British motives were fuelled by their continual refusal to supply his army with arms and he explained this to both General Mulcahy and Dillon in January 1941. They had been, according to Fisk, endeavouring in every possible way to get the British to make a declaration that they did not intend to invade this country. 'If you don't intend to invade this country why not supply us with the arms we want?' asked de Valera. He therefore took it that the non-supply of arms meant that the British intended to invade. He believed that, even if the British promised not to attack Ireland and if Ireland helped them to concentrate on any German danger, it still did not rule out a British invasion. One could argue that his attitude fostered the old Irish distrust of British motives (a form of *timeo Danaos et dona ferentes*).

Fisk adds that de Valera could not shake off the idea that Britain might have some long-term ambitions in Ireland, and that he developed this theme in May 1940 when conscription was once again proposed for Northern Ireland. Mulcahy and O'Higgins believed de Valera's concern bordered on paranoia. Fisk expresses the opinion that, under these real or imagined pressures, de Valera maintained the sort of hard-faced neutrality that Aiken espoused. O'Higgins wrote his own somewhat bloodthirsty assessment of this policy, outlined to him by de Valera's ministers in March 1941.[66]

At a briefing de Valera gave to Mulcahy and Dillon in January 1941, Dillon asked if it was not likely that Éire would find herself 'at war with the United States, Great Britain and Germany combined'. This amazing supposition was apparently taken quite seriously by de Valera, who 'could see the danger of getting into that position'.[67] Despite the government's fear that invasion could come from either of the two belligerent powers, both it and the army were pragmatic enough to know that the only chance the army had to defend the country was by means of guerrilla tactics. De Valera's belief in his own hedge-fighters' rhetoric, however ill-advised, found an empathy with most of the Irish Cabinet, who had been guerrilla fighters against the British between 1916 and 1921.[68]

Fisk mentions in particular Tom Barry, the legendary guerrilla leader who established the IRA's West Cork flying column and attacked the British army with devastating effect in 1920 and 1921. Barry volunteered his services in 1939 and allegedly became Costello's operations officer in the 1st Division.[69] By way of asterisked footnote,[70] Fisk states that on Barry's death in 1980 Costello praised his shrewd judgement and remarkable insight into the capabilities and weaknesses of possible invaders. Costello's account, however, was contradicted by Seán Cronin, a former editor of the *United Irishman* and later Washington correspondent of *The Irish Times*, who claimed that the army treated Barry like any other recruit in 1939, that the old IRA man packed his gear and returned home to Cork. Fisk omits to mention that Barry had been chief of staff of the IRA as late as April 1938. He resigned on their adoption of a motion backing the dissident Seán Russell's policy of what transpired to be a calamitous bombing campaign in mainland Britain,[71] a factor that cannot be ruled out in relation to his abbreviated service in the army. Cronin's account, to a large extent, lacks accuracy; Fisk's suffers from lack of substance.

FOUR

The Irish Army Intelligence System: Role, Methodology and Strategic Planning during the Emergency

G2: Its Role and Methodology during the Emergency

The intelligence branch of the army, G2, was pathetically debased following 1925, and continued so until 1939. Radically minimalised, it continued to function with virtually two officers – its Director, Colonel Archer, and the chief staff officer, Lieutenant Colonel Dan Bryan. By the end of the Emergency, however, the organisation had changed significantly, being largely manned in accordance with Table 104W of the Army Emergency Organisation (see below). Lieutenant Colonels

Table 104W[1]

	Int Duty	Central Control	East Sector	Cork Sector	Limerick Sector	West Sector
Capts	9	1	1	1	1	1
Lts	30+	3	1	0	0	0
Sgts	5	4	4	4	4	4
Cpls	5	5	5	0	0	0
Ptes	0	0	19	10	10	10

Addition 1: 6 Press Officers, 8 Intelligence Police Officers

Douglas Gageby (courtesy of the Honourable Supreme Court Justice Mrs Susan Gageby Denham).

Childers and de Buitléir, Captains Henry and Leonard, Commandant Quinn, Lieutenant Ruairí de Valera and Second Lieutenant Douglas Gageby played prominent roles as intelligence staff officers. Its personnel rose to sixty-five all ranks, with an additional thirty-four intelligence officers. Table 104W outlines the numbers in question, either under direction for intelligence duty or both under direction and attached, for administrative purposes, to the various elements of the army in which they were dispersed.

By 1944 G2 included the Director, Colonel Bryan, promoted from chief staff officer, his personal staff officer, Captain Healy, the executive officer, Major Guilfoyle, and three other officers. It also comprised seven subsections, as follows:[2]

A. Administration and regulations: gazette; war establishment; and map requisitions. The officer commanding had the rank of captain. One civilian, Mr Wing, was attached, in addition to five NCOs, three sergeants, two corporals and one private.
B. Information general: combat intelligence; books, requisitions. The officer in charge, Captain Kelly, had in his establishment two officers and two others attached (from wherever Colonel Dan Bryan chose to pick them), three sergeants, one corporal and one private.
C. Security – external: postal and censorship. This subsection, among the most sensitive and important, had a staff of three commandants, two captains, five lieutenants, one of whom was from the Naval Service. (Dr Richard Hayes was attached to them on part-time duty, his main concern being cryptology, a discipline at which he excelled. Additions included a Mr Smith and a quartermaster sergeant.)
D. Security – internal: The subsection was manned by one commandant, one lieutenant and two NCOs.
E. Coastal and air defence security: This was restored in April 1943 after a lapse of many years. The Air and Marine Service had a minimal staff of one lieutenant and one sergeant.
F. This subsection was concerned with publicity, press censorship, press liaison, photography – aerial and

ground – permits and film censorship, and press cuttings. Its officer in charge was the same Captain McCaul who had been sent by de Valera, under the guise of a Red Cross representative, to report on the conduct of the Spanish Civil War. Attached were Lieutenant Kelly, and a Mr O'Sullivan, whose speciality was the photography permits and film censorship aspect of the subsection. The private kept the press cuttings filed in the various journals.

G. Signals security: In charge was Commandant Neligan, with a Captain O'Sullivan as his staff officer. In addition the branch had the availability of three lady typists. In 1945, the system of reporting had changed for the better, and one centre, in Cork, catered for all reports to be passed to G2 in army headquarters. These embraced information on post-invasion France, and references to overland flights. Messages were handled as stated, in G2. Aircraft flights, convoys, including numbers of ships passing the Irish coast, were reported, and the work was considered most satisfactory.

Training in combat intelligence, especially up to the first major exercise in 1942, was of concern.[3] Correlation of intelligence reports exposed the following: Intelligence staffs on both sides were aware of the composition of the forces opposing them. In spite of this knowledge, which might not be available in war, the information on the enemy available at higher formations' headquarters was often both vague and unsatisfactory. Intelligence staffs were relatively large. The failure of the intelligence staffs to secure accurate information was attributed to faulty working of the intelligence system, and failure to verify and evaluate information received. Evidence from umpire reports stated that intelligence staffs on many occasions identified units at places where they had never been, and that these false identifications were accepted as evidence of the presence of units. More energetic steps on the part of the intelligence staffs to verify reports should have eliminated some of these errors. In one case, the intelligence report at the close of the exercise gave a very inaccurate picture of the situation, and did not give information which was available to subordinate formations and units. Had this intelligence staff been functioning farther forward and sent liaison officers to the headquarters of these formations and units, a more accurate picture of the situation could have been obtained. The intelligence plans were too elaborate, and better results might have been obtained by confining requests for information to more specific matters. In another case, although the terrain offered excellent possibilities for observation, no ground observation posts were established by the intelligence service. There appears at times to have been lack of liaison between G1 and G2 staffs. For instance, G2 report stated that one of their battalions had crossed the River Blackwater the previous day and had been repulsed. In fact, no crossing was made by the unit concerned.[4]

Even where the information available to G2 staff was reasonably accurate, there was often failure to analyse and evaluate it properly. One brigade was issued with an operation order, a list of the names of the principal commanders, staff officers and units on the opposing side; such information would rarely be available in war. On exercises, such action tended to divert the attention of intelligence officers from the collection and evaluation of the information obtained by contact with the enemy, which was their main task.

In most cases situation maps and work sheets were kept and G2 reports were submitted regularly.[5] The main lessons for the intelligence service were the need for prompt verification and analysis of reports, restriction of requests for information, and frequent visits by intelligence officers to headquarters of higher formations and units.[6] It was also recommended that message centres be improved because rechecks had to be made frequently.[7] Too often there were delays in the deciphering of messages, due to lack of practice by the personnel involved.[8] To what extent Bryan held responsibility for such lapses is debatable. He was responsible, however, for at least persuading both the Military College and each command to train its officers properly in the intelligence cycle and methodology.

Dr Richard Hayes, G2 Cryptologist

Richard J. Hayes was born in Abbeyfeale, County Limerick, on 26 June 1902, and his early childhood and youth were spent in Claremorris, County Mayo. Following graduation from Trinity College Dublin in 1924 with three honours BA (Mod.) degrees, in Celtic Studies, Modern Languages and Philosophy, he joined the staff of the National Library of Ireland (NLI) as assistant librarian in 1924, and succeeded Richard Irvine Best as librarian (director) in 1940. Shortly after the outbreak of war he was seconded to the Irish army to work on code-breaking. O'Halpin mentions that Hayes was a War of Independence veteran, a fact unknown to any of his family. Given Hayes' penchant for not revealing any service matters to his family, this is not too surprising. He continued during the war years to administer the library, returning full-time in 1945. He died on 21 January 1976. Among his plethora of literary publications is *Clár Litrídheachta na NuaGhaeilge 1850–1936*, compiled with Brighid Ní Dhonnchadha (3 vols).[9] This seems paradoxical, given that one of his alleged idiosyncrasies was a distaste of the Irish language.[10]

Throughout the war Hayes quantified the salient features of his work for G2, in chronological sequence. Little was achieved in 1940 other than a report by Hayes on the simplistic task of decrypting German agent Preetz's code, using the documents, system, book and keywords found in Preetz's room following his capture in August 1940.[11] Hayes' scathing summary of the (temporary) abandonment of his cryptological work in June 1941 alludes to the blasé approach of the army in allotting him two officers of clerical grade, even though he had requested two or three officers with good university qualifications in mathematics or science.[12] All transmissions to and from the German legation were monitored and logged from February 1941 by an army wireless section, to no cryptological benefit.

Following his arrest in November 1941, Goertz, another German agent, was questioned repeatedly in Arbour Hill prison. Allied to eighteen cipher messages found in German agent Held's house and others in agent

Dr Richard Hayes (courtesy of the National Library of Ireland).

Deery's possession, Goertz's cipher system was solved by Hayes and its mathematical implications studied. In addition, agent Marschner, who had escaped but was soon recaptured, had his cipher broken also. In 1943 Goertz's futile attempt to confuse Hayes by using a new code word from his Athlone military prison failed; Hayes broke the cipher after three weeks. A repeat attempt by Goertz in October 1944 also failed and Hayes decrypted all such ciphers until March 1945 when the series ended.

From August to October 1944 Hayes and his cohorts failed to decrypt codes based on a machine system, although Hayes felt sure that such was mathematically possible using a staff of four or five competent mathematicians over a period of three to six months. However, the process was abandoned due to time constraints and lack of skilled assistants. In 1945 a British cipher to the German resistance movement was broken in two days.

Hayes felt that they were inexperienced in the early war years and wasted some effort. He also admits the incurable optimism of his section, as against the British equivalent service whose vast resources simplified their cryptological methodology to a major extent. At the end of the war Hayes issued some stern advice to the government.

> We must not enter the next emergency without a nucleus, however small, of experienced staff. If we do, the danger will be over and the war lost or won before the necessary preliminary experience has been obtained. We must start in the next war where we left off in this, not surely from scratch again. The solution of many codes and ciphers

> depends on unremitting watchfulness and research waiting for the mistake to be made by the other side which is generally necessary to make success possible.
>
> For months they worked in England on double substitutions of great complexity until one day a horrid enemy operator forgot to make the second of the double substitutions and the whole system was split open in a few hours. For months also they worked on another cipher until one day an agent repeated a message in which he had previously made an error. From that moment the secret of all the disc-type ciphers was open. The whole success of a cryptographical department depends on this unending vigilance, waiting for the lucky break. An immense amount of mathematical research is necessary and it must be of the highest standard both of accuracy and imagination, but without the lucky break it is not enough. The ciphers of today demand the best brains available in quantity and all the time.[13]

Both Hull[14] and O'Halpin's[15] research supports Hayes' comments on the development of codes and ciphers. Hayes wrote that it was possible to view in retrospect the development of codes and ciphers during the war and to trace their history of ever-increasing complexity from the simple single transposition to the doubly transposed and substituted ciphers based on mathematically connected keywords used towards the end. While the greater part of the information available related to ciphers used by secret agents and transmitted by wireless, some facts concerning diplomatic and other codes were also included. Because of Ireland's geographical position, the ciphers with which Hayes and his staff had been concerned were nearly all German, apart from one British cipher and a comment on the Irish army cipher. Hayes continued:

> Ciphers have been of far greater importance in the present war than ever before in history. This was due to the universal use of wireless as a means of communication. Wireless has provided an extremely rapid channel for the sending of reports from agents to their headquarters and for the sending of instructions from the intelligence services to agents in distant countries. It has been used to a great extent as a method of communication between air, sea and land forces and their bases, and it has even been used by agents wishing to exchange information with one another in enemy country . . . secrecy can only be achieved by using really good ciphers . . . it became of vital importance to have the best ciphers possible and . . . to have the best cryptographical department . . . to enable ciphers to be broken . . . quickly . . . the British and American Governments expanded . . . cryptography services into vast organisations . . . staffed by combing the Universities for their best linguistic scholars and mathematicians. Calculating machines were used . . . capable of recording a hundred thousand sets of numbers and making fifty simultaneous calculations . . . Machines were . . . used to construct codes and ciphers as well as to decipher them. It

> may be asked how this unseen war of brains between the cipher makers and the cipher breakers ended . . . the cipher breakers won.[16]

Contextualising Hayes' work requires both comparison and contrast with his British counterparts in Station X, Bletchley Park, the Government Code and Cipher School (GC&CS). It was a catchment area for brilliant mathematicians, chess players, distinguished academics and linguists. The British used their talents and scholarly precision to break the German Enigma code, dubbed the 'Ultra Secret'. Churchill's description of Russia, 'a riddle wrapped in a mystery inside an enigma', can equally apply to the Enigma code, in Irene Young's view.[17]

Peter Calvocaressi describes the principle of Enigma as succinctly as possible: 'The Enigma was an encyphering machine that produced a highly variable scramble of the 26 letters of the alphabet by passing electric current through a set of movable rotors, each of which by its internal electric connections contributed to the overall scramble.'[18] Outlining the problem facing the code breakers, Michael Smith elaborates: 'There were 60 possible orders in which the wheels could be placed in the machine, with a total of 17,576 different position settings for each wheel. The plugboard allowed 150 million changes of circuit. The total number of possible settings for a basic German Enigma machine was, therefore, 159 million million million.[19]

Against all the odds the gifted cryptologists in Station X achieved the almost impossible and broke the Enigma code. Coping with even greater difficulties they broke Shark, the U-Boat Enigma and Fish, the cipher system used by Hitler to talk to his generals. Smith claims that the success of the code breakers arguably shortened the war by three years.[20] Bletchley staff grew from several hundred in 1939 to over 3,000 by 1942, and over 5,000 by the following year.[21] Although comparisons are considered spurious by some, this author believes the volume and quality of Dr Hayes' work for G2 during the war, with virtually no qualified staff, bears more than favourable comparison in relative terms with the work of Bletchley cryptologists.

The ciphers used by German agents varied. In the early years of the war they were mainly transposition ciphers. Having proved unsafe, however, they changed to substitution ciphers during the middle period, and double substitution combined with double transpositions towards the end of the war. The educational standard of the agent and the importance of his mission were factors to consider when selecting a cipher for him. The relative complexity of an agent's cipher was a measure of the relative importance of his mission and rank. One could find, in 1940, an agent using an absolutely first-class cipher equivalent to the best used towards the end of the war.[22]

Preetz, Hayes points out, came to Ireland in 1940 with a single transposition cipher, while Marschner was sent over in 1941 with a similar type of cipher. Single and double transpositions were the type in use for ordinary agents in these years and on through 1942. On the other hand, Goertz arrived in May 1940 with a cipher which, according to Hayes, the British cryptographers described as 'in the very first class and amongst the best three or four used in the war'. Towards the end of 1942 James O'Neill was sent out of Germany with a single substitution cipher. The following year Codd was trained both in transposition and substitution ciphers and at the end of 1943 O'Reilly came equipped with a substitution cipher operated by a disc. In 1944 and 1945 no agents reached this country. Had they arrived, they would have been equipped with substitution combined with transposition ciphers. Hayes' analysis of the various ciphers is instructive.

Preetz's Cipher

Wilhelm Preetz, married to an Irish girl from Tuam, was arrested following G2 surveillance shortly after the start of the Second World War. He fled bail but G2 traced him to Dublin, where both he and an Irish accomplice were arrested on 6 August 1942.[23] Preetz's cipher was a transposition in a cage twenty spaces wide based on the pages of a novel. The page was determined by adding the day of the month, the month and a constant. The preamble to his message was based on a numbering of the letters on the first unindented line of the page, and the letters at the beginning of each line for twenty lines down from the top formed the keyword for the transposition in the cage. A certain number of x's were used as nulls placed in a pattern in the cage. This letter was also employed as a full stop and emphasising sign with names. This kind of cipher is not difficult to break. If the language is German the c's and h's and the c's and k's can be tested in different links. In fact, an even easier method was available because a few of the messages contained the letter 'q' in the word 'frequenz'. The fact that 'q' was present made it clear that unless 'q' was a null it must form part of the sequence 'equen', as was in fact the case. Preetz made the foolish mistake of ending all his messages with the same word, 'gruesse'. Preetz had also, as all agents have, an emergency cipher to be used if he lost his book. The emergency cipher was a transposition based on a keyword which he carried in his head. The nulls in the cage, which was also twenty spaces wide, were fixed in position by the numbers of the letters of the keyword.[24]

Marschner's Cipher

Hans Marschner, a German artillery officer, was stationed in Hamburg on intelligence duties at the headquarters of a formation of the German army. He parachuted into County Wexford on the night of 12/13 March 1940. He was arrested on 13 March.[25] His cipher was also a simple transposition of the same type as the Preetz cipher. The keywords were obtained from the bottom of the page of a periodical. The cage was twenty spaces wide. (In fact nearly all German transpositions throughout the war were in cages twenty spaces wide.[26]) This illustrates the difficulty Germans had in avoiding 'method' where method is a disadvantage. If they had adopted variable widths in their cages it would have required a staff four times as large to produce the same results in the countries that were trying to break their ciphers. Marschner's emergency cipher was based on a fifteen-letter keyword. If any of the German agents, such as Preetz and Marschner, who were sent out with these simple transpositions in the first two years of the war had read Herbert Yardley's book *The American Black Chamber*, they would have realised that an efficient system for breaking their ciphers was in use in 1916. Apart from this book, of course, the ciphers would have been broken by any competent cryptographer in a few hours. The amazing thing is that the Germans made no attempt to conceal the 'ch' digraph by substituting another symbol for it or placing some agreed nulls in a position to split it. The lesson to be drawn from this is that there should be continuity between the cipher departments from one war throughout the peace to the next war. The colossal blunder the Germans made can only be explained on the assumption that the cryptographical staff in 1939 had no continuity with the staff of 1914–18.

Codd's Transposition Cipher

John Codd was trained as an agent but never sent to Ireland.[27] One of the ciphers in which Codd was trained was a transposition, again in a cage twenty spaces in width. By his time (March 1943) certain variations had been introduced into the single transposition. The variation consisted in Codd's case in numbering the horizontal columns and writing the clear text in each column across only as far as the space which had a corresponding number at the top of the column. This made the cipher somewhat more difficult to break – at least until the system was first discovered. Another variation on the simple transposition which was much favoured in 1941 and 1942 was to insert a very great number of nulls which might be any letters in the alphabet. Hayes had no experience of this variation but had been informed that at one stage the Germans were using 30 per cent nulls in their ciphers. This was no doubt abandoned because it must have led to a great number of mistakes in messages, rendering them uncertain or unintelligible. Codd was trained in 1943 in a substitution cipher based on a twenty-five letter square created by writing a keyword followed by the rest of the alphabet. The first figure in the substituted text is switched to the end and the figures are then substituted back into letters to give the final cipher text. This is a double substitution of which the Goertz cipher may be regarded as a further development.

O'Neill's Substitution Cipher

James O'Neill allegedly arrived in Ireland at the end of 1942 with encoding materials;[28] Hull, however, categorically disagrees with the allegation.[29] Recent research by this author, however, resulted in confirmation of O'Neill's capture while serving as a merchant seaman serving on the British ship SS *Duzesa* in the South Atlantic and subsequent internment in Germany. His return to Ireland in December 1942, and the fact that the military authorities, presumably G2, were looking for him is documented in excerpts from an army boarding and search report of SS *Kyleclare* in Dublin, a Garda file, a Foreign Affairs file and a censored account by the *Irish Press* dated 3/1/43.[30] O'Neill's cipher was a substitution cipher operated by a sliding rule and using a poem to give a series of letter positions for fixing the relative positions of the rule before enciphering each letter. It is of a type described in all standard works on cryptography and calls for no further comment.[31]

O'Reilly's Substitution Cipher

J. F. O'Reilly parachuted into County Clare on 19 December 1943 and was detained the same day.[32] A pair of discs with two jumbled alphabets were used in making this substitution cipher. The relative positions of the discs were designed to be altered before each letter was enciphered in ten positions corresponding to the numbers 0 to 9. There were two systems in use for providing a long series of numbers to control the alteration of the positions of the discs. The first and simplest was to write down a number followed by the date of the month and number of the month and continued by adding each figure to the figure immediately after it to give an endless series. O'Reilly was not intended to use this system. He was provided with a later invention – a microphotograph containing 400 sets of five-figure groups which were to be used from an agreed point. One of the defects in the type of disc used by O'Reilly was that the alphabets on the discs were originally created from a keyword instead of being chosen at random. This is another example of the German insistence on a systematic method where a hotchpotch mixture would have been more successful. One of the most interesting and valuable discoveries made in the O'Reilly case was a hitherto unknown method of turning letters into figures on a keyword in such a way that some letters were represented by a single figure and others by a two-digit number. This was discovered in the rough work in O'Reilly's cell when he was asked to prepare specimens of messages with his disc cipher. O'Reilly tried to fool them by combining this keyword substitution with his disc cipher. He then abandoned the attempt and refused to do any specimens but the method was seen before he destroyed his rough work.[33]

During the last year of the war the Germans developed an entirely new system of substitution and transposition ciphers. This single and double digit substitution system, which was unknown to the British and Americans, would never have been solved without the vital piece of information culled from O'Reilly's rough work, which appeared of quite minor significance at the time. In fact for a period of three months towards the end of 1944, the British were unable to read the ciphers in general use by the German High Command. After terrific efforts during which the fullest use was made of calculating machines, all the ciphers were finally broken. The 'black-out' coincided with Von Runstedt's counteroffensive through the Ardennes (the Battle of the Bulge), which lasted from 16 to 26 December 1944.[34]

Goertz's Double Substitution and Transposition Cipher

Arguably Hayes' work in decrypting Goertz's cipher was his most important, both to G2 and MI5/MI6. This was the best cipher used in Ireland by the Germans during the war. A full account of all its intricacies and the mathematical methods devised to break it is to be found on the Goertz file.[35] It was evidently reserved for very special purposes because, although the Germans knew of it in 1940, no agent except Goertz was trained in its use and other agents were sent out with third-class ciphers even though this first-class cipher was available. The Goertz cipher required no book or equipment; the whole system with the keywords could be memorised. A keyword is written into a twenty-five letter square. This forms a basis for turning the clear text into two-digit numbers. The set of numbers is written into a cage horizontally and the vertical columns of numbers are then transposed on the basis of the original keyword. The transposed vertical columns of figures are then substituted into letters by the original square to give the cipher text.[36]

In the interim, Richard Hayes and his staff, working with G2, managed, in collusion with their British counterparts, to break the German Legation code, and were thus in a position to inform G2 of the operations of the German consulate. Some difference of opinion exists among historians as to who actually broke the code. Helen Lytton maintains that it was not deciphered by the British Government Code and Cipher School but was deciphered by Hayes and shared with MI5.[37]

In contrast to the high volume of German material, only one British cipher was picked up, in March 1945, from a British transmission to a resistance group inside Germany. A few messages were picked up from each leg of the transmission. The cipher was a double transposition, each transposition being based on the same keyword. The first messages had a cage with a width of fourteen spaces; the subsequent messages were based on a keyword of thirty-one letters.

In contrast again was the low-secure Irish army cipher. In effect this cipher was a single substitution which repeated itself every thirty-two letters. Its security was very low. One must always distinguish between ciphers that require some kind of equipment and those that can be memorised or are based on an apparently harmless novel. Much higher security is to be expected from a cipher that requires equipment. Judged by this standard the Irish army cipher was very inferior; O'Reilly's disc cipher with its small and simple equipment was far safer.

The cipher used by the Irish army was based on a card that could be changed from day to day. The general system was a substitution based on thirty-two alphabets. The weak point in this system is that there are always thirty-two alphabets, never more or less. For short messages or a small number of short messages, the cipher is perfectly safe. However, as Hayes pointed out, the Irish army operated with a gaping hole in communications. It must be assumed that belligerents already discovered the type of cipher used. If twenty-four messages of about sixty words were picked up at various points, a central enemy unit would have between 6,000 and 7,000 letters to work on. These, written in columns of thirty-two, would give about 200 letters for each alphabet and the application of ordinary frequency tables to these 200 letters would quickly break the cipher. Bigram tables could also be applied to all the alphabets taken in pairs, while expert cryptographers would probably break the cipher with an even smaller amount of material available to them. With five or six assistants, two experts would deal with the material in an hour or two and the work could proceed from the moment the first message arrived.

The cipher could, however, be made relatively safe by adopting a simple device that loses none of its value even if the general order enforcing it were disclosed to the enemy. A general instruction could be issued, that those using the cipher should decide before enciphering any message to use a certain number of the columns of the card only – any number between twenty and thirty-two.[38]

Hayes also worked on deciphering German naval codes. These codes and ciphers came into Irish possession in March 1945 after the sinking of a submarine off Cork and the failure of the crew to take adequate steps to destroy the ship's papers. The codes were very elaborate and involved two substitutions after the original encoding from a code book. The substitutions were based on pages of figures and letters that were changed every day.

During 1940 some fragments of decoded messages were recovered from a crashed German aircraft. They seemed to be worked on a code book very similar to the naval code but without the substitutions. The naval code showed a great improvement on the air force code, being safe unless any of the code books were found or copied. The air force code was not unbreakable, although a large amount of material would be required on which to work. From a purely theoretical point of view, the fundamental idea of the Goertz cipher, the substitution from letters into figures and back again into letters, was used in the naval code.

Diplomatic codes were usually based on code books or machines. These were so designed that statistics compiled from thousands show an almost perfect uniformity of the figures or letters used, making them unbreakable unless the instructions for their use are not complied with or information from inside is available. Hayes believed that diplomatic codes were purchased or copied on a wider scale than generally believed:

> We have much to learn in this respect. Matters of this kind must, of course, be prepared years in advance. A great deal of effort was expended on the German diplomatic code without success. It should be noted that on any given occasion or for any special reason, an inside source could have been used to get copies of messages from the German legation in Dublin.[39]

One cannot discount the possibility that Hayes' analysis may have been correct. Neither can one be absolutely sure that Bryan did not have agents within a protagonist's legation.

In an unpublished account of his activities during the war, Dr Hayes recalled the following, which throws even further light on the ingenuity and resourcefulness of Irish intelligence services during the Emergency:

> After Goertz had been captured and put into Arbour Hill Prison I used to visit him once and sometimes twice a week and chat to him to try to get information from him. We built up a very friendly relationship. I began to work on his cipher and after several months finally solved it. The 14 or 15 messages finally proved to be practice messages

> relating to what happened to Goertz from the time he left Frankfurt to be dropped by parachute into Ireland and what happened to him for some months afterwards. He had evidently prepared these in order to send them whenever he could to Germany as he had no means of communicating after he escaped from Held's house because he had no wireless set. He lost his set when it was thrown out of the plane before he parachuted out and the wind took it away and he was never able to find it – that is, his transmitting set. It was a very complicated cipher going through 3 stages, 2 substitutions and 1 transposition.[40]

Hull has already outlined broadly Hayes' role in all G2 interrogations of spies.[41] However, Hayes' own account gives a greater insight into the range of challenges involved in cryptology:

> While Goertz was in prison, an Irishman who wished to work for the Germans, for money I would say, evidently had been given Goertz' cipher (by Goertz, I assume). He began to send messages to the German High Command in Lisbon. These were photographed by British Intelligence in Lisbon because the man, who was a cook on an Irish ship [Christopher Eastwood, motivated by Joseph Andrews[42]], instead of going to the Germans got frightened and decided to ask a Portuguese docker to deliver the messages and bring back the answers. The docker decided that there was money in this and went first to the

> British Embassy and handed over the messages to them. They told him to come back in a few days and that they would then give it to him to deliver to the German Embassy. They photographed the messages and the photographs were sent to London. Immediately there was considerable trouble and British Intelligence sent us over copies of these photographs and said that they were coming on an Irish ship to the German High Command in Lisbon.

One can at least assume from the foregoing passage that contact remained extant between G2 and its British counterpart.[43] Dr Hayes continued:

> I examined the messages and found that they were in Goertz' cipher, so we informed London that they were in a cipher the same as Goertz' system but that there was a different key word to the key word found in the messages from Held's house. We also said that if they sent over one of their cipher experts we would show him the method by which I had broken the Held messages. I had as a matter of fact worked out a system for breaking any cipher no matter what the key word was in the system. The British agreed and sent over the head of their Cipher Department from Bletchley in England to work with me for 2 or 3 days and study the method of reading the cipher. This event was of great advantage to Irish Military Intelligence because the people in London, while believing that we were doing our best to prevent the destruction of our

> neutrality by German agents working from Ireland, had the feeling that we probably were not competent as we had no experience in Ireland of this kind of international espionage. From then on, they treated us as their equals in this particular field.[44]

This author has seen no reference to Dr Hayes' specific recollection in wider literature, and sees no reason to doubt James Hayes' statement that the relevant document remains unpublished. Dr Hayes also recalled how they managed to get access to Goertz's code in the first instance:

> Perhaps I should now mention an experience I had with Goertz while he was in Arbour Hill Prison because it is a very amusing story. One day when talking to Goertz, I noticed that he had a bunch of papers in his hip pocket of his trousers – a rather thick bunch of papers. He was allowed to have papers in his cell because he passed the time reading and writing a play and therefore had all the materials for writing. I was very intrigued to know what was in this bunch of papers which he had in his pocket because I had suspected him for some time of being able to get messages out to the I.R.A. through some of the guards in the Prison who were Military Policemen. In fact this proved to be true, but we were unable to prove it at the time. I said to myself how can I possibly get at these messages or whatever they were in his pocket. I used to search his cell regularly when he was out on exercise but

> never found anything there which could have helped, and I asked myself how I could get at these papers which, being in his trousers pocket, went out with him when he went for exercise. It would have spoiled the friendly relationship we had built up with him if we had searched him, which of course we had a perfect right to do. He was searched when he came first after his arrest but there was no subsequent search afterwards.[45]

This statement must pose a question as to the lack of attention to vital aspects of security within the military prison. Hayes further recalled that Goertz

> ' . . . himself provided me with the solution of how to get at the papers without his knowledge. He happened to remark that his old ulcer pain had come back, he had a duodenal ulcer, and it was giving him trouble. I arranged for the prison doctor to have him x-rayed, determining to go through his clothes while he was being x-rayed. The doctor agreed, visited him and said that he needed x-rays and that it would be arranged during the following week. He was therefore brought to St. Bricin's [military hospital] under armed guard. I had gone there in advance so that Goertz would not see me there and remained in the doctor's private room downstairs while Goertz was brought upstairs to a waiting room. The idea was that I would go through his clothes while he was being x-rayed, copy the documents and replace them before he came back from the x-ray. I should mention that

> Goertz took the idea of being x-rayed in good part as he felt that great attention was being paid to his health. However, when I searched the clothes (he had been given a dressing gown only to wear while being x-rayed) in the ante-room there was nothing in the trouser pocket so that I knew that he must have forgotten to remove the documents when he changed into a different suit to come up for his x-ray. I rushed back to his cell therefore, found the papers in his other clothes, and rushed down to the General Post Office where we had machinery for photographing documents – very slow machinery which first made a negative from which a print had to then be made. There were about 15 pages in the documents and we worked as quickly as we could to photograph them, but this had taken a good deal of time – what with not finding it in the trousers in the hospital and having to go back to the cell and so on. Finally the phone rang (I should mention that of course Goertz could not be let back into his cell until I had replaced the documents in his other suit which he had not worn) and the doctor said that this man had been x-rayed in every position known to medical science, and in most positions had been x-rayed twice, he was blue with cold and for God's sake to hurry up. I asked him to give us 5 or 10 minutes when we would ring him and he could release him. The doctor agreed to this and I replaced the papers in his trousers in the cell.[46]

One wonders how Goertz, an officer of undoubted intelligence, did not become suspicious at the delay and question the reason for it. Much to the surprise of Hayes and de Buitléir, they did not find the codes but something almost equally interesting:

> What we had got was a complete account of how he proposed to escape from the Prison, very ingenious and something which nobody had thought of before. Arbour Hill Prison was a two-storey building and Goertz was not in an ordinary cell but in a store-room with barred windows on the first floor. Immediately above him was an attic, but the ceiling between him and the attic was an ordinary lath and plaster one. Goertz had conceived the brilliant idea of breaking into the attic through the ceiling and then moving a few slates, climbing out on the roof and sliding down to the parapet on the end of the roof. This was a distance of only about 6 ft. and the parapet was about 3 ft. high which would conceal him from any of the outdoor sentries posted around the prison. His plan was to crawl behind the parapet right round the prison, and having worked his way around the prison behind this parapet, Goertz meant to jump into a field in the back where he hoped to be assisted by an I.R.A. contact. The papers in his pocket went on to explain where he would go after he escaped – he would make his way to Glendalough to the house of Mrs Stuart, a Nazi sympathiser, and he arranged that the people in the house should walk across a clearing in the wood beside the house and drop a red handkerchief on the ground if the Police were at the house. On the

> other hand, if it was all clear, the person walking across was to drop a white handkerchief. Goertz would be hiding in the wood beside the clearing.[47]

The modus operandi employed by the authorities proved equally interesting, as Hayes continued:

> The following day the Commandant of the prison interviewed Goertz and said that he was rather ashamed of the state of the room in which he was imprisoned and he would like to repair it. He also asked Goertz if he would mind going down to an ordinary cell with the other prisoners adjacent to their cells while the room was being repainted which would only take 2 or 3 days. Goertz was very pleased at all the attention being paid to him and thanked the Commandant and agreed to go down. He was transferred downstairs and while the room was rapidly repainted (in a horrible shade of Board of Works brown) the upper side of the plaster in the attic had sheets of galvanised iron laid on it and these were fixed to the laths with 2 inch long screws. This meant that anyone who went through the ceiling from below would hit galvanised iron. Nothing happened for about a week and then one morning when the Military Police came in with Goertz' breakfast, they found him sitting on his bed blushing like a bride with plaster on the ground (white plaster). They went out, got a brush and pan and swept up the plaster and gave him his breakfast. Nothing was said by them or by Goertz. He had succeeded during the night in breaking a

> hole in the ceiling and then found the galvanised iron on the other side and so had to abandon his plan.[48]

Hayes also recalled that a message burnt by Goertz in the grate of his cell on 29 June 1943 was collected by Commandant de Buitléir and given to him. He continued:

> I brought the remains to the technical bureau, Kilmainham for chemical treatment. A door was carelessly banged in the dark room at Kilmainham while I was examining the document and it was blown to pieces on to the floor. I collected the parts and brought them away . . . I sought the assistance of an expert chemist in Trinity College, on whose discretion I could rely, for the chemical treatment of the particles. We procured a bottle of ink of the type actually used – Swan fountain pen ink, blue black. The ink was analysed to determine the iron content and experiments were then made with pieces of paper written on and burnt. It was found that the most suitable treatment was to place the burnt particles on glass slides and allow drops of solution to fall on them, the surplus after thorough immersion being poured off. The solution used was Potassium Ferrocyanide 2 per cent solution with the addition of a few drops of hydrochloric acid. The solution reacted with the iron in the ink and gave Prussian blue. All the particles became fairly legible, the greatest difficulty being to rearrange them in their correct positions. A certain number

> of particles were missing. In most but not in all cases the missing parts could be deduced. On the day that these burnt remains were removed from the cell a new cipher message headed 'KA-TFC DE . . . 5165' was found amongst Goertz's papers. It was naturally assumed that the burnt paper was the intermediate work of this cipher message. This was not the case. The real cipher message was in the burnt paper and it would seem that the message found in the papers was left as a blind and has no meaning.[49]

Hayes then outlined some of the technical aspects of the craft on deciphering work, something akin to working on a jigsaw from the reverse side:

> The burnt cipher message has been deciphered. It is of 126 letters and comes out on a keyword which is new to us – Cathleen Ni Houlihan. Unfortunately particles are missing in two parts of the first line of the message where a name is mentioned. Because of the nature of the cipher I can say with certainty that the missing letters can only be one of five letters. The text is as follows, omitting the two letters which are not available. Every other letter in the message is as enciphered by Goertz.
>
> 'Ask-EGP-X whether prepared to put money at disposal immediately (sic) after success the more chances x IRA must not know of it x discret x, Way up to you xx'.

> The name of the person in the beginning can only be
> C C
> A A
> *T EGP T* *Presumably x is an abbreviation sign*
> *H H*
> *L L*
> One possible interpretation is HEGPL. Assuming that Goertz made a mistake in enciphering and that G should be M meaning Hempel.

Hayes deduced the following from all his work on this cipher: that Goertz was able to get messages out from his cell; that there was someone outside who knew the keyword 'Cathleen Ni Houlihan' and could act on the message when received (Andrews? Mrs Andrews?); that a reply to the question asked in the message could be given perhaps by a carefully worded insertion in *The Irish Press*.

He had not yet tried this keyword on various unsolved messages; he felt it would take several days and doubted very much if it would solve any of them. Their letter frequencies seemed inconsistent with such a keyword.[50]

The contribution of G2 to the Emergency army was greater than the sum of its parts, many of whom were scattered throughout the country. Credit for such is shared by de Valera, Colonel Dan Bryan, Director of G2, his predecessor, Colonel Liam Archer and Lieutenant General Dan McKenna, chief of staff. Among its major achievements were its capacity to liaise successfully with MI5, the American OSS and the British army in

Northern Ireland. With regard to the army in the North, commanded by General Franklyn, de Valera did not seem to be averse to a certain amount of nepotism. The appointment of his son, Major Vivion de Valera, as liaison officer to General Franklyn ensured that in addition to Colonel Dan Bryan and the chief of staff, Lieutenant General McKenna, the Taoiseach was also kept informed of anything he needed to know by a member of his family. Such cooperation as existed between G2 with the Garda Síochána rendered the German infiltration and attempts to organise a spy network involving the IRA futile.

Every German spy was captured and interned very soon after landing, with the exception of Hermann Goertz. He eluded capture from 12 May 1940 to 12 November 1941, and eventually committed suicide rather than face repatriation to Germany at the conclusion of the war. G2 was also aware of Irish collaborators operating from Ireland, Germany, Spain and Italy. Colonels Liam Archer and Dan Bryan played major roles in reorganising G2 from 1938 onwards. Following victory in the Civil War, the army maintained a domestic intelligence system under its Director of Intelligence. It is interesting to note that its activities included the penetration of republican and communist organisations as well as internal army security work.

O'Halpin found little evidence regarding liaison on intelligence work between the Irish and British before 1938, but the wartime period saw significant cooperation between both intelligence services, considerably more friendly than that between the two governments.[51] The promotion of Dan Bryan to Director of Intelligence was of major significance. O'Halpin outlines some of the glaringly inaccurate views held by MI5 as regards the extent and efficiency of Irish counter-intelligence operations against Allied agencies in Ireland. The British assumed that the Irish were starting from scratch in forming a counter-espionage section in G2 in 1938.

This viewpoint failed to note, however, that the key Irish figures – Archer, Bryan and Hayes – had extensive War of Independence experience as clandestine operators. The MI5 Irish Section history paid generous tribute to Archer, Bryan and Hayes. MI5 had a misplaced fear that cooperation would be withdrawn if the Irish uncovered British covert operations within Ireland, but G2 had already penetrated the British Special Intelligence Service (SIS-UK) organisation in Ireland in 1940 and kept it under surveillance thereafter. Richard Hayes' codebreaking expertise for G2 proved of invaluable help to Bryan in his dealing with MI5 during 1943–44, prior to Operation Overlord, the Allied landings in Normandy.[52] The dictum, 'There are no friendly intelligence agencies; there are only the intelligence agencies between friendly states' remains valid. Bryan's cooperation was, like de Valera's neutrality, expedient rather then doctrinaire.

Passport control liaison provided a means to monitor alien visitors/possible international revolutionaries to Britain from the Dominions. The British gave the Irish a list of undesirables, the 'Passport Office Blacklist', carefully omitting the names that Scotland Yard and MI5 did not want included.[53] The appearance of a name on the blacklist did not necessarily mean that the individual was to be refused facilities. An application in that name should be dealt with in the light of additional information contained in records of the department.

The departure of the ultra-left for the Spanish Civil War to fight in the International Brigade meant that republicans no longer had to face the embarrassing charge of associating with communists as well as marginalising their standing in Catholic Ireland. In 1930 the government secretary, a former army Director of Intelligence, was conscious of the danger of cultural subversion, a matter that caused concern to the Cosgrave administration and its successors, leading them to introduce more draconian legislation. The IRA was therefore well rid of its International Brigade contingent, despite the latter's principled stand for democracy in Spain.

The IRA's next significant initiative in alliance building was its development of links with the Abwehr. This was to provide the Irish government with its gravest security problem when the Second World War broke out, because it threatened to compromise Irish neutrality. The strategic importance of Ireland to Britain has been adequately documented in Bryan's paper of 1936 ('Fundamental Factors').

It was not until 1938 when the naval installations in Ireland were handed over by the British to de Valera's government that the British took any interest in Irish affairs. For instance, a diplomatic representative was not appointed to Dublin until 1939, and for much of the interwar years ministers and officials seemed to know little and to care less about political conditions in Ireland.

O'Halpin believes the police Special Branch and MI5 kept a close watch on Irish republican groups in Britain. The Irish proximity to Britain may also have made British officials assume that in an emergency they could find out what was going on in Ireland simply by paying a visit, by consulting the government of Northern Ireland or by asking trustworthy parties in the country to keep them posted. Such parties included: British Petroleum, which regularly supplied the SIS (British) with material on the Russian oil products company in Dublin; Maurice Hanky, the accepted authority of inter-war British defence policy, who once obtained an estimate on Ireland's arms manufacturing potential from a Dublin firm of consulting engineers; and the remnants of the ascendancy, such as Elizabeth Bowen, who were only too happy to pass on information on the state of the country, the morale of its people, and anything else they felt would help the British government.

British recruits wishing to join either the navy or the army were screened lest the IRA tried to have its men enlisted. O'Halpin states that the authorities in Britain entrusted with such screening went about it in different ways, most of which he considers hare-brained, naturally attracting attention in Ireland. It was abruptly abandoned in 1936 when the IRA murdered one of those involved, the elderly Vice-Admiral Somerville, for allegedly supporting the application of some youngsters in west Cork to join some element of the British forces. This methodology was used by a gentleman known as 'Blinker' Hall, the wartime director of naval intelligence in the First World War. The War Office, using a practice explicitly approved by the Irish Cabinet, one much less provocative, more private, and probably more reliable, resolved the problem to the satisfaction of both the British and Irish authorities. They simply requested confirmation of character of applicants from the local civic guards.[54]

Security Organisation and Liaison, 1938–45

After the handover of the ports in 1938, so resented by Churchill, de Valera made a public pledge that Ireland would never be used by hostile powers as a base of operations against Britain. However, he was soon plunged into an abyss of potential treachery when he received a warning, passed to the Irish Diplomatic Mission in London, that the Abwehr was planning to use Irish nationals for espionage against Great Britain.[55] He was, of course, alarmed by this information and realised that Ireland needed a counter-espionage service. Responsibility was given not to the police but to army intelligence, G2. The Irish Director of Intelligence, Colonel Archer, travelled to Britain for discussions with MI5, and there followed a notable period of cooperation during which MI5 encouraged G2 to be the main security agency in Ireland. An official from the Post Office Special Investigation Branch was sent to London to be briefed on the various postal methods of assisting counter-espionage, and while there he also brought himself up to date on telephone supervision. As Ó Drisceoil points out, a postal interception unit was quickly set up within the Investigation Branch[56] and was operating efficiently before the war broke out.

O'Halpin outlines the rapid increase in cooperation in the area of security organisation and liaison between

1938 and 1945. The Investigation Branch unit reported not to the civil authorities but to G2, an arrangement that brought the army back into internal security work, since one of the principle objects of the system was to look for evidence of communication between the republican movement and foreign powers. MI5 also advised G2 to find a reliable man of the rank and capacity of a police inspector to make enquiries independently of the police, but the army considered this impracticable because it would lead to friction with the police and the Department of Justice. However, G2 became the conduit for information from MI5 concerning the movements of suspects into Ireland, while the police established an aliens section to supervise and report on suspicious characters. This collaboration quickly bore fruit. After a tip-off from MI5, a German visitor to Ireland was shadowed, and he left rather suddenly; it later transpired that he was an emissary from the Abwehr. Despite being trailed, he had managed to make arrangements for further contacts which resulted in two undetected visits to Germany by a senior IRA officer. A German woman in Dublin, to whose address a French naval officer was sending information, also left abruptly once the police put her under surveillance. In pure counter-espionage terms these matters were clumsily handled. Bryan felt the police bungled by watching suspects too closely. Nevertheless, the fact that the Irish authorities displayed such zeal was probably of importance in establishing their bona fides with MI5.[57]

Incompatibility within G2

Difficulties existed at the highest levels in G2. Relations between Bryan and his second in command, de Buitléir, were strained. Indeed, Hayes' work in cracking the Goertz code surprised Bryan, because he was not informed of such until a year after the code was broken. Bryan's remonstration with Hayes over such tardiness led to Hayes informing the G2 chief that de Buitléir had refused to transmit this information to his superior, cautioning that Bryan would only run hotfoot to the British with it. In the event de Buitléir was correct. As he had predicted, Bryan immediately passed on the breaking of the Goertz code to the British, for which he got very little in return. It would never have occurred to Bryan that he would be classed as pro-British simply because his job was to get on with his British counterpart in accordance with government policy. This rupture affected the transmission of vital information, such as the year-long delay in Bryan learning that the Goertz code had been broken. Bryan's description of de Buitléir's disloyalty does not differ significantly from Duggan's, who states that the subordinate, de Buitléir, had perfected his German in pre-war Berlin and Bryan considered him 'anti-British to the point of irrationality'. De Buitléir held the exact opposite view from Bryan. Duggan believed that both were 'good loyal officers with rather different ways of looking at things'. He adds: 'In a business where MI5 and SOE [Special Operations Executive] hated MI6; where the competing Abwehr agencies came to regard each other as the enemy; where the OSS, later to become the Central Intelligence

Agency (CIA), was riddled with hatreds, it is not surprising to come across incompatibilities in the Irish intelligence services.'[58]

Bryan may indeed have borne in mind de Buitléir's value as an interpreter.[59] De Buitléir was not overtly censured, despite an act of disloyalty that warranted severe censure.

Duggan maintains that Hayes never comprehensively broke Hempel's codes, but that the British did and lost no opportunity in putting the information to work, to make trouble for de Valera and to denigrate the effectiveness of his neutrality.[60] However, it is difficult to fully accept Duggan's claim, considering the amount of cooperation that existed, with de Valera's connivance and knowledge, between the security services of both countries. A large number of Irish citizens worked in Britain, and many thousands served in the British forces. The economic dependence that Ireland had on Britain was reciprocated to no little extent by Britain's reliance on Ireland with regard to agricultural produce.

Bryan realised how much the British and Irish had in common historically. He was devastatingly critical of IRA plans that projected German troop concentrations in impossible places, stating of Plan Kathleen that 'they were got up by an ex-teacher or an ex-customs and excise man, and . . . the Germans plan to bring warships where you couldn't even bring a row boat.'[61]

Bryan considered the breaking of the Goertz code to be quite important, insofar as the British picked up another line from Lisbon which originated in the code. The British admitted that they had not broken the Goertz code at that stage, and Bryan admitted later that

Hayes had broken it. De Buitléir evidently did not approve of the way Bryan was implementing government policy in contacts with London. Bryan did admit that sometimes G2 knew things that the British were after, but did not pass on the information. He also maintained that this happened in all intelligence organisations. Bryan stated that as soon as he took over from Archer as Director of Intelligence, he drove his section very hard, ensuring that nothing would happen to Irish security or to British or US security. He admitted that this policy was pro-British and insisted that G2 cooperated fully with the British and Americans on security matters that might affect them. He maintained that as the years went by he took a definite pride in the fact that his successful handling of the British and Americans on various issues resulted in their agreeing that the Irish G2 organisation did an excellent job. He also asserted that the chief of staff, Dan McKenna, was on the best of terms with the GOC in Northern Ireland, General Franklyn.[62]

Army General Staff Strategic Planning, 1944

The proscription of the 1944 document detailing what is regarded as the most important strategic planning to emerge from the army general staff towards the end of the Emergency, 'COS Memo – 23 August 1944', left a lacuna in historical research until recently. Its availability to the author now allows a more detailed account of the specifics mentioned.

COS Memo – 23 August 1944, submitted by chief of staff McKenna to the Minister for Defence, stated that the views expressed represented the considered opinion of the Council of Defence, general officers and senior officers of the general staff. It was a comprehensive, strategically oriented consideration of how the army of the future should be organised. It outlined in the starkest terms the total lack of preparedness for defence in 1939 and the possibility of voluntary induction of Irishmen to the Irish forces. It noted that during the Emergency, then coming to an end, the maximum strength of the army in permanent service never exceeded 42,000. Despite the efforts of the government, supported by all parties in the Dáil, the country found it impossible to increase the 1939 strength by more than 24,000, although during the same period an estimated 150,000 Irish citizens served in the British forces. The consequential defects inherent in the voluntary induction system – local covering forces with tactical reserves, no strategic reserves with influential striking power, high age profile and low medical standards – are all outlined. The voluntary induction system is condemned as a viable mobilisation method in favour of a partly compulsory national military training scheme with its attendant planning process. The memorandum literally sought a restated government response to a detailed strategic military plan for the future, and recognised that the nation as a whole had no realisation of the problems arising from the adoption of neutrality or the threat of invasion that arose during the previous four years. Such was the total belief of Major General McKenna and the general staff in the intelligence available to them from

Bryan's sources that the memorandum contained a detailed synopsis of both the British and German planning intentions for invasion.[63]

COS Memo, 23 August 1944[64]

In COS Memo – 23 August 1944 McKenna argued that the advent of the Second World War and the crisis of May 1940 found the country almost defenceless. The defence forces were inadequate in size, and neither trained nor equipped for war. The nation as a whole had no realisation of the problems arising from the adoption of neutrality nor of the imminence of a threat of invasion. Showing remarkable objectivity, the general staff raised two pertinent questions. The first concerned doubts as to the necessity for a defence force in the country, and the second was the value of any defence force which Ireland could afford to maintain. Before the Emergency, the general staff had the experience of front bench deputies seriously contending in the Dáil that 'disarmament was our best policy' and 'any forces we could afford to raise would be useless'; that 'if the Germans landed here other people will land to wipe them out'.[65]

The memorandum also questioned the viability of defence without a navy; while toying with the idea of arrangements with a naval power, the memorandum noted that during the Emergency there was general approval of neutrality and the idea of resisting any invader. Accordingly, then, defence should be bolstered. The general staff felt that there was no doubt that had the government not acted promptly in the summer of 1940, and had the people not responded, the country would have been occupied.

Recounting wartime experience, the memorandum pointed out that on 4 July 1941, two senior officers of the general staff obtained definite information that the army commander in Northern Ireland had been asked to formulate a plan for the invasion of the South. Also, they had in their possession definite evidence that in 1941 the Germans were considering the possibility of invading the country. The German plans had advanced to the stage where, in conjunction with 'Fall Gruen', a military handbook on Ireland was completed in Berlin on 15 October 1941 by the German general staff.[66]

The Irish general staff had recognised, therefore, that even though neither the British nor German plans were implemented, a real threat existed. They argued that it was not possible in 1944 to predict the positions of the great powers, but there was no doubt that whatever form the peace settlement would take, it would probably result in future war. McKenna felt that Irish neutrality created problems for Britain in the war, and their anticipation of Irish involvement following the Americans' entry had not materialised. Therefore, Britain would try and ensure Irish involvement in a future war.

The memorandum assumed a neutral position in future wars and planned operations, staffing and equipment on that basis. Such forces would be sufficiently strong to defend the country, obviating any basis for a pre-emptive strike by Britain. And although Britain's possession of the six counties complicated planning, the main consideration that would deter Britain from invading the South was the belief that it would cost them more than it was worth. Nonetheless, the problem of countering British aggression was much more difficult than the that of countering continental aggression, as the six counties provided Britain with a secure and ready base for operations against the South, while Britain's huge naval and air resources meant it could invade Ireland at any point.

The recommended 'Scheme of Defence' should provide for a number of key elements. Air and coastal defence required a small naval or marine service, a coast-watching service, fixed coast artillery defences, and protective units for aerodromes and other vital landing fields. The availability of tactical forces at strategic centres was necessary, particularly on the south and southwest coasts, the border, and a strong striking force centrally disposed. A small airforce would cover and operate in conjunction with ground and sea forces, and in the event of air attack would give a measure of protection to Dublin and other cities. Local defence forces would mainly provide relief for field troops for operational commitments. The general staff maintained that this scheme could deter continental aggression, and act as a counter to British allegations that Ireland was too weak to defend itself.

All such assumptions leave plenty of room for argument, particularly the following one in relation to strength, where one's immediate analysis tends towards a mindset of pious aspiration on behalf of the general staff. They estimated that a defence force of approximately 100,000 supported by a local force of about

150,000 was necessary. This would involve a regular army approximately double the size of that which prosecuted the Civil War, and the financial cost of maintaining that establishment was the chief reason for the hasty demobilisations in 1923–24. The 1944 plan was, therefore, highly ambitious.

Nevertheless, they envisaged a phased growth of the army. The first 'transition' phase would see a force of approximately 60,000, with local defence forces of at least equal strength. It was estimated that it would take at least three years to rebuild, equip and convert the current full-time Emergency army into the desired force. The general staff outlined two distinct elements forming both field forces and separate garrison units, and recommended that the strength of the permanent force would depend on whether the government adopted a compulsory or voluntary system of training. Assuming compulsory training, the permanent force would be about 15,000 strong, consisting of 9,500 field forces and 5,500 garrison troops. The plan outlined in detail the structure of the envisaged future army and the tasks allotted to each element. It included the caveat that, should it be decided to continue the voluntary system, 'it should then be decided to form a much stronger permanent force as required'.[67]

The great weakness inherent in such a voluntary system was that it was based on the principle of maintaining a small permanent force, which in time of Emergency was to be expanded to provide a defence force capable of defending the country. No such expansion is possible within a limited period, unless the officers and NCOs are already trained and the reserves available. Failure in this case was due to an impractical government policy in relation to the army from 1925 onwards.

While the government on the one hand held laudable objectives in relation to training a small army corps, in which every man should be trained to a level beyond his rank structure and every NCO to officer standard, it seemed to have failed on the basis that the general staff specified. A lack of sufficient education, a pernicious finance arrangement, excessive guard duties and low rates of pay deterred the better type of man from enlisting. Such circumstances made it impossible to provide from the permanent defence forces a sufficient proportion of trained officers and NCOs for the forces, which had to be raised rapidly during the early days of the Emergency. Not surprisingly, chaos ensued. The various classes of reserve – Class A, Class B, the volunteer reserve, the volunteer force, the first line reserve, the second line reserve and the third line reserve – were in effect a collective failure. This was due to lack of finance, since virtually 1925, for building the necessary infrastructure and having the necessary training staff available.

The general staff observed that, during the period of acute crisis, they never obtained the number of men necessary to ensure strategic mobility. At best, they could not provide much more than local covering forces, with tactical reserves. They also conceded other defects: with a high average age, the medical standards had of necessity to be low; otherwise it would have been quite impossible to organise field formation to meet any threat. Incredibly, some 8,003 officers, NCOs and men had to be medically discharged, unfit for service, over a four-year period during the Emergency.[68]

The memorandum could not visualise how a necessary defence force could be built up and maintained under a voluntary system, and posed questions relating to the planning for compulsory national military training. Noting the historic antagonisms towards conscription in 1917–18, the staff nevertheless felt that the threat during the Emergency would have changed public opinion. That was of course a political consideration, well beyond the brief of the military. However, national service was possible, and the scheme they envisaged would see all medically fit men between the ages of seventeen and twenty undergo a continuous period of not less than four months' initial training at a military depot. A reduced period of three months was envisaged for Local Defence Force (LDF) personnel who, prior to reporting, had attained a prescribed standard of fitness. Working on census returns, the staff calculated it would take three years to raise the initial force of 60,000 and that the higher number of 100,000 would be achieved within seven years.[69]

The memorandum challenged the government to either endorse the plan, including national service, or indicate an alternative. Perhaps more importantly for policy formations purposes, the memorandum questioned whether agreement for provision of an annual instalment of equipment would automatically allow the Department of Defence the power to initiate purchase action, without further sanction from the Department of Finance. It also queried whether the proposed munitions factory would proceed. These problems were very real for the army. The general staff noted the complete lack of modern equipment as the most serious problem during the Emergency. The organisation of practically every field unit in the forces had to be drawn up on the basis of available equipment, but it was impossible to secure advance information on assets. Therefore, organisation frequently changed when fresh consignments became available, while training programmes had to be similarly rearranged and amended on the basis of equipment availability. The general staff also noted that the supply of new equipment had an invigorating effect on morale.[70]

Some aspects of the pre-war procedure were unsatisfactory for the general staff. For example, the British suggested in the years prior to 1937 that the Irish army send their equipment particulars to them for inclusion in the overall purchase of equipment for the following year so that they could include Irish requirements in their contracts and thus ensure delivery to the army within the appropriate financial year. This could not be agreed to, however, on the grounds that the Irish army could not incur expenditure before the Dáil approved the necessary finances. Embarrassingly, when danger threatened, the army had to ask the British and Americans for equipment for a defence force, including local, of 250,000, irrespective of what financial provision had been made. The general staff was pragmatic enough to state that they could not expect this to continue in normal times, but at least the finance procedures of circumvention should not again be allowed to deprive them of essential equipment.

Despite all such recommendations, the end product was nil. One of the most cogent and far-seeing documents produced since 'Fundamental Factors' in 1936, the memorandum to all intents and purposes gathered dust on shelves in civil servants' offices in Defence and Finance, proscribed until recently under the Official Secrets Act. What chance, then, that the army proposal, included in the plan, that a munitions factory, which was under consideration since 1926 and which had been deferred by the contracting firm Imperial Chemical Industries in 1939 until the end of the war, could now become a viable enterprise? The army made it clear that the operation of such a munitions factory in peacetime was not alone a necessity but an essential part of defence organisation. One's overall reaction has to be one of total castigation of the government's penchant towards crisis management, as adopted in relation to the army.

Accepting that the general staff were close to breaching their role in relation to commenting on Dáil speeches, they entered the caveat that care had been taken, even though it was essential to keep such statements concise, to give a reasonably comprehensive picture of events. The document contained, inter alia, the recommendations in relation to the provision of military training after the war, which, it states, the Cabinet Committee on Economic Planning, at a meeting convened on 13 December 1943, requested the Department of Defence to furnish.[71] General McKenna signed the plan for government consideration, and concluded by drawing their attention to the desirability of early decisions being given so that the problems of demobilisation and post-war development could be approached in a methodical manner and on a basis that would fit in with future plans.

FIVE

Case Studies of Individuals Involved in Pro- and Anti-Irish State Security and Maintenance of Neutrality, 1939–45

COMMANDANT-GENERAL TOM BARRY

Tom Barry's army record shows that he enlisted on 12 June 1940 and was discharged just twenty-eight days later on 9 July. The defence forces number allotted him was E410364. Barry's discharge poses the question as to whether he was cashiered or covertly seconded to Florence O'Donoghue's Supplementary Intelligence Service (SIS). The 'cause of discharge', as listed in his discharge certificate, is given as 'His services being no longer required', and the authority for such is given as DFR A/10 (Defence Force Regulation), Para 5(u) and DFR 30/1940, Para 14.[1] This was essentially catch-all military bureaucratic phraseology used, often without due cause, to discharge a soldier at the whim or idiosyncrasy of a commanding officer. It has since been amended.

Tom Barry was one of the first IRA men who had not alone fought during the Civil War on the anti-Treaty side but had continued within the IRA ranks, reaching the position of chief of staff, from which he resigned in 1938. He stepped down when the Northern-based members of the IRA, who had taken over control of elements of its headquarters staff, proposed a bombing campaign in England. Barry was joined by many other Southern comrades with whom he had fought during the Civil War and who had remained loyal to him throughout the post-Civil War period up to 1938.[2]

On his arrival in Collins Barracks Tom Barry was interviewed by the then Colonel Michael J. Costello, later Major General Costello, general officer commanding 1st Division, who congratulated him on his spirited action in coming forward and suggested to him that he would be of great help in the Operations branch of the command. Among other matters, Costello was anxious that Barry undertake a short commissioning course. Barry disagreed with this and stated that he preferred to remain as a private soldier, but in reality his preference would have been for a quick commissioning as accorded Frank Busteed, Tom Crofts, Florence O'Donoghue and others.[3] Costello agreed to defer the matter for a short time, during which Barry was detailed to appear in the Curragh along with other men from the South to attend a commissioning course. He assumed that some plans he had been ordered to prepare for Costello were a cause for ridicule at army headquarters. This is certainly a possibility, as Barry was not trained in staff work to any extent whatsoever, neither during his British army days nor his War of Independence or Civil War involvement.

Barry was a great leader of men, who could hatch schemes and achieve success by personal valour, charisma and his very careful preparation for the type of guerrilla warfare in which he had become an expert. Within days of his arrival at the Curragh, trouble brewed. Whereas the norm for personnel who neither continued on nor took any part in the officers' course would have been to return them to their units, Barry was discharged from the army, effective from 9 July, arguably without due cause. This was done as a result of a very peremptory investigation into alleged drunken behaviour, evidence of which failed to be corroborated by witnesses of any substance, one of whom refused to state in writing what he had already alleged verbally. Barry's discharge was ordered by the Adjutant General on foot of an application from the commandant of the Military College. Barry proceeded back to Cork, where he had an interview with a high-ranking army officer, possibly Colonel James Hanrahan. This can be adjudged from a careful study of the initialled copy of his communication to the chief of staff and the mode of his address to the latter on behalf of Barry. This was not couched in the normal obsequious phraseology associated with the time.

Barry, who had also communicated with de Valera on the matter,[4] asked, having given the facts of the case from his perspective, to have his name and his reputation restored. The chief of staff took immediate action and ordered an enquiry, and Barry's discharge prevailed. The question remains as to whether Barry was treated unfairly, by virtue of his previous record in the IRA, or whether the then general staff simply mistrusted one of their greatest foes in the Civil War. The matter has never been cleared to anyone's real satisfaction with the exception of Costello, whose introduction to Barry's book,[5] in 1948, lionises him.

Commandant R. W. McIntyre, in an interview with the author, casts more than a scintilla of light on the close liaison that Barry maintained with senior members of the army in both the Southern Command and in Costello's division for the remainder of the Emergency.[6] It begs the question as to whether Barry became a member of the SIS. Most members received an Emergency Medal in 1951 (some refused it), but, as far as can be established, Barry did not receive one. However, more evidence has been shed on Costello's continued liaison with Barry throughout the Emergency and it was a real possibility that Barry became involved with the SIS.

McIntyre states that, in 1942, A Company of the 13th Infantry Battalion was tasked to take over the General Post Office (GPO) in Cork towards the concluding stages of the Blackwater 1942 manoeuvres; all GPOs would have been designated vital installations. The platoon commanders in A Company were Lieutenant R.W. McIntyre, Lieutenant Peter Nelson, Lieutenant John O'Boyle and Lieutenant Mossy Condon. Their company commander was Michael Connolly, and their CO was Lieutenant Colonel Jack Murphy. They were stationed in Cahir as 1st Division troops, a division commanded by Major General Costello and wearing the lightning flash as a badge of designation. The company was detailed to simulate a German parachute drop, and to this effect an Air Corps aircraft flew over Cork and dropped items accordingly. The company reached Cork after two days' march from Cahir. Their operational objective, within the bounds of the exercise, was to capture the 'vital installation', the

GPO. The intelligence part of their briefing included an instruction to the then Lieutenant McIntyre to lead his platoon to meet a man posing as a fifth columnist, at St Patrick's church. At the appointed rendezvous they met the man, who, to their surprise, was Tom Barry, who duly led them to the GPO.[7]

This incident allows one to assume that Barry continued a relationship with Costello after his (Barry's) discharge. It also poses the question whether he operated as a covert member of the SIS as organised and controlled by Major Florence O'Donoghue, whom Barry so much admired. O'Donoghue was by then the intelligence officer of the Southern Command. Costello's introduction to General Barry's book would indicate that it is quite reasonable to make such assumptions, while Commandant McIntyre made an unequivocal statement to the author that: 'Micky Joe [Major General Costello] and Jimmy Hanrahan [Colonel James Hanrahan] were in touch with everyone.'[8]

Meda Ryan quotes various examples of Barry's consistent liaison with Costello throughout the Emergency, and the latter's implicit trust in Barry's vision and capacity to size up situations which, in Costello's estimation, could not be surpassed. Ryan points out that as a direct result of Barry's advice, Costello arranged to have 400 lbs of gelignite planted in the basement of the City Hall, 'a strategic building in the city, on the water's edge'.[9]

General Costello's introduction to Barry's book pays some very singular compliments to Barry's capacity as a leader. He states that, in war, Napoleon insisted: 'It is not the men who count! It is the man!'[10] Tom Barry exemplified the Napoleonic aphorism. Costello adds that the book is remarkable for the fact that, unlike other books on the period, it is uninfluenced by the bitter divisions of the Civil War, and free from attempts to belittle or ignore the opinions of men who opposed him in it. It is a measure of Barry's quality that, after arriving on the scene in 1920, he quickly established his pre-eminence among the galaxy of leaders which west Cork had already produced. Costello extolled Barry's qualities in detail during the War of Independence.[11] A man of the utmost integrity, it is highly improbable that he would have concocted such an introduction for any other reason than to identify Barry's qualities as both an officer and a combat leader. The assertion that Barry was wronged in being discharged in 1940 is arguably right. One could also logically argue, based on McIntyre's statement to this author, that Barry, despite his discharge, continued his liaison with Costello and Florence O'Donoghue, possibly as a covert agent of the SIS.

As for Barry's desire to receive the same merited conditions as others in rapid commissioning to officer status, military records of the individuals reveal the following: Florence O'Donoghue enlisted in the army on 12 June 1940. In accordance with the normal procedure he was discharged on 7 July 1940 for the purposes of being commissioned as an officer, on 8 July 1940. Tom Crofts enlisted and was discharged on the same dates for the same purposes. One must assume, in both their cases and in Frank Busteed's, who enlisted on 19 December 1940, was discharged on 21 January 1941 and commissioned on 22 January 1941, that any potential officer's course they completed was of a cursory nature. The same applies to the man Barry named as O'Mahony; Frank John Mahony enlisted on 3 July 1940, was discharged on 28 July and commissioned on 29 July 1940. He resigned his commission on 13 June 1942.[12] He was one of the Mahonys who owned Blarney Woollen Mills. It is incongruous to think of a Mahony of Blarney joining the Irish army rather than the British army; the family would have been considered virtual landed gentry, empathising with the British. One other such individual was one of the Williamses, owners of the Tullamore Dew distillery.[13] The short time served between the enlistment dates and the commissioning of Florence O'Donoghue, Tom Crofts, Frank Busteed and Mahony would indicate that all had empathy with Fianna Fáil prior to the Emergency.

Florence O'Donoghue and the SIS, Southern Command

Florence O'Donoghue had been a Volunteer since 1916. Tom Barry's character analysis of him is as follows:

> He had filled many offices in his brigade at different periods. Shrewd, calm and capable, I rated him as one of the ten best officers I met during my membership of the IRA. An all round officer, his speciality was intelligence, and he can be bracketed justly with Michael Collins, the director of intelligence, as the outstanding IO in Ireland. I was to get to know Florrie well, for he was to be the first appointed Adjutant of the 1st Southern Division,

> while I was to be the 1st appointed Deputy Divisional Commander of that Unit. So for some time we worked close together. Not the least of his good qualities were his pleasant easy ways and his loyalty to brother officers.[14]

The following statement of evidence on the importation of arms from Italy in 1921 illustrates the attitude of Major Florence O'Donoghue:[15]

> I cannot recall at what time in 1920 I first heard of the project . . . I am unable to fix the date, but think it was about October or November, 1920. There was, of course, no intention of keeping it a secret from General Headquarters: what I wish to emphasise is that Southern Brigade Officers felt impelled to consult together at that stage on the best methods of developing . . . The two principal matters considered were: The need for more arms – particularly rifles; Means of spreading the fight so that the enemy would be unable to concentrate against the active areas.
>
> My recollection is that it was decided to press GHQ to endeavour to procure arms, and to urge . . . the co-ordination of activities in neighbouring brigades . . . the germ of the Divisional area . . . In January, 1921, Cork 1st Brigade was informed . . . that GHQ had a project for the importation of arms – a single cargo of some considerable quantity being envisaged . . . Liam Deasy, Adjutant, Cork 3rd Brigade, joined me in Cork about 11 December, 1920, and we travelled by train to Dublin . . . We

> attended a meeting at Barry's Hotel, Gardiner's Row, at which a number of GHQ Officers were present . . . The project was discussed . . . and the landing place settled . . . at some selected point on the West Cork Coast in Cork 3rd Brigade area.
>
> The question arose of sending of Officer to Italy . . . and of piloting the ship to the selected landing place . . . I suggested Comdt. Michael Leahy . . . we regarded the project as the most important effort to obtain a substantial quantity of arms undertaken since 1916. The recommendation was accepted . . .

O'Donoghue concludes his statement:

> . . . near Glanworth on 11 January, 1921 . . . Some plans were made for the distribution and security of the expected arms . . . discussion of plans in connection with the project . . . took place after the formation of the 1st Southern Division. [At] . . . a conference of Cork 1st, Cork 3rd and Kerry 2nd Officers, held in Shanachrane . . . on 7 April, 1921. Liam Lynch presided . . . Cork 3rd Brigade had by then completed arrangements for the actual landing at Myross Strand, near Glandore Harbour . . . Dumps capable of holding the whole expected quantity were made in each Brigade . . . It was intended that Cork 1st and Cork 3rd Brigade Columns would cover the landing, and that all Battalions on the line of movement northwards would be mobilised . . . Some portion of the arms was to go to Kerry . . . Humphrey Murphy and John Joe Rice, Commandant and Vice Commandant of

> Kerry 2nd Brigade attended . . . Lynch and I met them, and Seán O'Hegarty, O/C. Cork No. 1, at Gougane on the night before the conference . . . we did not have any definite information about the complete failure of the project at the Italian end until after the Truce . . . It was after the Truce that we learned that Commandant Leahy actually arrived back in Dublin on the day we met at Shanachrane. I do not know why the project failed in Italy.[16]

John Borgonovo's recent work as editor of Florence and Josephine O'Donoghue's memoirs of their dual leading roles in the war of independence, and Florence's role as a peace broker in the Civil War is a riveting study.[17] Lee's foreword includes the following significant comments:

> The War of Independence was first and foremost an Intelligence war. The poorly equipped IRA had no hope unless they could compensate for their grossly inferior gun power not only through greater will power, but through superior Intelligence. The role of IRA Intelligence officers was crucial in levelling up the odds.

He adds:

> It is the judgement of John Borgonovo, the editor, that O'Donoghue, a farmer's son from Kerry, was as crucial to the struggle in Cork as Michael Collins, a farmer's son from Cork, was to the struggle in Dublin, different though the quiet O'Donoghue was from the flamboyant Collins . . . Florrie's

> character, as one of the most thoughtful members of the IRA and IRB, enables the restrained realism of his approach, reflecting rather than declaiming his underlying idealism, ignited by the impact of Easter week, to carry more conviction than would a more egotistical account.[18]

Borgonovo depicts contemporaries' descriptions of Florrie as shy, restrained, pensive, and Jo as outgoing, outspoken and passionate. He believes that both typified IRA activists that emerged during the War of Independence – highly intelligent, competent in their professions, and dedicated patriots. Their relationship resulted in a direct flow of sensitive information concerning planned British military movements throughout Munster. Josephine had access to such information through her position as head of clerks/typists in the British 6th Division headquarters. Borgonovo puts Jo's contribution on a par with those of the most important IRA intelligence sources of the conflict, David Neligan and Éamon Broy. He views Florence's self-reflections as nonconformist with the stereotype IRA guerrilla, believing that O'Donoghue revealed more empathy and morality than expected of an 'IRA murder gang assassin', an image portrayed by some commentators. The O'Donoghues' account of their part in the War of Independence helps people to understand the surprising success of the Irish revolutionaries against what was then the world's reigning superpower.[19]

Formation of Supplementary Intelligence Service

Florence O'Donoghue answered the call to arms once again in 1940; he was commissioned on 8 July 1940 and soon after was co-opted into G2 as a captain in the Southern Command. He was personally responsible for setting up the Supplementary Intelligence Service in the Southern Command, on 10 March 1941.[20] Unlike other normal security activities during the Emergency, the SIS proved itself a unique asset to Bryan's organisation. O'Donoghue issued Instruction No. 1 on 10 March 1941, outlining the area of responsibility for operations, the main objective or purpose of the organisation, and their methodology of carrying out such duties. The SIS operational areas corresponded roughly to the 1921 battalion areas, embracing a number of battalions within each county. Their main purposes were as outlined in Florence O'Donoghue's letter dated 10 March 1941.

The SIS was required to secure continued sources of information after an enemy occupation of Ireland, which seemed at certain stages inevitable during the Emergency. Accordingly, absolute secrecy was accorded to personnel and to their activities. Members, unlike the remnants of the very likely defeated Irish army, were to remain in their areas and maintain contact, through an agent, with the command intelligence officer. Only the chief of staff had the authority to allow either the person in charge or indeed any member of the organisation to evacuate an enemy-held area. If the evacuation of a member became absolutely essential at short notice, the chief of staff was to be immediately notified at his telephone number – Cork 851 – known only to those entitled.

The officer commanding the forces in an area was to ensure that all members maintained area contact. All enemy activity, post invasion, was to be noted and again conveyed to the command intelligence officer. Such activity included combat intelligence on the enemy's environment and also the enemy's methodology, for instance their use of parachutists, their use of sea plane bays, long lakes, harbours, beaches, roads, rail, bridges or important junctions that would convey an advantage to the enemy and be a handicap to Irish forces. The SIS was also required to inform all changes in enemy activity and equipment. Lists of instructors were compiled to inform members of roads, paths and byroads in their operational areas, which they would learn to travel by day, and by night without lights. They were required to keep all information on such data up to date. This was later regarded by cavalry troops as 'reviewing the going map'.[21] The SIS was also responsible for a constant review of all inhabitants in its area, the outlook and action of such inhabitants, and was also required to tabulate all who would likely help either the British, the Germans or the Italians. The next part of its duties involved notes on all visitors, tourists, cyclists, hikers, caravaners, photographers, sketchers, map users and anyone taking notes in its area of operation.

Any urgent enquiries were to be made directly to the chief of staff, while other reports were transmitted verbally or in writing by all agents. Their signals, presumably at night, were to be either by light and/or sound, and they were to prepare special ground markings for their own use. The SIS was an intelligence organisation whose mission was to observe and report; its members were specifically prohibited from taking any action. From July 1940 onwards the SIS network in the Southern Command was fully operational, and complying with both its initial instructions and periodic instructions as issued by O'Donoghue.

O'Donoghue demanded complete and accurate accounts, and brevity was to be observed as far as was humanly possible. Agents were also required to express their opinion on the reliability of sources, dates and times, and were only allowed to submit one subject per representative. They did not sign names to reports, but used a number code instead. They were regarded as a special intelligence force of the LDF but, paradoxically, they remained unattested within the same organisation.

The SIS was organised in groups of ten to twelve. An appointed group leader maintained contact between individual agents and the army intelligence staff of the Southern Command. Each agent was required to give a solemn verbal undertaking, in the presence of an army intelligence officer, to carry out the duties as specified and explained; he was to maintain essential secrecy regarding the existence of the organisation and their activities. No records were to be kept beyond minimal usage. All members were to be protected. They were made aware that the strategic value of their area of operation, its anti-tank and other forms of defence, particularly vital roads, railways and potential landing areas such as lakes, piers, harbours and beaches were all within their area of activity and as such they should be totally and thoroughly acquainted with the topography of their area. Furthermore, they should maintain absolute knowledge of the Post Office, the telephone and telegraph facilities, and hotel and petrol supplies within their area of operation. The reason for monitoring the inhabitants and visitors to the areas specified was to gauge their potential for harbouring and assisting the enemies of the state before, during, and after any invasion. Other reports, post invasion and occupation of their area, were to include the type of collaboration by locals and awareness of the difficulties and danger posed to the state and the army.

One report, signed K104,[22] described a visit to Tralee by the American OSS officer Spike Marlin, who admired Bryan's work in serving both Irish and American interests during the Second World War. As an example of SIS surveillance, he cites a succession of reports from an agent in Fenit which alerted O'Donoghue to the efforts of the renegade Special Branch man Jim Crofton to get a seaworthy boat for the escape of the German spy, Hermann Goertz, in February 1941.[23]

De Valera's recruitment of the Broy Harriers to deal with large-scale demonstrations by the Blueshirt movement attracted hundreds of republicans to its ranks who would otherwise have joined the IRA. Some of these were given permanent posts in the Special Branch. They were not used to police procedure and discipline, and because they were effectively political recruits, senior officers in the Garda Síochána had difficulty in controlling them. In 1940 many of them were passing information to the IRA, while one of them, Jim Crofton, helped the IRA to plant a bomb in Special Branch headquarters. He was eventually arrested as a result of good surveillance by army intelligence, Florence O'Donoghue and his SIS, while trying to organise the escape by boat of the Abwehr agent Hermann Goertz. Despite this embarrassment, relations between army intelligence and the Special Branch did not suffer. Bryan felt that it made the police more security minded and consequently more efficient than they had been.[24] O'Halpin's description of Crofton's attempt to facilitate Goertz's return to Germany[25] is corroborated by Coogan's sparse comment on the incident[26] and Bowyer-Bell's more detailed account.[27]

Bryan commented on the action of O'Donoghue, who obtained details of the proposed boat escape of Goertz, and what happened when the local police arrested Jim Crofton. Crofton, who was still a member of Special Branch, apparently deceived his fellow detectives and police who arrested him into believing that he was on some duty. O'Donoghue had heard about this and had to use his influence in G2 to ensure that Crofton was detained. Bryan understood that Crofton was not merely searching for a boat but that he had Goertz with him, and evidently had a boat ready. He also knew that Crofton was sympathetic to the IRA and that several other members of Special Branch were also sympathetic to and aiding the IRA.[28]

In February 1951 a special memorandum was submitted to the government recommending all 140 members of the Southern Command for the award of the Emergency Service Medal and certificates to the Supplementary Intelligence Service (SIS) Southern Command. The minister for defence, Dr T. F. O'Higgins, was highly impressed with his written brief on the matter, and regarded the SIS as having been of much more value to the state than the LDF.[29] A difficulty arose initially with the issue of the medal in that the necessary requirement of a 60 per cent attendance rate was not recorded, and the SIS personnel were not enrolled or attested to the Local Defence Force (LDF). Given the necessity for secrecy, however, the difficulty was overcome and the medals and certificates were sent by post to the individuals. Such was the end, as far as is known, of the Emergency Supplementary Intelligence Service.[30]

It is interesting to note that on 20 September 1940 Eastern Command informed G2 that the gardaí were responsible for internal security and maintained liaison with the Local Security Force (LSF) and thus it was the view of Eastern Command intelligence staff that the SIS would cause friction between the gardaí, the LSF and indeed G2. They suggested that more agents should be seconded to assist the gardaí in special areas of operation, adding: 'It is more than likely that Bryan already had this contingency well covered.' G2 Eastern Command observed that combat intelligence matters were referred to by General Murphy in discussions with Garda superintendents on 13 July 1940. Murphy comments that the gardaí awaited definite instructions as to what their role would be post invasion. These observations were signed by a Captain R. L. Daly, who was on the G2 staff of the Eastern Command.

A scheme that worked so well under the aegis of Florence O'Donoghue, within the Southern Command, was unacceptable to Eastern Command intelligence. One could reasonably argue that secret organisations such as the SIS, reporting directly to the G2 of the Command, was considered unnecessary by Major General Hugo MacNeill and that the viewpoint of the Eastern Command was that they would run their own show.[31] There has always been sensitivity in army/Garda relationships in respect of areas of operational responsibility. The institutional balance was an irritant at times to both forces during the Emergency, although O'Halpin believes it provided an appropriate check on both forces given the exceptional powers they enjoyed.[32]

Bryan and O'Donoghue maintained contact with SIS and other informants. Outside the Southern Command there was nothing comparable to the SIS. McIntyre's assertion that 'Micky Joe and Jimmy Hanrahan kept in touch with everyone' is not in the slightest bit far fetched. Bryan, Archer and O'Donoghue had their own methodology of keeping in touch with old comrades and old adversaries, principally because they agreed, at this crucial stage in the country's difficulties, that it was time to 'step together' on behalf of the state.

German Agents and Related Activities in Ireland, August 1939 – December 1943

The German spies who succeeded in entering Ireland during the course of the Second World War, twelve in all, were, with the exception of Hermann Goertz, quickly captured and detained. This illustrates the awareness of G2, the Garda force and the populace at large to remain alert to possible German infiltration. It also shows the German underestimation of Irish intelligence agents' capacity to prove so effective throughout the war. The outstanding incidents affecting the counter-espionage section related to German activities. 'Fall Gruen' comprehensively illustrates Germany's plan to invade Ireland (see Appendix VII for an excerpt from the plan),[33] and Lytton's work includes a contemporary map of possible invasion routes from a German-controlled Ireland into the industrial heartland of Britain in the Midlands and Clydeside.[34]

Activities of German agents despatched to Ireland from August 1939 to December 1940 and German sympathisers already living in Ireland were closely monitored by G2 and gardaí throughout the period. Examples of case histories are documented in Bryan's papers.[35] One should bear in mind that the material included in the Bryan papers was based on information supplied by G2 agents, the SIS, Garda contacts and to some extent MI5 throughout the Emergency. Bryan also had contacts of his own and was not overly disposed to sharing all the information available to him with either his own agents or anyone else, except when it suited him to so do; this practice is not unusual on the part of intelligence organisations or agents.

One such paper concerns intelligence that emerged from G2 at that time. The family of Michael Held was first investigated towards the end of 1938, but gardaí reported that none of the family had suspicious associations. Bryan, however, discounted this and remained convinced that Stephen Carroll Held, stepson of Michael, was one of the individuals involved in an attempt to use Ireland as a base for espionage and possible attack against England.[36] On 22 May 1940 the

Garda authorities raided the house of Stephen Carroll Held. Bryan's subtle inference of inefficient Garda planning is instanced by his mention of a lost opportunity on their part to arrest both Held and another man (most likely Goertz), who fled the house before the raid. One could also deduce from his insert in the Held file a similar criticism of the Garda laissez-faire attitude in failing to react to a report of a parachutist (probably Goertz), landing in Ballivor, County Meath, on 6 May 1940.

The subsequent search of the premises revealed articles normally associated with individual spies, or an attempted network.[37] Some articles were linked to Iseult Stuart, wife of Francis Stuart, then known to be in Germany, while documents found confirmed Bryan's suspicions of an espionage plot at that time, and current literature complements the basis for this.[38] Bryan's contention that the cipher messages found were in no known cipher may have been true at the time, but Dr Hayes subsequently discovered the methodology to decrypt both Goertz and Held's codes during the course of the war.[39] Of particular interest are references in these documents to agents' information gathering of military significance relating to Northern Ireland, including position and strength of the enemy; landing places from which seaborne or airborne troops could land and suitable places where parachute troops could be dropped; military geography in general; and own forces outside (presumably German sympathisers) and inside Northern Ireland. It considered the possibility of propaganda and directing common opinion in an effort to encourage empathy with the German cause. Other information included the possibility of sabotage; of cooperation with German forces inside Northern Ireland with forces from here (presumably Éire); march routes; and a large-scale map, 1 inch to a mile, of Dingle Bay and Ventry Harbour; analysis of Ventry Harbour as operation base; and Dingle fishing boat station. The latter request may have been of value in respect of submarine operations in the Atlantic but does not conform to any aspect of the invasion plan outlined in 'Fall Gruen'.

Bryan believed that the documents found in Held's house were written in Ireland by someone who had a good knowledge of Irish topography and who was evidently more than merely a radio operator. He also believed that the writer was Goertz, whose mission would seem to have been of an organising or directing kind. Goertz remained free until his arrest on 12 November 1941. He should of course have been aware of the danger inherent in paper trails and might well have taken a lead from arch-Machiavellian de Valera. Raymond[40] was queried by Bryan: 'When can historical researchers hope to have in Ireland, in the National Library, microfilm of all war papers relating to Ireland?', to which Raymond replied: 'I very much fear the answer to your question may be never . . . The major problem is that de Valera simply put little diplomatic or security information on paper from 1940–1944.'[41] G2 agent Commandant de Buitléir was instrumental in the final identification of Walter Simon, a German agent of importance sent from an espionage bureau in Hamburg which dealt with English and Irish affairs. Arguably Simon's internment ended a period of inept bungling by gardaí, who, up to his positive identification, were inclined to believe a series of contradictory statements made by him. Academic research confirms G2's stance.[42]

Hans Marschner, Parachutist

The German agent Marschner, according to Bryan's account, was an officer in the German Artillery employed on intelligence duties at the headquarters of a formation of the German army stationed at Hamburg. He landed by parachute from a German aircraft at Ballycullane, County Wexford, on the night of 12/13 March 1940. He had at one time lived in German southwest Africa and was in possession of a South African passport issued in Berlin which would not, however, be recognised by the British authorities for most purposes. Stephan's comprehensive account identified Marschner as Sergeant Gunther Schutz, a budding officer trained in the Oldenburg Artillery Regiment and claimed for service as an agent by the Abwehr.[43] Current research uses the name Schutz rather than Marschner.[44]

Bryan's account, although mainly accurate, does not include all the aforementioned details. His resumé continues: 'Marschner (hereinafter called Schutz) landed in uniform and flying kit but concealed those together with his parachute.' Bryan omits to state that Schutz also possessed an English overcoat, civilian presumably. Unable to fix his position, dropped in County Wexford, far from Newbridge and Dublin, his planned destination, he was arrested on 13 March. He almost immediately admitted his identity and the fact that he had landed from a German aircraft. The normal spy paraphernalia immediately compromised him to such an extent that he admitted under interrogation his purpose to meet and liaise with Werner M. B. Unland, a dormant agent, in Dublin.[45] The ease with which German agents were compromised and detained causes a doubt in this author's mind as to the agents' training, lack of cunning and general capacity to absorb Garda and G2 interrogation without revealing the true purpose of their presence in Ireland. The question also arises as to whether their German handlers in the Abwehr cared about the successful completion of their missions or otherwise. Recent literature confirms my doubts by casting similar suspicion as to the true purpose of 'Fall Gruen'.[46] Both Stephan and Hull's research elaborate and verify Bryan's account of Schutz's truncated attempt to become an active German agent in Ireland.[47]

Werner M. B. Unland

Bryan's detailed account of Unland's connection with Schutz is an example of a suspect against whom, by a process of continuous investigation, an exceedingly strong case had been built up prior to his arrival. The case had involved G2, Postal Censorship, Post Office Special Investigation Branch and the gardaí. O'Halpin's 1999 study correlates with Bryan's contention.[48] Bryan illustrated the procedure followed in dealing with suspects who came under notice, which led eventually to Unland's arrest and detention. Hull's recent study castigates Unland in no uncertain terms:

> . . . he was the German version of Graham Greene's character in Our Man in Havana: he succeeded in

> convincing a remote German Intelligence headquarters that he had a fully functional network established in Ireland . . . Unland's network was wholly notional . . . Unland's messages can be classified into several different categories: whining requests for money, fictional descriptions of his intelligence contacts and attempts to dissuade the Germans from sending to Ireland more agents, who could expose his tissue of deception.[49]

In this author's opinion Unland would have self-destructed whether Schutz had compromised him or not. He would almost certainly have been apprehended, largely through the efforts of two men, Colonel Dan Bryan and Detective Garda Michael J. Wymes, later Garda commissioner, and the organisations they controlled. Schutz considered that Unland had been inactive in Ireland for some time prior to his arrest.[50]

The Unland Case

Bryan's continuing account of the Unland case poses an immediate question as to the legality of both Bryan and G2's disregard for the letter of the law in respect of wartime censorship. Ó Drisceoil comments that G2 'had a far broader remit and were far less constrained by law, custom, by civil government or by rival institutions than the British or American security agencies'. He continues: 'Very little occurred in wartime Ireland without its knowledge; politicians, public services, political activists, aliens, Allied and Axis diplomats, journalists – none escaped the attention of G2.'[51]

Ó Drisceoil's thesis confirms this author's view that Bryan was more concerned with creating a public image of preserving Ireland's half-armed, pro-Allied neutrality than with maintaining stifling legalistic boundaries.

Bryan stated that shortly before the inception of Postal Censorship in September 1939, letters were first observed by G2 going to the Dansk Import & Export Company, PO Box 105, Copenhagen, Denmark. G2 became suspicious at the content of the letters, typewritten in English and either unsigned, signed with a scribble or signed 'Walsh' or other names; they were generally posted in Dún Laoghaire and no address of sender was given. G2's examination of all their records of aliens in the Dún Laoghaire district led to the eventual reduction of the number of possible suspects to one.

Werner M. B. Unland, a German who arrived in Ireland on 27 August 1939 from England and who resided at Greena House, Dún Laoghaire, was the most likely suspect. An examination of Unland's registration card at Aliens Branch, Department of Justice, increased suspicion as it revealed a strong similarity between his signature and the scribbled signatures on the 'Dansk' letters. The gardaí were asked to supervise Unland, who was eventually detected posting a 'Dansk' letter. The gardaí reported regularly on his movements until the beginning of June 1940; these reports, however, furnished weekly to G2, do not show Unland as having any associates or moving about more than to cinemas, post offices, etc., and indicate no evidence of suspicious activities on his part.

Bryan's Unland report continues to delve into the minutiae of the latter's series of letters known as 'Dansk' and some correspondence with alleged clients in Northern Ireland and Spain. One wonders why such time and resources were spent on a whining wastrel when he could have been apprehended at will. In this author's opinion the only possible reason is that there may have been a bigger fish in the pond to net, unlikely as that may seem; Bryan did not clarify the issue. In any case Unland was arrested on 21 April 1940 and duly interned for the remainder of the war.

Obed, Tributh and Gartner

Bryan's account of these three agents is significant in that it exposes their short-lived freedom as a symptom of their pathetic mental preparedness, stupidity and general ineptitude to rate as efficient agents. All three arrived in Castletownshend on the west Cork coast on 7 July 1940, and were arrested in Drimoleague on the day of their arrival – Tributh and Gartner were Germans and Obed an Indian. Found to be in possession of currency, explosives, detonators and bombs, they had come from Brest and their alleged mission was to get to England where they were to engage in sabotage coincidental with the German invasion. They disclaimed any intention of action against Ireland. Their behaviour exhibited a lack of appreciation of the mental capacity of the Irish security forces. The two Germans were poor examples of allegedly trained saboteurs from, arguably, the most outstanding military fighting force in the world at that time. All three were given penal servitude for seven years.

Wilhelm Preetz

Bryan described Preetz as a German national of somewhat cosmopolitan experience, married to an Irish girl from Tuam. He attracted the attention of G2 in 1939 by the rather considerable amount of currency he was allowed to bring from Germany on a trip to Tuam, ostensibly to his in-laws. Investigation showed that he had made previous visits here unaccompanied by his wife. G2 surveillance heightened their considerable suspicion of him, yet the gardaí could find no reason to be of similar mind. Soon after the outbreak of war, however, Preetz was arrested in the house of his in-laws in Tuam. While on bail awaiting prosecution, he disappeared, and eventually succeeded in returning to Germany. The foreign correspondence of his family and of an associate of his, a grocer's assistant named Joseph Donohue, was kept under observation. Bryan does not indicate whether such correspondence surveillance was strictly covered by the letter of the law; one suspects that neither did he care. His attitude was directed towards achieving results, irrespective of the methodology used, in this author's opinion.

Continued investigation led to the suspicion that Preetz was again in Dublin accompanied by Donohue, and the two were eventually traced to a flat at 23 Westland Row. On the evening of 6 August 1940 Preetz and Donohue were arrested by detectives. A search of the flat revealed a suitcase, the dimensions of which fitted a rubber case found at Minard; it contained a radio receiver and transmitter. Later a passport was found, while a number of sheets of squared paper bore various figures, letters, calculations, certain phrases in English, and rectangles containing sentences in German. Among some cheap novels and periodicals, a book, the title of which purported to be *Hide in the Dark* but which turned out to be the diary of Katherine Mansfield, aroused interest and was examined in connection with other papers found in the flat. This examination disclosed that the book *Hide in the Dark* was a key in which Preetz was sending and receiving messages in cipher. All items were submitted to G2 for scrutiny.

The messages referred to his location in Dublin with Donohue, to weather conditions, and to difficulties in the operation of his set. Incoming messages asked for information regarding troops in Northern Ireland. Preetz was found to be in possession of a passport which had been issued to him in Ireland prior to the outbreak of war in the name of P. J. Mitchell, a person from Galway living in Australia. This passport was intended to deceive any authorities into whose hands Preetz might fall. It contained his photograph but the particulars also suited Mitchell. The conditions under which he obtained it indicated gross neglect of duty on the part of the Garda concerned.[52] Once again Bryan castigates a Garda for what he regarded as ineptitude, despite many instances of successful parallel investigations involving G2 and the gardaí. Intensive research in contemporary literature does not dwell unduly on alleged Garda ineptitude, with the exceptions of Hull, who finds the seemingly naive reaction of Sergeant Gantly of the Dublin Metropolitan Division to Simon's contradictory statements as 'unbelievable',[53] and of both Hull and Stephan's mention of the irregular circumstances of Preetz's acquisition of his Irish passport.[54]

Walter Hermann Christian Simon, alias Karl Anderson

This man evidently landed about 13 June 1940 on the Dingle Peninsula from a boat or submarine; he later attracted the attention of detectives on the train from Tralee to Dublin. On arrest, he was found to be in possession of a considerable amount of English sterling and US dollars and gave an account of himself which was false. He was later identified as Simon, who had served a sentence in England prior to the war for a breach of aliens regulations and was suspected of espionage. In this author's opinion, he was yet another example of a German agent who grossly underestimated the ability of the Irish security organisation. Simon, alias Anderson, would appear to have drunk too much whiskey after landing and then talked foolishly.[55] Hull describes his performance as underwhelming.[56] The same might apply to the professional performance of all German agents who tried to outwit the Irish intelligence system during the Second World War.

IRISH-BORN GROUPS

Irish Friends of Germany

Bryan admitted that a nebulous series of groups which existed in Dublin gave G2 an amount of trouble during the war. They belonged to two organisations known as The Irish Friends of Germany and Cumann Náisiúnta. Bryan believed that many in these groups were quite 'harmless'; the organisers, however, were either persons known to have been for a considerable period in touch with German propaganda organisations and advocates of Nazi views. They had been prominent in the Blueshirt movement or O'Duffy's Spanish Brigade episode and were also imbued with either fascist or Nazi ideas. Bryan did not envisage trouble from the groups – unless, that is, a German invasion of Ireland materialised. And he was even more concerned that a number of military personnel might be foolishly influenced by them.[57] He wrote: 'At the present moment the personnel likely to be affected in the army are not a problem, and with a few possible exceptions are loyally performing their duties, but under different circumstances and influences, they would require careful attention.'[58]

Bryan's thinly veiled inference implies that G2 had already commenced surveillance on the unnamed military personnel and that the army was not exempted from suspicion of treasonable activities during the war. It also allowed him the accolade of retaining a sense of balanced judgement in precarious times for the nation; he was no more averse to criticising army personnel than he was gardaí.

Such is seen in the report compiled by G2 on the counter-espionage section, which depicts the general working of the section during the Emergency. The amount of what may be described as routine work of such a section tends to increase continuously during a period of war. Bryan believed that the Held case and others, combined with the development of the war in Europe, meant a huge increase in the volume of both highly important and routine work. He also asserted that, prior to the Held case and the relatively sudden change in the operational state of the European war, almost nobody was prepared to believe that Ireland might be directly affected by espionage and the like. This beggars belief; surely Bryan and G2, which more than any other element of the army were prepared, even prior to the war, to delve into all aspects of intelligence, were more than ready to forecast the probable German and Allied courses of espionage. Current literature would have us believe so.[59]

Bryan described the volte-face that ensued among Irish people. Spies, parachutists, suspects generally and illicit radio sets were being reported in large numbers. Such was the volume of these reports, indeed, that work tended to get out of control. Bryan makes the general point that additional officers who were procured for the section had unfortunately to be diverted to field duties, and the work of collation, evaluation and dissemination was largely neglected. Realising its value, however, he reorganised his resources to cope with the problem, only too aware that the Held, Karl Anderson and Preetz incidents – as well as that of another agent, Ernst Weber-Drohl – indicated significant German activity within the country. These activities, with the possible exception of those of the three men who landed in Cork, he attributed to the operation of a secret German organisation or series of groups in this country. He believed that these groups were concerned with the direction of espionage, sabotage and propaganda either within Great Britain and Northern Ireland only or within those territories and Southern Ireland also. Bryan maintained that the extracts from the Held papers plainly indicated that while the purpose of 'Plan Kathleen' was the invasion of Northern Ireland, the plan obviously also envisaged the use of Southern Irish territory.

Current literature refutes Bryan's contention as being somewhat inaccurate; both O'Halpin and Hull are largely in agreement on the details.[60] One of Hull's most interesting comments is: 'However, G2 surveillance had missed the one significant event of [German agent] Pfaus' visit: the link-up between Germany and the IRA.'[61] G2, like Homer, sometimes nods! Such activities resulted from individual correlation rather than that of groups or secret German organisations.

Illicit Entry and Exit

Bryan was concerned about uncontrolled entry or exit from the country. Weber-Drohl, Karl Anderson, the three men in Cork and Preetz succeeded in entering Ireland without detection. It was only afterwards, sometimes owing to accidental circumstances, that detection took place. It seems that during the darkness of winter the principal deterrent to illegal landings were the long periods of unsuitable weather and possibly the effectiveness of British anti-submarine methods. Judging by G2's experience in previous cases, it would seem that if persons landing from submarines, on the coast, had effective arrangements made to be met and transported away, the prospects of their being detected were not good. One might question whether Bryan and his G2 agents were beginning to exhibit a lack of confidence in their own ability at that stage. Has the time now arrived for historians to indulge in a smattering of revisionism?

Ireland as a Base for Espionage

Bryan commented on the consequences of the occupation of most of western Europe by Germany. All contact between Great Britain and western Europe, except Spain and Portugal, had been severed. His analysis of the situation was logical. He believed that while Britain might make illicit touch directly with the continent by landing persons from submarines or small boats, it was exceedingly doubtful if, except possibly in remote parts of Scotland, there was any prospect of Germany making illicit contact with Britain except by radio. While invaluable for certain limited purposes, radio is not of itself sufficient for the conduct of espionage, sabotage or propaganda over a period. All traffic and contacts between England and the continent were carefully supervised. Such supervision was not possible between England and Ireland and did not exist between North and South. In addition, the wartime restrictions were not as rigidly applied in Ireland as in Britain, and it seemed reasonable to believe the claim that Ireland was being primarily used as a base for espionage operations against the British. Documents captured indicated that Ireland was more than such a base.[62]

The IRA and German Organisations

Bryan's contention that there was no evidence of association between the IRA and German organisations is not borne out by modern researchers.[63] His papers state that the gardaí, who dealt with the IRA, had obtained no evidence of such association, and concluded: 'It seems probable that in the event of a long war, common policy may lead to mutual action in certain matters.' He continued: 'In this connection, it should be added that the groups referred to . . . include people from both the old Blue Shirt and the old IRA element.'[64]

Diversity of Recruitment and Treatment of Aliens

Other types of recruits posed new challenges to GHQ and to the army. Irishmen came with an alarming and dazzling variety of religious and cultural allegiances, and also experience. University graduates, not only from the National University of Ireland but also from Trinity College, made their appearance in uniform. Men considered incurably pro-British by breeding, class, education, and religion came forward to defend Irish neutrality. To an extent all were welcome, and yet at first were slightly suspect. According to O'Halpin, 'G2 was concerned about their attitude should Britain attack first. The presence of Protestants in the army, LDF and LSF was a source of some comfort to the British precisely because it was felt they would not bear arms against British forces.'[65]

The overall ethos and practice of religion during the Emergency was not favourable to non-Catholics. The army authorities yielded to the Catholic chaplaincy service's imposition of compulsory attendance at Church parades.[66] O'Halpin accurately reflected the concern within G2 caused by Jewish recruits and those of the Ailesbury Road and Killiney pro-British set – 'unreconstructed bastions of pro-British sentiment and Protestant affluence' – during the Emergency.[67] His reference to a G2 memorandum on Jewish church parades remains relevant.[68] G2's sensitivity to Jewish recruitment stemmed from 'the fundamental characteristic of the Jewish people . . . that they have no national allegiance and are described as . . . being supernational or international in character'. I agree with O'Halpin's citing the conclusions of unnamed authors 'who have studied the Jewish problem'.[69]

Continuing on this theme, it is well to reflect on the correlation as existed between G2, the government, alien immigration and recruitment of Jews. The attitude of the Irish authorities towards aliens and prospective immigrants, including Jews, reflected a mirror image of that held by Bryan and Archer, and through them G2. Bryan's attitude on Adolf Mahr,[70] who was closely watched by G2, is reflected in modern studies. Bryan concluded in December 1945 that Mahr was 'an open and blatant Nazi and made every effort to convert Irish graduates, and other persons with whom he had association, to Nazi doctrines and beliefs'.[71] Mahr was director of the National Museum and was in a position to observe Irish politics and society.

The leader of the local branch of the Italian Fascist Society, relatively small, was Count Eduardo Tomacelli, who had come to Dublin in 1935 and taken up a position at Trinity College as a teacher of Italian. G2 had two intelligence sources in the Dublin universities, codenamed 'Rome' and 'Paris'. Bryan knew that Mahr and Tomacelli's fascism and Nazism doctrine targeted radical culturalists and the IRA;[72] the latter was virtually destroyed during the Second World War by de Valera and his government. Mahr attempted to persuade Colonel Fritz Brase, the German director of the Irish Army School of Music, to accept group leadership of the Dublin branch of the Auslands-Organisation. Refused permission by his army superiors to join, his entreaties did not influence the military authorities' decision.[73] Duggan maintains that Fritz Brase left Auslands-Organisation as directed by army authorities.[74] There is no doubt that Fritz Brase showed a distinct naivety in thinking that his army superiors would believe the case he propounded. Such was the efficacy of G2 in relation to German personnel.

Otto August Reinhardt, who left Ireland on 18 August 1939, was described by G2 as a typical military man in appearance. He knew the country well and had a thorough knowledge of the eastern seaboard. G2 believed that he worked for German intelligence, the Abwehr, in Germany, during the war, as did Helmut Clissmann, another party member who left Ireland in August 1939.

Clissmann came to Ireland as an exchange student in Trinity College. While there he became a lecturer in German, and, according to G2, seemed to have exercised supervision and control over German exchange students in Ireland. By 1936 he was regarded with suspicion, and a permit for the renewal of his stay in Ireland was refused by the Department of Justice on 19 November 1936. However, through the intervention of the legation and the Department of External Affairs, this was extended to

June 1937 and thereafter to December 1938. He married an Irish woman known to G2 to have strong republican views. Both were followed, on one occasion to a rendezvous with a person allegedly known to G2 to be a senior member of the IRA. G2 also intercepted a letter to Clissmann from Adolf Mahr which began 'Dear Party Comrade Clissmann' and ended 'Heil Hitler, Dr Mahr, Party Group Leader'.

In addition, G2 had a report that Clissmann also sought to negotiate an exchange programme between Clann na h-Éireann groups and the Hitler Youth, but the plan was never realised. Clissmann returned to Dublin after the war, which he spent in Copenhagen, Berlin and Rome, and died in Dublin in 1997. G2 always suspected that he worked in intelligence, and quoted from an intercepted letter of his wife to her sister dated 23 March 1943: 'Helmut is away doing his bit in the South [of Ireland] but should be back soon.' G2 sources believed he frequently met Francis Stuart in Berlin. Bryan wrote on Clissmann's return to Ireland in October 1948: 'It is well to remember that he was, during the Emergency, connected with activities directed not merely against this country but also against Great Britain.'[75]

Keogh Scathingly Comments on the 'Last Chance' Scenarios for Saving More Jews

Between 1933 and 1945, about 250,000 refugees from Nazism had reached the United States, compared with 150,000 who entered Palestine. Éire's stance was similar to that taken by Canada, Australia, New Zealand and other dominions. Liberal euphemism describes their various policies towards refugees, and Jewish refugees in particular. All could have done much more. Keogh argues that Ireland, and other countries lost a chance 'to save many lives'.[76]

O'Halpin and Keogh agree in identifying G2's antipathy to admission of aliens, particularly Jews, during the Emergency. O'Halpin states that after war broke out, official opposition to the admission and naturalisation of all aliens hardened. G2's line was particularly clear: the more aliens let in for any reason, the greater the security and political risks incurred.[77] Keogh believes Archer's attitude was that of 'a beleaguered administrator determined to keep down the number of aliens in the country, particularly the number of Jews'. Bryan's recommendations in all individual cases had a decisive influence, mirroring those of Archer and the Departments of Justice and Industry and Commerce.[78] Problems arose during the Emergency which demanded Irish solutions to Irish problems, and non-acceptance of G2 recommendations. Realpolitik ignored both principle and prejudice.

Hempel's Transmission of Essential Elements of Information to Germany

While none of the German agents in Ireland contributed any substantial intelligence to their German handlers, the same was also true of the various Irish people who tried to gather information of use to Germany. O'Halpin believes that the most significant of these was the maverick Charles McGuinness, a Marine Service NCO who managed to pass certain information to the German legation on shipping that was picked up in postal and telephone surveillance and led to his being jailed for seven years in 1942. Duggan's account identifies McGuinness as a captain of the Irish Naval Service,[79] as against O'Halpin's Marine Service NCO.[80] On the basis of his research O'Halpin's identification of McGuinness is correct. Joseph Andrews, a close acquaintance of Goertz, managed to send enciphered messages to Portugal via a cook in a ship plying between Dublin and Lisbon. British and Irish cryptanalysts broke the cipher (the Goertz code),[81] which led to the arrest of Andrews and the courier in August 1943 and the text of all the traffic seized.

Given that neither German agents nor Irish sympathisers contributed anything of value to the Abwehr during the war, it is interesting to note Duggan's assertion that Hempel's reports incriminate him for breaching neutrality. Duggan gives examples of Hempel's proactive reactions to what were requests by the Abwehr for essential elements of information.[82]

The most important of Hempel's signals compromised a Canadian division's (Montgomery-planned) Dieppe raid, resulting in 3,369 Canadian casualties out of the 5,000 strong force involved, on 19 August 1942. Emboldened by his success, Hempel signalled vital elements of information to his German masters which resulted in disaster for the Montgomery-inspired Operation Market Garden in Arnhem in September 1944. Duggan comments: 'For all the sound and fury about him, Goertz had never supplied information remotely comparable in quality to the diplomat's cloaked contribution.'[83]

O'Halpin feels that the security policies and practices adopted during the Emergency were justified by the activities of indigenous subversives and foreign powers. He lauds Dan Bryan's courageous pre-war analysis in 'Fundamental Factors'. Bryan's forecast was borne out by events, as both main belligerents took a covert interest in Irish affairs as the IRA/German alliance took shape. He maintains that the preventive measures taken by the state took were crucial in containing subversion and espionage and providing a private balance to what was in public a volatile and acrimonious Anglo-Irish relationship. The acrimony was virtually minimal between Irish and British respective security agencies, except when Churchill took a hand in matters, about which it usually transpired his staff knew more than he did. The US minister Gray, possessing little if any diplomatic training, petulant . . . unhelpful . . . unbalanced',[84] 'an impossible man',[85] 'a malevolent influence',[86] sent alarmist and widely inaccurate diplomatic reports on Irish security which took precedence in Washington over the more measured conclusions of Allied security agencies. O'Halpin's thinly veiled and caustic criticism of the American is of note.[87] Draconian government interference and scrutiny culminated in an extraordinary level of domestic surveillance and censorship in all aspects of daily routine. Associations were investigated for traces of anti-national sentiment and intrigue.

Aliens were automatically treated as suspect. The rigid exclusion of refugees continued, with which G2 concurred. Security policy was made and decisions taken, almost entirely at administrative level, within the Garda, army and the Departments of Justice and External Affairs. O'Halpin suggests that the ministers responsible averted their eyes from even the most intriguing or salacious results of police and army enquiries and they did not read the transcripts.[88] To date, one need only study the paucity of factual information given on the yearly audit report of the comptroller and auditor general in relation to the secret service budget to understand the subtle insistence of the comptroller and auditor general in pinning responsibility on the minister for his department's non-contribution of detailed figures. The audit for 2005 is a mirror image of all such audits, virtually since the foundation of the state.[89]

The military tribunals became not only a supplementary judiciary to deal with political offences but the sole arbiters of life and death for people accused of the most serious subversive crimes. Ireland preserved its neutrality during the Second World War only by the partial abandonment of the key democratic presuppositions underlying its constitution. But as events since 1922 had demonstrated, that was nothing new.[90] Ireland, without sufficient military means to defend its neutrality, had to resort to the measures indicated by O'Halpin. In Duggan's opinion British intelligence obfuscation was the greatest threat to Irish neutrality: 'British intelligence, while technically accomplished, is not renowned for its finesse in interpreting Irish situations; a pre-conceived technical stereotyped approach and a congenital contempt seem to stunt their evaluation.'[91]

German and British Plans to Invade Ireland

In January 1942, G2 issued Intelligence Note No. 81 under secret cover Section A, Copy No. 1423, German Army Organisation. It cancelled Notes Nos. 4 and 49, and drew the attention of all officers to DFR A.8 Part 1, Section 3. Its table of contents gives minute details of a German infantry division, a motorised infantry division, a motorised infantry regiment, SS formations, armoured division, parachute troops, mountain regiment, and a description of armaments. It concludes with some tables of weights and measures, presumably of the equipment.[92]

Close liaison existed between G2 officers and MI5, with Irish officers sent on British exercises and courses in Northern Ireland. Details in respect of the British were either given freely to G2 and Army Operations, or gleaned by those sent on such courses. In respect of Intelligence Note No. 81 produced by G2, it can be taken without much doubt that it was designed for study in conjunction with the German plan to invade Ireland – 'Fall Gruen'.

The Irish military authorities had known as far back as 1942 of a German plan to invade Ireland, from an invasion route in the south and east of the country, and had prepared plans to engage such an invasion until the British army in the North, as per tacit agreement, would come to their assistance.[93] The meticulous detail of the 201-page 'Fall Gruen', as indicated in the glossary below, included photographic and geographic outline of areas from Mizen Head to Malin Head, and cast a most serious doubt on German claims as to their aircraft 'straying' into Irish territory during the bombing raids on Britain. The evidence would point more towards an operational plan to invade Ireland.

Some historians project a speculative view that Irish army resistance would have disintegrated against German or British invasions. Perhaps, but in my opinion not without the invading force sustaining unacceptable casualties and residual guerrilla conflict.

TRANSLATION GLOSSARY: 'FALL GRUEN'

For official use only.
Military geographical report about Ireland.
South and eastward (from Mizen Head to Malin Head).
Text and pictures with map layout.
Taken on 31 May 1941.
General Staff of the army.
Department for War Maps and Land Surveying Office, Berlin 1941.

The German map of Ireland depicts the following: the location and details of maps of the coastal strategic locations. The letters A, B, C give the sequence of maps of these coastal areas. They depict the following details of the relevant port areas: harbour basins, steel works, oil depots, barracks, lighthouses, rail lines, islands, loading slipways, large mills, breweries, storehouses, canal docks, port layout, power stations, chemicals factories, farm power station, gasworks. This applies mainly to Dublin and Cork, but all other photographic and profile detail contains similar accuracy. Coastal profiles depict lighthouses, towers, watch/guard houses, hill lines and heights, depths of water and distances of such from coast line, harbour entrances.[94]

Significant Contributors to the Security of the State and Maintenance of its Neutrality during the Emergency

Colonel Dan Bryan was Director of G2 from 1941 to 1952. During the sensitive years of the Emergency he controlled a very unobtrusive but efficient intelligence operation. While studying medicine at university he joined the Volunteers, later serving with the 4th Battalion, Dublin Brigade of the Old IRA. He joined the pro-Treaty army with the rank of captain in June 1922, a proactive decision on his part. Bryan's initial service with the Infantry Corps was a prelude to a military career spent almost entirely in intelligence work in army headquarters. He moved to the intelligence branch in 1924 and subsequent appointments were in plans division, in the assistant chief of staffs' branch, in G2 general staff, as executive officer G2 and as chief staff officer G2. Promoted to colonel and appointed Director of Intelligence in June 1941, he was renowned for his cooperation with Richard Hayes, director of the National Library, in breaking German codes. He transferred to the Military College as commandant in 1952 and retired from the defence forces in 1955.[95]

West's 1981 study features extensive coverage of Bryan's work with G2.[96] On becoming Director of the organisation, he continued to maintain the frostiness

Caption: Colonel Dan Bryan (courtesy of UCD Archives).

associated with his predecessor Archer, but a certain thaw was detectable by the end of 1943. G2 had put twelve Abwehr agents behind bars and the atmosphere between the Allies and Dublin had begun to thaw. De Valera rejected a US request for the expulsion of German diplomats in Dublin, but offered a compromise which the Allies found acceptable.[97]

According to West, de Valera authorised Bryan to invite a representative of the US Office of Strategic Service to Dublin and liaise with G2. In 1944 the Americans were worried that the Germans could discover some of the Allies' invasion secrets, and so a delegation consisting of Hubert Will, chief of the X2 counter-intelligence branch of the OSS in Europe, and a Lieutenant Edward Lawler flew to Belfast and caught a train south to Dublin. The Americans suspected that the German legation in Dublin was a centre of Abwehr operations and they were particularly anxious to discover if G2 was monitoring German wireless transmissions or tapping the telephone there. Bryan evaded all their questions, merely pointing out that the Germans no longer had their diplomatic pouch and their short-wave radio had been rendered unserviceable. Whenever Bryan was pressed on a point such as the placing of a G2 informant inside the legation or the interception of the cable traffic, the G2 chief replied that such action would be a violation of German sovereignty. The OSS men noted however that Bryan did not actually deny that his organisation had taken such precautions.[98] Bryan's attitude is reflected in Duggan's work: 'His bland, gentlemanly, roundabout way of getting to the point concealed a steely professionalism which won the respect of friend and foe alike.'[99]

Bryan and Hayes proposed to de Valera that a secret agreement between OSS and G2 be initiated, to which de Valera consented,[100] even though the wily statesman was, no doubt, aware of the risk he was taking in endangering Irish neutrality. Lieutenant Lawler, according to West, was allowed to remain in Dublin and study the security arrangements made by G2; the Americans agreed to respect the confidence and keep what they learned a secret. West adds that Lawler was satisfied that G2 had taken almost every possible precaution. The telephones at the German legation were tapped and every letter was intercepted. The only improvement he could suggest was the inspection of the Germans' waste paper. By April 1944, Lawler was satisfied he could find no flaw in G2's arrangements and was sure the D-day preparations would not be leaked via Dublin. One can assume that an Irish officer of Bryan's calibre and rank was not unduly perturbed at Lawler's scrutiny of G2's security precautions. Had he been so, he would not have made his original proposal to de Valera.

Bryan was also mentioned in another book by West, who claims that for the first time help had been obtained from Irish military intelligence.

> The head of G2 Colonel Dan Bryan consented to take the OSS [US Office of Strategic Services] officer Edward Lawler into his confidence on condition that Lawler did not pass information directly to MI5. Lawler abided by the letter on the pact. G2's intelligence was passed to Hubert Will of X2 [US counter-intelligence] who was then able to reassure Cecil Liddell that the Irish had indeed taken all the necessary precautions to control German espionage in Éire.[101]

Bryan reviewed West's books, was unimpressed and stated that the references to the Irish intelligence service were 'inaccurate and unreliable'.[102] The most telling tribute to Bryan, in the immediate aftermath of his death, was paid to him by America's most successful agent in Ireland during the war, E. R. 'Spike' Marlin. His compliment to Bryan and refutation of West's inaccuracies shows the extent of his knowledge and appreciation of Bryan's outstanding talent as Director of G2.[103]

Arguably the most ludicrous statement made by West in his 1981 work was as follows: 'Hayes and his five children spent hours deciphering the messages and gradually discovered the key.'[104] Had he bothered to contact any of Hayes' family, or the National Library, he would have known that three of Hayes' children were born post 1941, and that cryptography was not a matter for children. One wonders whether West had an ulterior motive and whether his inaccurate and unreliable account was deliberate. Marlin refuted West's other allegations, expressing his surprise that such works should be even considered as references in a review of Bryan's career, given Bryan's view that they were both 'inaccurate and unreliable'.

Lieutenant Edward Lawler did not take up his post at the American legation until after the Allied invasion of Europe started. Spike Marlin records that, but for the objection of David Gray, he was to have accompanied Lawler and Hugh Will to Dublin on 21 June 1944 to introduce them to Bryan. His refutation of West's assertions are unequivocal. He refutes as absurd the claim that Bryan insisted that Lawler should not pass information directly to MI5, and maintains that Cecil Liddell of MI5 was treated on the same basis as the OSS was by Bryan. Marlin also insists that a meaningful relationship had been proposed by the secretary of the Department of External Affairs, Joseph P. Walshe, early in 1943 and was officially concluded during a visit by Colonel David Bruce, OSS chief of mission, London, with Walshe in May 1943. Marlin was assigned to act as liaison officer with Bryan and performed this duty through personal visits to Dublin from London and through correspondence and contacts with the High Commissioner's Office in London.[105]

Marlin omits to mention that General Bill Donovan, Roosevelt's 'coordinator of intelligence', founder of the OSS, had despatched an agent to Kerry in 1942 whose mission was to develop a network around the southwest to collect information for transmission to the legation. Florence O'Donoghue of G2 uncovered the plot and G2 agents kept it under surveillance thereafter.[106] By 1943 all belligerents were realising that Bryan and his G2 operatives were a most reckonable organisation.

Marlin's direct liaison with Bryan continued until Lawler came to Dublin after the invasion. The wireless transmitter in the German legation had been removed by the Irish authorities long before Lawler's arrival on 21 June 1944. The statement that 'by April 1944, Lawler was satisfied he could find no flaw in G2's arrangements, and was sure that the D-Day preparations would not be leaked via Dublin' is an interesting comment, but one without practical significance. Hugh Will of X2 and Marlin came to Dublin from London to attend a tripartite conference on 2–4 May 1944 with the Irish and British authorities in order to discuss the security measures that should be taken by the Irish authorities to ensure as far as possible the security of the Allies' invasion plans.[107]

Marlin recalled meeting Nigel West in London about 1984 during which he pointed out the errors in West's books. West expressed his regrets that he had been furnished with inaccurate information but omitted the fact that he had never consulted Bryan in researching his books. Marlin's refutations can be interpreted as compliments to Bryan. He concluded his correspondence by expressing his thanks and appreciation to Colonel Bryan for the outstanding service he and his organisation rendered Ireland and the US during the Second World War by preventing Ireland from being used as a source of information that might have had disastrous effects on the Allies. Marlin regretted that Bryan's services were never sufficiently recognised during his lifetime, a sentiment also expressed by Duggan.[108]

A document issued to Ms Grace Tully, White House staffer, with attached memorandum, dated 30 March 1944 and signed by William Donovan, Director of the Office of Strategic Services, was transmitted to President Roosevelt. Even in sanitised form it is a grudging tribute to the extent of G2 cooperation with OSS agents during the war. Prior to its declassification on 19 April 1985, its content was not made available for historical research.[109] Donovan's memorandum informed the president in broad terms of the extent of Irish cooperation with the OSS. The OSS initiated the *démarche* in 1943, about which the undiplomatic diplomat Gray did not want to be concerned.

As a result of 1943 conferences, the OSS representative in Dublin was from time to time furnished with information by G2, requested or volunteered. Since, at the US minister's request, the representative (presumably Marlin) moved his base to London, some of the information he received was sent to the OSS London office. The balance was given to him either before he left or on subsequent liaison trips to Dublin. The memorandum lists the information received: German agents in Ireland, their training, instructions, equipment (including radio equipment) and ciphers; radio activity; illicit radios, interception, and direction finding; the Irish Republican Army; complete lists of Axis nationals, persons of Axis origin, and Axis sympathisers in Éire, their jobs and where possible their views and activities; Axis diplomatic and consular representatives and their known contacts; map of the coast-watching system; reports on shipping activities; Axis propaganda; submarine activity off the Irish coast to the extent known; Irish prisoners of war in Germany and known activities of Irishmen in Germany; political groups in Ireland with fascist leanings or ideologies; interviews with persons who had recently left the continent, including the Irishman recently parachuted by the Germans into Ireland; lists of German aviators interned; and lists of and interviews with survivors of a naval action off the Bay of Biscay picked up by an Irish ship. Donovan claims that the information contained in these reports was confirmed by other sources, and its potential was important. He adds that the Irish gave full cooperation in intelligence matters and points out that the OSS did not offer the Irish information in return and gave them little. He then mentions the delivery of the American Note, and claims it resulted in prompt Irish cooperation in adopting whatever security measures were recommended by the OSS.

Donovan's memorandum was couched in truths interspersed with half truths. One could interpret it as having administered a cautionary smack on the hand to de Valera and Bryan, who would immediately fully disintegrate under US pressure. He obviously did not understand the strength of character of both men.

Fulsome tributes were accorded to Colonel Bryan on his death by Lieutenant-Generals M. J. Costello and G. O'Sullivan, and by Colonel Ned Doyle, military historian. Lieutenant-General Costello said he was 'a man of outstanding intellect with a remarkable intuition and memory . . . one of the best practitioners in the Irish intelligence service'.[110]

Bryan's surviving papers in University College Dublin Archives embrace aspects of Ireland's foreign policy during the Emergency, G2's constant development of the Irish military intelligence system and British, American and German intelligence contact with Ireland. They reveal the enormity of the tasks facing Bryan and his staff throughout the Emergency.

Military Information and General Section

During 1940–41 intelligence notes were issued on a number of subjects, including British army organisation, German army organisation, anti-tank tactics, anti-aircraft tactics, obstruction of aerodromes, and airborne and parachute troops. These notes were issued for general information of officers; notes were also prepared for limited circulation among senior officers on the present situation of Ireland, possibilities of invasion and its nature. Bryan's papers show that, owing to lack of staff, it was not possible to supervise combat intelligence training in commands. Drafts for an intelligence handbook suitable for other ranks and the Local Security Force were in preparation; nevertheless, G2 did not escape censure for poor unit level intelligence cell operation in the 1942 manoeuvres. On the positive side the section did arrange for the printing of modified (military) editions of the half-inch Ordnance Survey (OS) map with a 5,000-yard grid, as adopted for operational purposes. These, together with modified 1-inch OS maps and romers[111] on a large scale were of great value to operational forces.

Given de Valera's stated policy that the Irish army would fight whatever antagonist invaded, G2 took prudent measures to obtain and circulate reports on the dispositions of British troops in Northern Ireland. In addition, it maintained a constant liaison with the chief press censor's office. The section was also tasked to ensure that 'no item affecting the Defence Forces or Defence questions is passed for publication until this Branch is circulated'[112] – surely an understatement!

The Bryan papers indicate that numerous problems affected the defence forces in relation to the Emergency Powers Order and its application to censorship, publicity, distribution of information, control of means of communication, photography and maps. Without going into specifics, G2 simply declared that 'Defence measures have been dealt with in cooperation with other Branches and Departments affected'. It seems clear to this author that G2 took every opportunity to highlight its own problem areas. For example, the collection, evaluation and distribution of military intelligence was seriously affected, due mainly to insufficient numbers of trained personnel. Sources of information that existed in peacetime had almost completely dried up; the lack of trained observers and/or military attachés abroad was seriously felt.[113] The file does not specify what measures were taken to ensure the appointment of military attachés. The army was, and remained for many years, aware that the Department of External/Foreign Affairs had always attempted to block such appointments. This trend has been modified in recent years and army officers have been posted to appointments in United Nations headquarters, New York and to European Union military appointments in Vienna.[114]

Coastal and Aerial Intelligence Section

Information collected by this section covered the movements of belligerent aircraft seen or heard in the vicinity of Irish shores or over Irish land boundaries, naval surface belligerent craft in Irish territorial waters or adjoining waters, and submarines. The section was also responsible for monitoring of mines floating or dropped inside territorial waters, vessels in distress, survivors, attacks on shipping and sinkings and matters relating to unusual happenings on Irish coastlines or inland that might be associated with either aerial or marine activities of belligerents. While it was the function of the Infantry, Engineers, Ordnance, Air Corps and Air Raid Precaution services to collect fragments of missiles dropped from aircraft in Irish territory, the responsibility for the correlation of information and the identification of the country of origin rested with G2. Such incidents were reported speedily, and interim reports submitted to enable the government to issue special bulletins.[115] After full investigation detailed statements of evidence accompanied by photographs and samples of the principal exhibits were sent to the Department of External Affairs, while summarised reports were circulated daily to the Minister for Justice. Matters of outstanding importance were reported by telephone direct to the Minister for Defence, the Minister for External Affairs and Minister for Co-ordination of Defensive Measures as soon as possible following receipt of the information.[116]

Military Information: Foreign Armies

G2 operatives encountered difficulty in obtaining accurate information about foreign armies after the commencement of the war, and particularly after France's capitulation. Studies carried out by G2 officers and data compiled in relation to foreign armies before the war proved useful as the basis for the work in progress at that time. G2's work in regard to foreign armies in 1940–41 was almost entirely confined to the two main belligerents. Such restriction is difficult to believe, since Bryan did not reveal all activities of G2 operatives, even in documents classified as confidential and circulated only at the highest level. Most of the information committed to paper was fairly routine reporting of current incidents and future routine planning. Information on the two main belligerents was updated as available, presumably on a need-to-know basis.

Since practically all sources of information on the continent were closed to G2, its intelligence on the German army was mainly obtained from reports published in Britain and the US, supplemented by what Bryan might guardedly call 'unspecified items'.[117] Details of the organisation of the German army (early 1940) were circulated together with information on tactics employed by parachute and airborne troops. With regard to the British army, air force and navy generally, many of the documents such as war establishments, training pamphlets and periodical notes, and army lists, previously obtainable by G2, were no longer available.

As was usual at that time, the report contained a reminder to its readers of G2's staff shortage, that the collection, evaluation and distribution of information about the British and German armies was unsatisfactory owing to a lack of trained staff officers and because it was not possible to fully utilise limited sources. Most of the information referred to was widely circulated in the army through intelligence notes.

Work continued apace in G2, however. Estimates of the situation were prepared as required in connection with the work of the general staff and the plans and operations branch. The nature and compilation of the data on which these estimates were based was dealt with in a separate report. Provisional manuals on combat intelligence were reissued for the instruction of the defence forces and the local defence forces. The duties and establishment of the brigade intelligence section were revised and reissued pending their publication in a brigade staff manual.

Personnel: Intelligence Service

Headcount grew as the workload did. The growth areas were appointments outside the Department of Defence, in press, postal and telegraph censorship, as command or divisional press officers and as brigade intelligence police officers. A course was arranged at the Military College for twenty-eight officers to be trained to fill appointments on the intelligence staffs as division liaison officers, brigade liaison officers (four brigades) and assistant brigade intelligence officers (four brigades). The formation of additional brigades necessitated the running of similar courses. The object of these courses was to ensure that officers employed on combat intelligence work would have received adequate training.

Bryan's papers include an incomplete section of an undated report compiled by G2 outlining matters affecting British and Irish relations, aid to the British war effort and the activities of the US within Ireland. Despite the omission of the specific date, the incomplete report is important, illustrating the obvious covert surveillance of named politicians – James Dillon and Frank McDermott – and their association with both the US legation and UK representative's office.

It focused on information of considerable importance, including the views and associations of Irish people who thought that Ireland should associate itself more actively with Britain in the prosecution of the war, information that G2 passed to External Affairs. Senator McDermott appeared to be on intimate terms with the staff of both the UK representative's office and the US legation, who seemed to be fully acquainted with his views as to the war, while Deputy James Dillon, a member of the Defence Council, was named as being on friendly terms with the US legation, where his views on Ireland's attitude to the war were known. Other persons prominent in political circles, including another member of the Defence Council (unnamed in the section of the document), also expressed views indicating that they did not approve of complete neutrality. They obviously were unaware that neither de Valera nor Bryan approved of such a course either and practised what Lee described as 'half-armed' neutrality.[118] G2 felt that the presence of those named persons at lectures gave a platform for propaganda to the British belligerents which would not have otherwise been available to Britain in this country.

The report also analysed Irish aid to the British war effort and commented on both British and American subterfuge. G2 knew that numerous recruits for the British forces came from this country and that they had been assisted to proceed to Northern Ireland. Action was taken against officials of the British Legion who were assisting in this work on a large scale and who were prepared to assist deserters from the defence forces to join the British army.

G2 was aware that many Irish enlisted in the British forces for better pay and allowances and also because married men were not at the time accepted in the defence forces. Significant voluntary financial aid in the form of collections was secured to buy aircraft for the British forces and to provide comforts for the troops. After a certain amount of data had been collected from postal censorship and otherwise, the government issued an order to limit these activities. The report mentions that a number of British intellectuals, socialists and 'war dodgers' had fled to Ireland. And although, with one or two possible exceptions (unnamed), they merited no serious importance, they still warranted G2 investigation because of large numbers of reports made to G2 agents.

The report added that no evidence existed that the US had indulged in any espionage activities during the previous year. Inevitably, evidence of a growing and intense interest in Irish affairs on behalf of US representatives and official visitors to Ireland was unearthed. There were two reasons for this interest in Irish affairs. Firstly, a very definite view was held by both 'official' and 'unofficial' Americans (whatever an unofficial American might be) that Ireland should support England to the fullest extent in the war, including the use of air and port facilities. Secondly, Ireland should, because of its geographical position, effect measures that the United States would later take to maintain communications with Britain. The type of action is neither stated nor forecast in the report. The legation was probably a greater centre of pro-British influence in Ireland than the office of the UK representative, who evidently felt himself restricted in a way that the US minister did not.

Intimate relations were maintained by the legation with prominent politicians, such as Dillon and McDermott, who advocated an attitude more favourable to the British. G2 believed that some of the politicians mentioned kept the legation fully informed as to happenings in Ireland, while the legation of course maintained the most intimate relations with the UK representative's office. It was possible to supervise US activities here in a way that British activities could not, probably because mutually acceptable covert relations already existed. G2 surveillance of US representatives, however, threw considerable light upon British activities. Such surveillance unearthed an unfavourable reaction from the US legation to the neutrality policy of the Irish government.[119]

Prior to Bryan's appointment as Director of Intelligence, his predecessor, Colonel Liam Archer, held the post with distinction. Although his reputation is somewhat overshadowed by Bryan's, the latter nevertheless valued Archer's work to such an extent as to retain copies of significant documents, issued by Archer, in the Bryan Papers. Among these is a copy of Intelligence Note No. 15. Issued by Archer on 10 July 1940, it details current activities of foreign agents and their likely tasks, pre, during and post invasion of their countries.[120] In Holland and Poland fifth columnists were blatantly active, while espionage, sabotage and other subversive activities abounded. In Denmark and Norway covert preparations and operations were kept as secret as possible.

Archer asserted that because such preparations were not generally known or overt did not mean that secret plans were not proceeding, and he specified activities in which agents were likely to engage based on experience of the war to date. These were wide-ranging, embracing all aspects of the army establishment and civil government, national infrastructure and communications systems, as well as all shipping facilities.[121] Archer's second category highlighted probable fifth columnist activities in the event of invasion, and how they would attempt to assist the enemy by sabotage or utilising assets to spread confusion among the civil population, and other subterfuges. Archer reminded his address group that such activities were carried out in accordance with pre-arranged and detailed plans and often directed by some central agency.[122]

Archer's work output was prolific during 1939–40, during which he gave an insight into the amount of detail prepared by G2 in relation to the ongoing tactical and strategic methodology as it evolved during the course of the war.[123] The German generals had learned of the futility of First World War tactics and strategy. Consequently, their army embraced the Blitzkrieg concept of rapid movement of combined forces to break through static enemy defence systems, flank and rear encirclement forcing their opponents to capitulate or be destroyed. Intelligence Note No. 19 relating to German airborne troops was hugely important, outlining their organisation, equipment and armament, supplies, training, suitable landing areas, landings, action on landing, losses incurred, troop-carrying aircraft, use of gliders and air transportation of armoured fighting vehicles.[124]

Other intelligence notes included details of anti-tank tactics and weaponry of various armies, irregular warfare and the shock tactics of Blitzkreig.[125] Archer's notes made Irish operational commanders aware of the perils they would face in the event of a successful German invasion, and its implication of death, destruction and punitive occupation for the Irish populace. He should not be overlooked by historians' study of those who made quality contributions to the fledgling Irish state during dangerous times.

Operation Ireland

On 2 September 1948, Kathleen Stout, civilian no. 25978, a duly appointed translator for the German and English languages in the office of chief of staff McKenna, certified that she had made a true and correct translation of document No. NG-5760, 'Proposal for Ireland Operation' dated 24 August 1941.[126] The German document, classified 'top secret', included details of proposed timings, landing places, personnel selected and mission details.[127] Bryan, typically, does not indicate the date on which the document came into his possession. One could draw an analogy with Joe O'Carroll's concluding contention that MI6 had a network of informants in Ireland during the war, but its files may never be opened.[128]

The German plan envisaged the latest possible time for the operation as 15–25 September 1941; prerequisites stipulated dark clear nights before the autumn storms set in. Lieutenant-Colonel van Harlinghausen, Knight's Cross with Oak Leaves, stated at Lorient on 11 July that he was prepared to airlift the three persons intended to carry out the operation, and foresaw no particular difficulties in the undertaking. A suitable Heinkel 59 was prepared and an experienced pilot appointed, who had already carried out similar operations successfully. The proposal was submitted to Gesandtschaftsrat Weber in the Reich Foreign Ministry by Veesenmayer, and included the following details: the landing was to take place only if a landing place was clearly visible and there were no particular dangers; the approach would be made from a great height; disembarkation would be made via rubber dinghy; all three agents would receive English collapsible bicycles for greater ease of movement on land.[129]

After careful investigation Brandon Bay was agreed upon for the landing. A bay on the Dingle Peninsula, it had the following advantages: easy flying reach of Brest, where the flight was to start; sheltered position, safe for disembarkation; numerous possibilities of safe refuge on the Dingle Peninsula for the persons to be landed, within an hour's walking time at most; the possibility of being transported quickly to Dingle Peninsula with the aid of friendly fishermen; Lough Gill, an inland lake situated near the landing place, offered favourable hiding places for equipment (radios and money); Dingle Peninsula very popular with tourists, so the agents would not attract attention.

The participants in the operation were named as Irishman Frank Ryan and two former members of the Brandenburg Training Regiment, Corporal Clissmann and Pfc [Private] Rieger. Frank Ryan had already taken part in an aborted operation with Seán Russell, and after the latter's death (a cause of disputed rumour-mongering) he returned by U-boat in accordance with instructions. Ryan, an Irish republican and member of the Leadership Council of the IRA, had participated in numerous actions against England. In 1929 the British secret service made an unsuccessful attempt on his life, and since then he had often been imprisoned. It has been said that he had extensive connections with Irish republicans, even within de Valera's immediate circle and with de Valera himself; he also had connections with the Irish regular army, Irish nationalists in

Northern Ireland and, especially, leading Irishmen in America.[130] These contentions were mainly true, with the exception of the reference to de Valera.

Veesenmayer misjudged de Valera as much as the British chiefs of staff's planning subcommittee did in 1936. De Valera's mailed fist had bludgeoned the IRA since his party attained power in 1932/33, yet he sent a telegram to Franco asking that Ryan be spared from execution, a fate suffered by many members of the International Brigade captured by Franco's army during the Spanish Civil War.

Of the men selected by Veesenmayer for the planned Irish operation, Clissmann lived in Ireland for more than five years (1933–34 and 1936–39); he was married to the daughter of a well-known Irish nationalist and had been a close friend of Frank Ryan since 1930. He had German military training, had already taken part in one operation against England, spoke perfect English (with an Irish accent) and had numerous contacts in Ireland. Rieger also had military training, spoke perfect English and was a trained radio operator. The undertaking was instigated and prepared in conjunction with the Supreme Command of the Wehrmacht, Abwehr Division II, and was submitted for approval with mutual consent.

The tasks allotted to Clissmann were listed in a letter of 23 August sent by the OKW (Oberkommando der Wehrmacht, German high command) to the Foreign Office. If Ireland should be occupied by the English or the Americans, the following should take place: preparation of guerrilla warfare; establishing contact with the IRA and activation of work of the IRA in Great Britain, and at the same time delivery of the funds anticipated by the IRA; establishment of radio communication; transmission of military intelligence and weather reports, since in accordance with de Valera's orders radio traffic between the legation and its Foreign Office was cut to a minimum. The latter assumption is not correct, however. The German legation radio operated until December 1943 when the set was surrendered by Hempel to Fred Boland of the Department of External Affairs and Commandant Neligan, the G2 signals expert. O'Halpin's research confirms my viewpoint.[131]

In addition to the above military tasks, the following political tasks were assigned to Frank Ryan and Clissmann: establishment of a general, effective liaison with the IRA; transfer of urgently necessary financial assistance for the IRA, for which the Reich foreign minister made £40,000 sterling available; and establishment of agreement between IRA and de Valera – if such was expedient. Veesenmayer felt that Frank Ryan was particularly well suited for just that task – a misjudgement of de Valera's policy and gross exaggeration of Ryan's capacity. De Valera did not need Veesenmayer's advice with regard to the Irish policy of neutrality nor to encourage the Irish will to resist an invader.

Veesenmayer was correct in stating that Ryan had a particular influence on the Irish in America which could be used politically for propaganda purposes. His planning advice continued: exerting influence on conduct and policy of Irish nationalist activities through Clissmann; to provide the Reich with a clear picture of the internal and external situation in Ireland; careful observation of England and American endeavours in Southern and Northern Ireland; and if Ireland should be occupied by

England or America, organisation of resistance movement and closest possible contact with enemy forces.

Veesenmayer also suggested factors that adversely affected 'Operation Ireland', and it did not seem advisable to keep Frank Ryan in Germany any longer. The concluding communication in respect of the operation issued from Wehrmacht Command simply reiterates the military tasks already specified as Clissmann's responsibility. Recent literature depicts Veesenmayer as a coup d'état expert who was responsible for the deaths of 825,000 Jews, and exposes his aborted collusion with Ryan, Russell and Clissmann as an abject failure, comparable to Casement's.[132]

De Valera, well versed in the craft of ruling and the exercise of power, proved himself an enigmatic figure to both British and American statesmen and politicians during the Emergency. Not only did he maintain a pose of exercising a policy of strict neutrality but also a continuous, though covert, brief on the military intelligence system. That he managed to do so proved him a statesman of both Machiavellian and Herculean stature. Ryle Dwyer attributes the following grudging tribute to de Valera, allegedly accorded him by Gray, in respect of his cunning use of the Irish-American platform on the thorny matter of access to Ireland's Atlantic ports.

> He is probably the most adroit politician in Europe and he honestly believes all he does is for the good of the country. He has the qualities of martyr, fanatic and Machiavelli. No one can outwit, frighten or blandish him. Remember he is not pro-

> German nor personally anti British but only pro-de Valera. My view is that he will do business on his own terms or must be overcome by force.[133]

General Michael Collins, Major General M. J. Costello, Colonels Liam Archer and Dan Bryan, and Major Florence O'Donoghue all played outstanding roles in the foundation and continuing evolution of G2 from its inception, while Commandant-General Tom Barry was acutely aware of its singular importance to field commanders. It is imperative also to consider General Dan McKenna if one was to decide which of those renowned soldiers contributed most during the fledgling state's most singular years of danger. It becomes essentially a judgement choice.

The McKenna papers, with the exception of his lecture notes for an address delivered in the Military College on 12 October 1967,[134] have not yet been reposited in any archival institute, and remain in the possession of his family. Should a decision be made to reposit them in an archival institute, I am assured that Military Archives would be pleased to index and care for them.[135] Until then historians must rely on political and military comment from those who were closely associated with McKenna to outline his character and contribution to his country. McKenna was responsible for the military direction and control of the defence of Ireland from January 1940 until 1945. A native of County Derry, he played an active role in the War of Independence, enduring the difficulties, dangers and hardships of war in an area where sections of the local population were actively hostile. McKenna's career followed the normal pattern of diverse military appointments. Although not chosen to undergo any of the training courses associated with the military mission to the US in Forts Leavenworth, Benning and Sill, he was appointed a member of the revived Military Tribunal in 1931, an onerous and dangerous task which was testament to his mental toughness. Recent literature corroborates this.[136]

The defence forces' phoney war period was ended ingloriously at Christmas 1939 by the IRA raid on the magazine fort, in which a large portion of the reserve ammunition was taken. This led to a realisation of the need for strict control, discipline and security before the greater threat of possible invasion. McKenna was appointed chief of staff with effect from 29 January 1940, at a time when the state was ill-prepared and sadly deficient in arms and field forces. McKenna convinced de Valera of the need for instant military and national mobilisation, and the immediate organisation, training, officer selection, arming, equipping, clothing and housing of the greatly enlarged forces involved intense and extensive staff and administrative work. Because of the paucity of warlike stores, the manufacture of explosives, grenades, mines and armoured cars was undertaken. Simultaneously, plans for national defence and the employment of the improvised forces were made lest the then feared invasion should materialise.

McKenna directed all activities by continuous conference and inspection and, when necessary, his formidable drive was applied with full force; he did not suffer fools gladly. He had far-reaching military powers, and continually travelled the country attending training exercises and inspecting progress; these tours were often climaxed by parades and inspections by the Taoiseach or other members of the government.[137] When the military situation seemed ominous, McKenna was the first person to whom de Valera turned. As the person who carried the supreme responsibility, de Valera had the best opportunity of appreciating his qualities. McKenna won the complete confidence not only of the Taoiseach and the government but also General Franklyn, commander of the British troops in Northern Ireland, with whom he would have had to cooperate in the event of a German invasion or confront in the event of a British invasion. When the threat of a British invasion no longer existed, Franklyn, during one of his meetings with McKenna, stated semi-jocosely to him: 'Now McKenna, we will never know.'[138] Franklyn's brevity suggests confirmation of contingency British plans for invasion.

As the person who carried the supreme responsibility, de Valera had the best opportunity to appreciate McKenna's qualities. De Valera stated that:

> I have already said that our thanks were due to providence for sparing us from the horrors of war during the last conflict. Next to providence we should thank the army. We should particularly thank the chief officer of the army, whose service to this nation will never be fully recognised. He was a man who knew his work, a man of ability, and a man of great commonsense. No matter how skilful a person may be in professional or particular matters, if he fails in that quality of general commonsense, he can be a danger. We had the

> great blessing of having at the head of the army a man who was loyal and true to the country, a man whose commonsense was exceptional. He enabled us to get through a very difficult period, and in dealing with problems that arose with various people he was able to gain their confidence and make them realise he was a man of his word and that he represented a government that was also of its word.[139]

In the debate during the moving of the Estimate for the Defence Forces for the year 1949/50, Dr Tom O'Higgins,[140] Mr Frank Aiken[141] and Major Vivion de Valera[142] paid equally fulsome tributes to McKenna, lionising his characteristics of 'support, sound advice and loyalty', 'fine service, full satisfaction, service to the country', 'foresight and forethought'. The survival of Ireland's neutral status during the war was ensured through the interface of the Taoiseach with the specified officers, all of whom played significant roles in Irish army intelligence, G2.

CONCLUSION

From 1918 to 1945, the experience of Irish army intelligence was in some respects unique, but broadly comparable to that of other western states. Between 1918 and 1923, the Irish state evolved from a guerrilla war against British forces and a bitter civil war. Post-Civil War demobilisation and attendant fiscal severity led to military discontent that lingered for many years; indeed, by 1939 the army had plunged to a professional nadir. Irish army intelligence, not unlike the peacetime experience of intelligence services in other countries such as Britain, receded in importance and the resources it could command. Yet the government and army, shocked by the audacious and successful IRA raid on the magazine fort in December 1939, engaged in crisis management policy designed to maintain Irish neutrality.

Post-1919, the IRA realised the absolute importance of organising a systematised structure of intelligence throughout Ireland. The IRB, unlike the Fenians who were riddled with spies, based its organisation on a cell system. Treachery met fast retribution, and spy rings were eliminated. The IRB, headed by Michael Collins, infiltrated the IRA and effectively controlled it and the armed struggle. Collins ruthlessly eliminated British agents throughout the war, and the IRA/IRB neutralised the RIC. The IRA then won the battle for the hearts and minds of the Irish people and formed another link in its intelligence structure. Although vastly outnumbered by the British army, the IRA forced the British into negotiations with Sinn Féin in 1921. The intelligence gap was not alone equalled, but superseded by Collins and Florence O'Donoghue's agents in the War of Independence.

Having realised the importance of building such structures, Collins and O'Donoghue became the principal architects of intelligence organisations within their area of operations. Such was the success of the IRA intelligence system at that time, mainly in Dublin and Cork, that it enabled ruthless IRA active service units and gunmen to assassinate enemy agents and meet terror with terror. Their methodology paid dividends in their overall campaign to persuade the British to come to a political solution with Sinn Féin. The IRA's greatest success lay in infiltrating the British secret service, which Collins succeeded in doing in Dublin and O'Donoghue in Cork. Their agents invariably produced timely information, allowing intelligence officers to brief commanders of the active service units who in turn could use such intelligence to eliminate their opposition.

One would not want to underestimate the capacity of the British intelligence service to infiltrate IRA formations. These spies more often than not were Irish men and women. Some had a sense of loyalty to the British Crown, as in the case of Mrs Lindsay in west Cork, while others informed on their colleagues as a result of being bribed by British agents. Lack of security appreciation led to IRA columns in Clonmult and Ballycannon being wiped out.

Both Townshend and Liddle Hart emphasise the vital role that intelligence played in all guerrilla encounters, working in the light of superior local knowledge combined with reliable news about the enemy's disposition and moves. Yet again, despite the vastly superior resources of men and equipment, the British failed to conquer the IRA or even to weaken it to such an extent that it would have no further capacity for warfare, guerrilla or otherwise. They failed because they lost the battle for the hearts and minds of the people, just as the anti-Treaty forces lost them in the Civil War. While the anti-Treaty side never formally surrendered, they were forced to dump arms and to cease fighting.

It is noteworthy that Dan Bryan's capacity to use intelligence, having joined the pro-Treaty army, was devastatingly destructive to the anti-Treaty forces in Dublin during the Civil War. One can indeed concur with Hopkinson's prognosis that the outlook for the IRA in the capital was to remain bleak throughout the Civil War because of Bryan's capacity to identify all anti-Treatyite safe houses.[1] Bryan's success as an intelligence officer caused battalions and company organisations in Dublin to fragment. Bryan, and the intelligence he delivered, was essentially responsible for this, confirming again, if confirmation were needed, the vital role of intelligence in war.

In peacetime, however, the role and resources of the army and its intelligence system suffered badly. The new state faced challenges of establishing legitimacy and adapting to stringent financial circumstances. For the army, this meant swingeing cuts throughout and the virtual emasculation of the military intelligence system. Such political tunnel vision lasted until 1939 when the government was forced to adopt a crisis management solution to attempt to rejuvenate the shattered remnants of an army that had plunged to its nadir.

Despite these cuts in the 1920s, Costello, Archer and, particularly, Bryan maintained covert contact with what would otherwise have become defunct – a military intelligence system. G2, which became a highly sophisticated and efficient counter-espionage organisation during the Emergency, had pre-war difficulties in common with all British intelligence agencies, mainly no recruitment opportunity for suitable personnel.

Intelligence alone, however good, cannot be responsible for victory. It does, however, make an invaluable contribution to the capacity of political and military leaders' efforts to understand the dilemma they face in adopting a particular stance. Ireland successfully resisted the efforts of greater countries, with vast military resources, to force it to adopt other than a neutral stance during the war. The British chiefs of staff Report 491 of July 1936 served as an ominous reminder to Irish army planners of a possible British pre-emptive strike at Saorstát Éireann prior to European hostilities. If Bryan had a copy of the paper,[2] one can assume that it acted as a catalyst for the rapid completion of his 'Fundamental Factors' in order to encourage the Irish body politic to commence thoughtful consideration of Ireland's precarious state of defence.

John Keegan reminds us that intelligence is a weak form of attack on an enemy. While accepting that conventional wisdom believes that knowledge is power, he asserts that knowledge cannot destroy or deflect the damage or even defy an offensive initiative by an army unless the possession of knowledge is also allied to objective force.[3] He accepts David Kahn's contention that 'there is an elemental point about intelligence which is a secondary factor in war.'[4] Keegan castigates intelligence as never being good enough; only force counts finally.[5] However, this is a highly debatable point, not just in the context of Irish developments but more generally.

Perhaps intelligence systems and the value of military intelligence are widely misunderstood and over-hyped. But one cannot underestimate their value to commanders and politicians in coping with problems that arise, either in war or during peacetime. Keegan maintains that the British and Indian troops repelled the Japanese attempt to invade India via Kohama and Imphal in 1944, not because intelligence had disclosed the enemy's plan but by stubborn relentless combat. Similarly, he cites the American capture of Iwo Jima in 1945 as not being due to any intelligence that had revealed the layout of the Japanese defensives.[6] Keegan emphasises that thought did not play a major role in victory but rather courage and unconsidered self-sacrifice. He deems the fall of Crete in 1941 to an inferior German force as an unnecessary disaster, the fault ultimately of 'PhDs in higher mathematics' in Bletchley Park. For although the comprehensive guide to the German airborne assault was decoded, General Freyberg, commander in chief of the Allied force in Crete, was not informed, on the basis that he would not understand the raw decrypts. Consequently, the British suffered the needless embarrassment of total defeat and were forçed to withdraw what remained of its formations back to Egypt.[7]

Keegan changes his philosophy to fit circumstances, however. For instance, he did not mention Operation Market Garden, Montgomery's ill-conceived plan to capture bridges over the rivers Maal and Waal, Arnhem being the most important. Montgomery deliberately omitted to inform the relevant formation commanders of the vital intelligence that two German Panzer divisions were deployed in the area of Arnhem. As a result the lightly armed British First Airborne Division was slaughtered, only 2,500 managing to escape out of 12,500 committed to the operation.

Intelligence can yield information, such as that which Bryan and his G2 agents used in Ireland during the Emergency, to keep both political and military leaders constantly focused on neutrality. Thomas Cleary considers that Sun Tzu's 2,000-year-old work, *The Art of War*, remains the most influential book of strategy of all time. Indeed, it is as eagerly studied today by politicians and business executives as it was by military leaders and strategists for the last two millennia. Sun Tzu considered that to win without fighting was best,[8] a dictum which gives added veracity to Bryan's 'Fundamental Factors', while his philosophy is also analogous to that espoused by de Valera and his military commanders and staff during the Emergency. The basis, of course, was good preparation.

As early as 1925 the army commenced strategic planning – a process that continued into the 1930s and 1940s. Strategic planning papers by both Costello and

Bryan also had significant influence on government censorship policy during the war. The general theme of Costello's memorandum was a proposal for the establishment of an overarching censorship bureau, headed by a director working in harmony with the general staff. The end product was that, during the Emergency, Ireland had a more stringent censorship system than any nation involved in the war. The Irish plan for censorship as produced in 1925 differed from the British one in that it identified censorship as a system embracing the protection of the country and its military forces. It unequivocally insisted on censorship of all news media, adding that censorship was essential for the maintenance of neutrality and would benefit the morale of both civilian and military forces alike and assist in the prevention of industrial and commercial espionage and malevolent publicity. Its objective was to prevent such leakages as would affect the life of the nation. It recognised, however, that to keep the people in blind ignorance was counterproductive, so the recommended course implied shrewd judgement on the part of those tasked with releasing relevant information.

The plan ensured that the Department of Defence had the primary vote in the forming of any regulation. In effect, pre-war planning such as that outlined by Costello in 1925 acted as a template for the censorship system introduced in Ireland from 1939 to 1946. Frank Aiken's memorandum for government on 23 January 1940 epitomised government policy in relation to neutrality, censorship and democracy for the remainder of the Emergency. It took the form of a pre-emptive preparation of the government to the opposition's expected attacks on the planned introduction of new draconian censorship policy, which in any case was enforced.

Dan Bryan's 1936 paper, 'Fundamental Factors', had a profound influence on military thinking and political action. The Bryan Papers suggest that he may have been aware of the British plans for Ireland as early as 1936 and that these may have acted as a catalyst for 'Fundamental Factors'. In that assessment, army intelligence officers quite reasonably concluded that it would be military suicide for the defence forces to make more than a show of organised resistance. The Irish army general staff were aware of Britain's ambivalent military intentions, that while Plan W was ostensibly the British response to an Irish call for assistance, it could also stand as an embryo plan for the British invasion of Ireland.

Bryan's document focused the government's attention on virtually the only policy that it could adopt: neutrality. Yet it took until the German invasion of Europe to expedite a typical crisis management response from the Department of Finance. Indeed, Finance's intransigent policy contributed to the half-armed neutrality surmised by Lee,[9] and was arguably a major factor in Bryan's prioritisation of counter-intelligence during the Emergency. On the political side, de Valera believed in neutrality based on political expediency and not on principle. Internally, army intelligence assisted in preserving the status quo. Despite the debacle of the magazine fort raid – which Bryan conceded as 'our Pearl Harbour' – army intelligence proved effective against the IRA. Not only did Bryan pursue the raiders, but he unearthed enough intelligence to recover more ammunition than was lost, as the trawl found dumps from the Civil War era.

At the beginning of the Emergency, Archer and Bryan, with de Valera's approval, co-opted Dr Richard Hayes to the staff of G2. This shrewd move gave the army one crucial additional resource. Hayes was a self-taught codes and cipher expert and an accomplished linguist. His personal papers tend to confirm O'Halpin's assertion that almost single-handedly he provided G2 with the capability for the informed analysis of complex signals intelligence issues, and crucially for breaking the only enciphered traffic which really mattered for the government during the war, the communications of individual German agents.[10]

APPENDIX I

Chronological Sequence of Events, 1918–46

1918

6 February: Extension of suffrage to most women over thirty

12 March: Dillon replaces Redmond (died 6 March) as chairman of Irish Parliamentary Party

9 April: Military Service Bill introduced by Lloyd George, with provision for extension to Ireland by executive order, enacted 18 April

18 April: Anti-conscription conference at Mansion House, Dublin, followed by meeting with Catholic bishops at Maynooth leading to coordinated declaration

21 April: Pledge to resist conscription administered in Catholic churches, with token but effective general strike

23 April: Most republican leaders, including de Valera, arrested as parties to a 'German plot'

11 November: Armistice agreed between Germany and Allies

14 December: General election, returning seventy-three Sinn Féin candidates

1919

18 January: Peace conference convened in Paris

21 January: Dáil Éireann convened at Mansion House, Dublin, approving declaration of independence and appeal for international recognition of Irish Republic

1 April: De Valera elected president of Dáil, after escape from Lincoln Jail (3 February)

11 June: De Valera begins campaign of propaganda and fund-raising in North America (arriving back in Ireland on 23 December 1920)

28 June: Treaty signed at Versailles between Germany and the Allies, Dáil's delegates having been excluded from the peace conference

7 October: Cabinet appoints committee to discuss Irish constitutional settlement

25 November: Membership of republican organisations proclaimed as illegal throughout Ireland, following proclamation of Dáil on 12 September

19 December: Unsuccessful ambush near Dublin's Phoenix Park of the viceroy, Viscount French

1920

2 January: First enrolment in England of temporary constables to reinforce RIC ('Black and Tans')

25 February: Government of Ireland Bill introduced in House of Commons (enacted 23 December, with provision for partition into two states)

4 April: Destruction by IRA of almost 300 unoccupied RIC barracks around Easter Sunday

June: Sinn Féin dominate elections for county and rural authorities (following qualified success at urban elections, 15 January)

19 June: Disturbances in Derry leading to eighteen deaths

21–24 July: Catholic workers expelled from shipyards and engineering works, and fatal rioting in Belfast

27 July: Formation belatedly sanctioned of force of ex-officers to assist RIC, later named Auxiliary Division

6 August: Boycott of Belfast firms inaugurated by Dáil Éireann

9 August: Restoration of Order in Ireland Act maintains and expands coercive powers under Defence of the Realm legislation

25 October: Death on hunger strike at Brixton Jail of Terence MacSwiney, lord mayor of Cork

1 November: First execution of rebel since 1916 (Kevin Barry); recruitment commenced for (Ulster) Special Constabulary

21 November: Assassination of fourteen British intelligence officers by IRA, followed by fatal reprisals at Gaelic football match in Croke Park, Dublin ('Bloody Sunday')

28 November: Sixteen Auxiliaries killed by Tom Barry's West Cork flying column at Kilmichael

10 December: Martial law imposed in four southwestern counties (extended to four adjacent counties on 4 January 1921)

11 December: Extensive burning and looting in Cork city by Auxiliaries and police, after ambush at Dillon's Cross

1921

1 January: First 'authorised' military reprisals against property, County Cork

13 May: All Sinn Féin candidates for Southern House of Commons returned unopposed

24 May: Unionists win forty of fifty-two seats in Northern House of Commons

25 May: Dublin's Custom House destroyed by IRA

7 June: Sir James Craig elected as first prime minister of Northern Ireland (parliament opened by George V on 22 June)

9–15 July: Belfast disturbances cause over twenty deaths

11 July: Truce implemented between British army and IRA

16 August: Second Dáil convened by Sinn Féin MPs, Dublin

26 August: De Valera elected president of Irish Republic by Dáil

14 September: Dáil elects delegates to negotiate with Lloyd George and ministers, following prolonged preliminary exchanges

11 October: Anglo-Irish conference opened in London

22 November: Control of police in six counties transferred to Northern government

6 December: Articles of agreement for a treaty signed in London

1922

7 January: Dáil Éireann narrowly approves Treaty, after acrimonious debate beginning on 14 December

14 January: Provisional government appointed under Collins, in tandem with new Dáil ministry under Griffith (who replaced de Valera on 10 January)

21 January: Ineffectual pact between Collins and Craig to end Belfast boycott and protect Northern Catholics

12–15 February: Belfast attacks cause twenty-seven deaths, attributed to IRA, followed by four months of renewed sectarian rioting, sniping and shooting

26–27 March: IRA convention establishes anti-Treaty Executive Council under Traynor, in defiance of Mulcahy's army staff

30 March: Second futile pact signed in London between Craig and Collins, along with Churchill; Treaty given force of law in United Kingdom on the following day

7 April: Civil Authorities (Special Powers) Act, NI, allows internment and other emergency measures for one year, the act being periodically extended and made permanent on 9 May 1933

14 April: Rory O'Connor's faction of anti-Treaty forces establish headquarters in Four Courts, Dublin

20 May: Collins and de Valera sign electoral pact to maintain balance of parties in Second Dáil at forthcoming election

23 May: Northern government declares republican organisations illegal

31 May: Royal Ulster Constabulary established in place of RIC in Northern Ireland; RIC in Southern state disbanded by 31 August

16 June: Pro-Treaty candidates dominate election for provisional parliament to approve draft constitution for the Irish Free State, following collapse of electoral pact

22 June: Sir Henry Wilson (military adviser to Northern government) killed by IRA in London

28 June: National army initiates open Civil War by attacking O'Connor's anti-Treaty force garrison in Four Courts. Garrison surrenders 30 June

22 August: Collins killed in ambush at Béal na mBláth, west Cork, following Griffith's natural death on 12 August

9 September: Third Dáil (provisional parliament) convened, and Cosgrave elected as president of Provisional Government

11 September: Proportional representation abolished for local elections in Northern Ireland

28 September: Dáil approves creation of military courts to try civilians

10 October: Catholic bishops issue joint pastoral excommunicating active anti-Treaty forces

25 October: Constitution approved by Dáil (ratified by British statute on 5 December); rival republican government constituted under de Valera, with support from IRA

17 November: First of seventy-seven anti-Treatyites executed

6 December: Cosgrave appointed president of Executive Council of new Irish Free State

7 December: Northern parliament votes to opt out of Free State (implementing Cabinet decision of 13 March)

1923

12 February: Cosgrave agrees secretly to payment of annuities, due from purchasers of Irish land, to British Exchequer

31 March: Customs control inaugurated between Free State and United Kingdom

24 May: De Valera instructs republicans to abandon armed resistance following suspension of anti-Treaty force offensive on 27 April

11 June: Anti-Treaty Sinn Féin reorganised at Mansion House, Dublin

8 August: Garda Síochána given statutory force (inaugurated 21 February 1922)

15 August: De Valera arrested in Ennis, County Clare. Interned until 16 July 1924

27 August: Cumann na nGaedheal victorious in general election for Dáil

10 September: Irish Free State admitted to League of Nations

1924

6 March: Army mutiny following announcement of reorganisation and reduction of national army on 18 February

10 March: Eoin O'Duffy (chief commissioner of Gardaí since September 1922) takes temporary command of defence forces until February 1925

2 April: Southern judiciary reconstituted by Courts of Justice Act, followed on 21 April by Ministers and Secretaries Act regulating civil service

10 May: Northern government declines to appoint delegate to Boundary Commission (MacNeill appointed by Free State on 20 July 1923)

6 November: Boundary commission convened in London, after legislation to allow appointment by British government of Northern delegate

24 December: Release of last remaining internees in Northern Ireland

1925

3 April: Unionists returned with reduced majority at general election, Northern Ireland; Devlin and nationalist colleagues take seats on 28 April

3 December: Under tripartite agreement in London, financial and constitutional settlement altered and boundary confirmed, after leaking of commission's report on 7 November and MacNeill's resignation on 20 November

1926

11 March: De Valera resigns as president of Sinn Féin

16 May: De Valera launches Fianna Fáil at La Scala theatre, Dublin

14 November: Two gardaí killed in attacks on barracks by IRA

19 November: Autonomy and equal status of dominions affirmed at Imperial Conference, London

1927

9 June: Cumann na nGaedheal narrowly retains power as minority government after general election, with Fianna Fáil taking oath and seats on 11 August
10 July: O'Higgins, Minister for Justice, assassinated by IRA
11 August: Further Public Safety Act in Free State provides for special courts with military members and suppression of associations
15 September: Cumann na nGaedheal again heads poll at general election, with reduced representation for minor parties
9 November: Electoral candidates in Free State required to declare their intention of taking oath if elected

1928

12 July: Constitution amended to prevent popular initiation of bills and restrict referenda
26 December: Further Public Safety Act in Free State repeals draconian legislation of 11 August 1927

1929

22 May: Failure of Labour and Local Option candidates in general election, Northern Ireland

1930

12 February: First censorship board appointed for Irish Free State.
1 April: Irish Labour Party separates from TUC
17 June: Northern Education Act gives greater state support for voluntary (often Catholic) primary schools
17 September: Free State elected to League of Nations council

1931

26–27 September: First conference of Saor Éire (republican socialists) in Dublin

17 October: Constitution amended to allow for military tribunal to suppress drilling and for proclamation of associations (effected 20 October)

18 October: Catholic bishops jointly condemn republican organisations

11 December: Statute of Westminster releases dominions from legislative supremacy of the imperial parliament

1932

9 February: Army Comrades Association (ACA) formed in Dublin

16 February: General election in Free State allows formation of minority government by Fianna Fáil and election of de Valera as president (9 March)

18 March: Suspension of act of 17 October 1931 sanctioning military tribunal

11 May: Nationalists leave Northern House of Commons over curtailment of debate

10 June: De Valera declines international arbitration over proposed revision of Treaty, following United Kingdom's objections to his proposal on 16 March to abolish the oath of fidelity and withhold land annuities payable to the British exchequer under the agreement of 12 February 1923

30 June: Free State suspends payment of land annuities to British Exchequer

15 July: Punitive duties imposed by British Treasury on goods imported from Free State, followed by retributive application of tariffs by Free State

26 September: De Valera addresses League of Nations assembly in Geneva as its chairman

4–13 October: Strikes and riots over lack of unemployment relief, Belfast

16 November: New parliament building opened at Stormont, Belfast

1933

4 January: Formation of Centre Party agreed, Dublin

24 January: Fianna Fáil gains small majority at general election in Free State

22 February: O'Duffy dismissed as Garda chief commissioner

24 March: Blue shirt adopted as uniform for Army Comrades Association

3 May: Oath of fidelity removed from constitution

9 May: Permanent force given to special powers legislation, Northern Ireland (repealed in 1972)

20 July: O'Duffy elected as leader of Blueshirts (renamed National Guard)

22 August: National Guard proclaimed as unlawful association following prohibition and abandonment of procession proposed for 13 August

2 September: United Ireland party (later Fine Gael) launched under O'Duffy, combining Cumann na nGaedheal with Centre Party and National Guard

2 November: Powers of governor general further restricted by constitutional amendment; appeal to the Privy Council abolished on 16 November

30 November: Northern general election returns Craigavon's Unionists to power as usual

1934

5 June: Electoral candidates in Northern Ireland required to declare their intention of taking seats if elected

21 September: O'Duffy resigns as leader of Fine Gael

21 December: Coal/cattle pact mitigates impact of economic war on Irish farmers

1935

12 July: Catholic families driven from their houses after renewed disturbances in Belfast

1936

29 May: Free State Senate abolished
18 June: IRA proclaimed in Free State as illegal organisation
20 November: O'Duffy leads 'Irish Brigade' to support Franco's nationalists in Spanish Civil War. Brigade arrived back in Ireland on 22 June 1937
11 December: Remaining references to the Crown and governor general removed from Free State constitution, but diplomatic functions of Crown confirmed in Executive Authority (External Relations) Bill enacted on following day
16 December: Irish republicans under Frank Ryan join International Brigade opposing Franco in Spanish Civil War

1937

1 May: Draft constitution for Éire published (approved by Dáil on 14 June)
1 July: General election in Free State returns Fianna Fáil to power with reduced majority; new constitution approved by referendum
29 December: New constitution of Éire implemented

1938

9 February: Northern general election returns Unionists to power with increased majority
25 April: Anglo-Irish agreement ends reciprocal tariffs and 'economic war' and provides for transfer of the 'Treaty ports' to Éire's control

26 April: British government agrees to maintain Northern social services at British levels through subsidies from exchequer

17 June: Fianna Fáil returned to power with slightly reduced majority at another general election in Éire

25 June: Douglas Hyde inaugurated as first president of Éire

12 September: De Valera again elected as president of League of Nations assembly

22 December: Internment reintroduced in Northern Ireland under Special Powers Act

1939

16 January: IRA initiates bombing campaign in Britain, abandoned in March 1940

4 May: Chamberlain announces the exclusion of Northern Ireland from Military Service Bill

25 August: Five killed in Coventry bombing by IRA

1 September: Reserve called out on permanent service

2 September: De Valera reaffirms intention to maintain neutrality in case of war, as previously announced on 19 February

3 September: Britain declares war on Germany; Emergency Powers Act in Éire allows wide range of restrictive regulations

24 December: Magazine fort in Phoenix Park raided by IRA

1940

28 May: Local Security Force established

7 June: State of emergency declared

10 June: Recruiting begins

3 September: Marine and Coast-watching Service established

1 October: Construction Corps established

1941

1 January: Local Defence Force established

1942

17 July: Marine Service established
17 August/September: Major manoeuvres at division level carried out by army

1945

8 May: War in Europe ends
1 November: Demobilisation begins

1946

2 September: Emergency ends

APPENDIX II

List of Principal Characters, 1930–46

AIKEN, FRANK (1909–83) was born in County Armagh and was IRA chief of staff from 1923 to 1925. De Valera's right-hand man, he served as Minister for Defence from 1933 to 1939 and Minister for Co-ordination of Defensive Measures from 1939 to 1945.

BEWLEY, CHARLES (1888–1969) was the maverick son of an established Dublin family. He succeeded D. A. Binchy in 1933 as Irish minister in Berlin. Before the outbreak of war, de Valera axed him and he retired to Italy. Captured by the Allies towards the end of the war, he was lucky not to have been executed as a spy.

BINCHY, D. A. (1900–89) was the first Irish minister to Berlin. A very distinguished scholar, he had little enthusiasm for diplomatic life, and he returned to academic life at the first possible opportunity.

BOLAND, FREDERICK H. (1904–85) was assistant secretary in the Irish Department of External Affairs, 1938–46. He later had a career of outstanding distinction in the Irish diplomatic service.

BRYAN, COLONEL DAN (1900–85) was the highly successful Director of Intelligence (G2) in the Irish army. He was single-minded in his professionalism and was highly regarded by his peers, particularly in Britain.

COSTELLO, LIEUTENANT-GENERAL MICHAEL J. ('Mickey Joe') (1904–86) commanded the 1st ('Thunderbolt') Division in the south of Ireland. A charismatic leader for whom down-to-earth soldiering became a religion, he whipped his division into a high pitch of combat readiness. He later had a highly successful business career.

DE BUITLÉIR, COLONEL ÉAMON (1902–81) was Bryan's assistant as Director of Intelligence. Differences of temperament and approach between the two men led to a strained working relationship.

DE VALERA, ÉAMON (1882–1975), the last surviving commandant of 1916, architect of the constitution, and implementer of neutrality, was Taoiseach and leader of the Irish people during the Emergency.

GOERTZ, DR HERMANN (1890–1947) was an Abwehr spy. He parachuted into County Meath in May 1940 and remained at large for eighteen months. His mission achieved little.

GOGAN, LIAM (1891–1979) was a veteran of 1916 and a relative of Patrick Pearse. He and Hempel were close friends during the envoy's time in Dublin and he was regarded by Berlin as an authority on the IRA.

GRAY, DAVID (1870–1968), a cousin of Roosevelt, was American minister in Dublin during the Emergency. He was not a career diplomat and his gauche assertive personality did not endear him to de Valera, who was more than able to adroitly manipulate Gray's unedifying diplomatic blunders. Gray was more likely to cause problems than to solve them.

HAYES, RICHARD (1902–74). Director of the National Library of Ireland, Dr Hayes was co-opted into G2 to organise and operate a cryptology section. His brilliant success rate saw him recognised as one of the foremost cryptologists of his time.

HEMPEL, EDUARD (1887–1972) was the minister plenipotentiary for the Third Reich to Éire, 1937–45. A formal and correct diplomat of the old school, the propriety of his conduct was in sharp contrast to that of Gray.

KERNEY, LEOPOLD (1891–1962) was Irish minister to Spain during the Second World War. He failed to keep in touch with the changing nuances of de Valera's neutrality policy and consequently assumed it to be less flexible and more Anglophobic than it actually was.

MACNEILL, MAJOR-GENERAL HUGO (1900–63) commanded the 2nd ('Spearhead') Division of the Irish army deployed along the border. An energetic and mercurial figure, his flirtations with Goertz were fraught with danger.

MAFFEY, SIR JOHN (LORD RUGBY) (1894–1969) was United Kingdom representative to Éire, 1939–49. An old colonial administrator, he was considerably less abrasive than Gray and his relations with de Valera were generally even-tempered. He did, however, vent his frustrations with the Taoiseach in private memoranda to London.

O'DONOVAN, JIM (1897–1980) was the chief Abwehr agent in Ireland. He had fought in the War of Independence and had taken the republican side in the Civil War. In 1941 he was arrested and interned for three years in the Curragh.

THOMSEN, HENNING (d. 1975) was Hempel's second in command at the German legation in Dublin and was commonly regarded as a Nazi overseer. He maintained a close professional relationship with Hempel.

VEESENMAYER, EDMUND (1904–77) was one of the Nazi party's most accomplished coup d'état specialists and was specially selected by Ribbentrop to foment rebellion in Ireland. He had proved his ruthlessness in liquidating Jews in Hungary and Czechoslovakia, for which he was sentenced to seven years' imprisonment by the Nuremburg tribunal. He constantly exaggerated the IRA's ability to precipitate a revolution in Ireland.

WALSHE, JOE (1886–1956) was the secretary to the Department of Foreign Affairs, 1922 46.

WARNOCK, WILLIAM (b. 1911) ran the Irish legation in Berlin from the time of Bewley's dismissal until 1944. In his quiet way he complemented Hempel's work in Dublin in keeping Irish–German relations on an even keel during an extraordinarily difficult period.

APPENDIX III

Extract from Siobhán Langford* Papers, Cork Archives Institute

IRISH REPUBLICAN ARMY
HEADQUARTERS
Dept . . . Intell. 1st Southern Division

Ref. No. D/1 16th April 1923.

To/
W.N.

1. Yours of 6th inst. Re., Magner, passed to me by Adjt. Information noted. I know all about this fellow. So do they in Cork No. 1.

2. Note information was received from a G.H.Q. Staff officer. I should like to have a report from you as to the possibility of getting further information from him. Give me all particulars if he is a willing informant.

3. Yours of 27th ult. Received yesterday, addressed O.C. Div. Info. Re., Seán Mac. (spy) removal of guard at Golden's noted.

4. There is a terrible delay in your communications reaching this H.Q. Could you suggest any quicker way of getting despatches to and from you, than through Brigade. What about a call-house for yourself.

5. Could you let me have a list of enemy guilty of murders, torturing, spying, burning, etc., as original lists appear to have been captured. Supply following details in each case:—

(1) Name in full
(2) Home address
(3) Where stationed or living at present

* Siobhán Langford acted as intelligence officer for General Liam Lynch throughout the War of Independence.

(4) Offence
(5) Record in B. and T. War.
(6) Full description, including any special places he is in the habit of frequenting, pubs, race-courses etc.

I am very anxious that you supply such particulars in the case of Seán Mac Swiney.

6. Wasn't the death of the Chief a paralysing blow. However, we must be prepared to meet with such terrible reverses.

____

DIVISIONAL I.O.

5th Battalion

Crown Forces

Full Name	William Phogdale
Rank	Constable Mechanic
Description	Height 5'11", brown eyes, dropped shoulders, medium build, thin face, London accent

Photo if possible

Last station served in, in Ireland	Gormanstown Depot
Present address	Gormanstown Depot

Offences

(1) Drove lorry load of police to Clogheen massacre and was present at same

Dates, places, and particulars in detail.

(2) Obtained information of this and other IRA matters in Cork, thereby assisting others in directing movements of immoral women specifically brought into the city as part of the Secret service (British) and also by constantly frequenting pubs patronised by IRA
(3) Admits he 'saw red' and opened indiscriminate fire on a crowd of people assembled round the corpse of a policeman shot in the city, because on his arrival in a lorry he thought he saw some people laugh at him.
Short survey of evidence available to support charges, giving names of witnesses.
(4) His own admission

APPENDIX IV

Army Intelligence Reports, 1924

<u>CONFIDENTIAL</u>

OFFICE OF DIRECTOR OF INTELLIGENCE
General Headquarters,
Parkgate,
DUBLIN, 14 Feb 24.

To/

<u>Each Member of the Army Council.</u>

Sir,

I have the honour to state that information has come to hand that the Irregular Director of Intelligence – Carolan – has asked his I.O's. to prepare a complete list of Demobilised Officers from the National Army. Carolan states that he can get in touch with these men quite easily, especially in the country districts.

I have the honour to be, Sir,
Your obedient Servant,

____________________ COLONEL.
FOR DIRECTOR OF INTELLIGENCE.

CJD/TM.

OFFICE OF DIRECTOR OF INTELLIGENCE
General Headquarters,
Parkgate,
DUBLIN, 4th January, 1924.

REPORT

We are in receipt of very definite information that the Irregulars in Dublin have commenced re-organising on a fairly big scale within the past fortnight.

Six whole-time organisers have been appointed and allotted a Battalion Area each. These persons will be paid. Their instructions are to look after the ex-internees first and to ensure that they are roped into the organisation again.

Copy to: M/D. (2).
C/S.
A/G.
M/G.

D.I.'s OFFICE,
General Headquarters,
Parkgate, DUBLIN.

REPORT

ACTIVITIES OF RELEASED PRISONERS

Every prisoner being released from Internment Camp is required to fill up a form, copy of which is attached, before the prisoner will be admitted to the Company or Battalion of the I.R.A. to which he belonged, or which he is joining.

Copies to:–

M.D. (2).	G.G.S. (1).
A.G. (2).	Q.M.G. (1).

CIRCULATED BY____________________

DATE____________________

RELEASED PRISONER'S STATEMENT

Batt ....

Dublin 1. Brigade.

The following particulars will be supplied by each released prisoner himself and will be signed by Coy. And Batt. O/Cs.

1. Prisoner's name and rank ....

2. Coy ....

3. Date of arrest ....

4. Where arrested ....

5. Names of places where interned ....

6. What Dublin Bde. Officers were in close touch with you while interned? ....

TREATMENT WHILE IN PRISON

1. Were you beaten, tortured or otherwise ill treated?

   ....

   ....

2. If so where and on what date?

   ....

   ....

3. Give name, rank and any other particulars you know of the F.S. officials concerned

   ....

   ....

   ....

4. Did any republicans witness the ill treatment? ....

   ....

   Give names and I.R.A. units of any witness

   ....

   ....

Signed .... Coy. O'C.

.... Batt. O'C.

D.I's OFFICE,
General Headquarters,
Parkgate,
DUBLIN, 22ND Jan., 1924.

LOT 200/1

Copies to:–	M.D.	2 copies,
	C.S.	1 copy,
	A.G.	1 do,
	Q.M.G.	1 copy,
	D.I.	1 copy,
	2nd S. Division	1 copy.

REPORT

A document recently intercepted in the post gives the following report of a Divisional Council meeting (Irregular) of 2nd Southern Division on 20–12–'23:

REPORT ON DIVISIONAL COUNCIL

2nd Southern Division 20–12'–23

Officers Present: Staff.

O/C. Division D/O/C. Division. Adjt. Division.
D/Org. Division D/Eng. Division

Bdes:

O/C. Waterford O/C. Tipperary No. 2 O/C. Tipperary No.3
O/C. Kilkenny No. 1 and O/C. Kilkenny No. 2

Meeting attended by C/S. and D/M/S

<u>AGENDA</u>:	(1) REPORTS FROM BRIGADES
Waterford Bde.	7 Bns. 150 men. 40 active. 38 rifles. 3 Thompson's. 1 L.M.G. All Staffs complete.
Tipperary No. 3	8 Bns. 350 men. 60 active. 270 rifles. 1 Thompson. 2 M.G. No Adjt. On Bde. Staff.
Tipperary No. 2	3 Bns. 150 men. 10 active. 18 rifles. Staffs complete.
Kilkenny No. 1.	4 Bns. 300 men. 60 active. 100 rifles. No Bde. V/C.
Kilkenny No. 2.	4 Bns. 230 men. 40 active. 23 rifles. 1 M.G.

(2) EMPLOYMENT SCHEME

Not working. Instructions issued to get Committees going through Sinn Féin Clubs.

(3) I.R.P.D.F.

Working fairly well on all Bdes. Committees and Staffs in Kilkenny and Waterford working most satisfactorily.

(4) EMIGRATION

Three cases from Tipp. 3., and nine from Waterford.

(5) MORALE OF PEOPLE

All Bdes. Report improvement.

(6) RELEASED PRISONERS

Morale good.

(7) CONDUCT OF VOLS

Excellent. There being no cases reported of robbery, etc., except in one district in South Kilkenny. There was no clear statement made with reference to the latter.

(8) QUESTIONS, ETC.

______________________________ COLONEL

APPENDIX V

G2 Cryptology: Reminiscences of Dr Hayes

Record of Work: 1940

Documents relating to Preetz's cipher were found in his room when Preetz was arrested in August 1940. The system used and the book containing the keywords were known from these documents and no work was necessary beyond writing a report on the system. There was no other cryptographical work done during the year.

Record of Work: 1941

In February 1941, after I left the Department, the transmissions of the German Legation were picked up and the incoming and outgoing traffic was recorded by our wireless section from that time onwards. Work was begun on the code in a room in Beggars Bush. I volunteered for this work and asked for the assistance of two or three men with high University qualifications in science or mathematics. The help requested was not forthcoming and I was given instead three lieutenants of clerical grade ability. These men did useful work in tabulating material and compiling statistics but had no special ability for cryptography. Three or four months were passed in establishing that the German code was not of the simple dictionary code book type. The work was then abandoned about June 1941 as there was not the slightest prospect of success with the staff available. No further cryptographical work was done during the year as there was no material available.

Record of Work: 1942

Following the arrest of Goertz in November, 1941, there was a considerable amount of time devoted to visiting and questioning him in Arbour Hill Prison. This revived interest in the eighteen cipher messages found in Held's house in 1940 which Goertz stated to be a diary of his experiences up to the date of the Held raid. Certain cipher messages found in Deery's possession were also available. After many months work the Goertz cipher system was completely solved and all the mathematical implications of this kind of cipher were studied. Early in this year Marschner was recaptured after his escape and a cipher message was found on him ready for transmission. This cipher was solved in one evening's work.

Record of Work: 1943

The discovery of the Eastwood messages to Lisbon early in 1943 led to a great amount of work which culminated in the visit of the head of the British Codes and Ciphers Department and the breaking by his experts of the cipher in April 1943.

From May to August cipher messages were found from time to time in Goertz' cell, and work on them went on continuously until the end of the year. It was found that nearly all the messages were fakes but one genuine cipher was found amongst them and this was solved. In November, 1943 the series of messages on a new code word were sent out from Athlone by Goertz. This cipher was broken after three weeks intensive work.

Record of Work: 1944

During Christmas week 1943 when it seemed that no further ciphers would appear and a period of relaxation might be hoped for, O'Reilly arrived with new types of ciphers in his possession. From January to April these ciphers were studied and the systems analysed. There were no messages in our possession in these ciphers but it took several months to correct all the false statements made by O'Reilly in relation to the method of working his ciphers.

The Goertz messages continued to provide frequent work throughout the year and in October, 1944 Goertz changed his keyword and tried to get in direct touch with the German Legation. After some weeks intensive study the new keywords were discovered and the ciphers read without trouble from then until March 1945 when this series ended. In all fifty-eight sets of messages passed to and from Goertz during the fifteen months when this line was in use.

In August, September, and October, 1944 a continuous investigation of the German diplomatic codes was carried out in an attempt to relate a message sent to Goertz through the German Legation to three telegrams which seemed with high probability to be the cipher text. The investigation was founded on the assumption that the code was based on a machine. An interesting mathematical system was worked out which made it possible to test the code for the more probable possibilities. Each separate test involved the solution of two hundred and nineteen equations for nine unknowns but it was found to be theoretically possible to break the code provided it was based on a machine. Work had to be abandoned through lack of time and skilled assistance. Each single test (and over nine were probable) involved three weeks intensive work which could not be interrupted for more than a few hours if the mathematical thread of the argument was not to be broken. Furthermore as the mathematical argument was continuous any mistake rendered the whole operation useless and it had to be started all over again. A staff of four or five competent mathematicians might have achieved a result in three to six months. In any case the theoretical value of the work done was of great interest and may at some future date prove invaluable.

Record of Work: 1945

Apart from the occasional passage of ciphers to and from Goertz during the first three months of this year, no new material became available until a British cipher to the German resistance movement was picked up in March and April. This cipher was broken in two days. In June, 1945 Codd was interviewed and a report on his ciphers submitted.

Lessons to be Drawn from our Experience

It will be clear from the preceding paragraphs that our success in dealing with cipher problems had increased with our experience and opportunities of discussion with others working in the same field. The most difficult thing for the inexperienced cryptographer is to know when to give up attempting the impossible. We had so very little material to work on during the first two or three years that our experience had nothing on which to crystallise and it was only towards the end of the war that it was possible to face up to the problems with confidence and without unnecessary wasted effort.

The British cryptographical staff tried to solve ciphers until there was at least two to three thousand letters of material available. They considered anything less as either impossible or depending on pure good luck and good luck will not appear unless there is a wide range of averages to produce it. Here weeks were spent on material of 200 to 400 letters. It requires incurable optimism to carry on with such impossible attempts.

After Goertz had been captured and put into Arbour Hill Prison I used to visit him once and sometimes twice a week and chat to him to try to get information from him. We built up a very friendly relationship. I began to work on his cipher and after several months finally solved it. The 14 or 15 messages finally proved to be practice messages relating to what happened to Goertz from the time he left Frankfurt to be dropped by parachute into Ireland and what happened to him for some months afterwards. He had evidently prepared these in order to send them whenever he could to Germany as he had no means of communicating after he escaped from Held's house because he had no wireless set. He lost his set when it was thrown out of the plane before he parachuted out and the wind took it away and he was never able to find it – that is, his transmitting set. It was a very complicated cipher going through 3 stages, 2 substitutions and 1 transposition.

Chronology, Goertz File

1890 Goertz born
1915 In German Air Force
March 1936 Goertz sentenced in London to 4 years penal servitude. Goertz in France before the War
March 1940 Goertz meets Tillmanns in Cologne
April 26th approx. Goertz left for Ireland but gave up over England for technical reasons
May 5th Goertz left Germany and landed at Ballivor 11pm
May 6th Goertz contacts Cooney and Reilly at Ballivor
Night of May 6–7 Goertz travelled from Ballivor to near Kinnegad
May 7th Goertz remained at the bank of a little river near Kinnegad
Night of May 7th–8th Goertz crossed the Boyne by swimming and reached NW of Prosperous
May 8th 12 noon. Marched by day from Prosperous towards Laragh
Night of May 8th–9th asked his way at police station at Poulaphouka
May 9th reached Laragh at 10am and slept there all day
Night of May 9th man called to Laragh to bring G to Dublin
May 10th G boarded with people in Dublin (Rathmines)
May 11th three men and women in car in Ballivor searching for parachute
May 12 or 13 G visited by his wireless operator from Belfast
May 14 approx met Stephen Hayes
May 19 approx. G removed to Helds
May 21 approx. met Hayes in Helds. Wireless set brought to Helds for G, also his parachute
July 1940–end of July 1941 Goertz at No. 1 Charlemont Avenue
End of Jan 1941 Miss Coffey says she took in Goertz to No 1 Charlemont Avenue, Dun Laoghaire
28 August 1940 Boat with engine purchased in Abbey Street for G and tried out.
Nov–Dec 1940 Radio set bought in Donnybrook for G
Before 18 Feb 1941 G in Tralee neighbourhood

February 1941 Goertz went to Kerry
Beginning of August 1941 Goertz went to Brittas
19th Sept 1941 Miss Coffey interrogated by police
About 19–21 Sept Goertz at 7 Spencer Villas, Glenageary
26 Sept 1941 Mullins and Peterson trying to get a place to hide Goertz
20 Aug 1941 Boat brought to Brittas by Miss O'Mahony
27 November 1941 Goertz arrested at Coffeys

Held Chronology

1938 Held and G. D. Hamilton on holiday in Whitley Bay
24 January 1939 police report Stephen Carroll held on managing business of Held from Dublin
January 1939 Hamilton and Held disagree. Legal proceedings pending. Held living at 13 Airfield Road, Rathgar
16 April 1940 Held visited W. P. Wrathall? 204 Rue Royale, Brussels
26 April Held in Berlin (according to Goertz)
9 May 1940 Mrs Stuart buys clothes for man
22 May 1940 Held seen on Home Farm Road, Drumcondra
22 May 1940, 10.15 p.m. Raid by police on Kronsvanz, Templeogue Road
23 May 1940 Held arrested 1.40am
25 May 1940 Mrs Stuart arrested
26 May 1940 Suspicious stranger in Ardrahan, County Galway
1 August 1940 O'Connor's Irish Friends of Germany stated that Seán Russell and a German staff officer had landed one afternoon at Kill, County Kildare

APPENDIX VI

Excerpt from 'Fall Gruen'

<u>**Nur für den Dienstgebrauch!**</u>

Militärgeographische Angaben über Irland

Süd- und Ostküste

(Von Mizen Head bis Malin Head)

Text- und Bildheft mit Kartenanlagen

Abgeschlossen am 31. Mai 1941

Generalstab des Heeres ·
Abteilung für Kriegskarten und Vermessungswesen (IV. Mil.-Geo.)
Berlin 1941

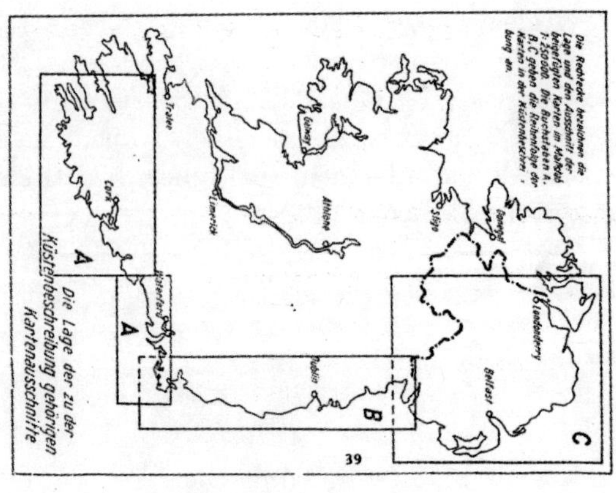

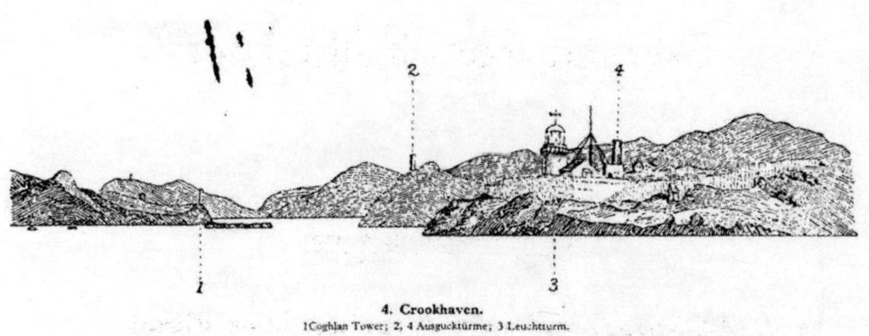

4. Crookhaven.

1 Coghlan Tower; 2, 4 Ausgucktürme; 3 Leuchtturm.

5. Küstenprofile zwischen Mizen Head und Roaringwater Bucht

1 Long Island; 2 Copper Point rw. 320° (mw. NzW ⅝ W) ½ Sm; 3 Skull Point; 4 Stadt Skull; 5 Mount Gabriel; 6 Cosheen Point; 7 Cosheen Crag in Eins mit (8) Barnacleeve Gap in rw. 0° (mw. NzO ¾ O). — Abschnitt 1, Karte A.

56

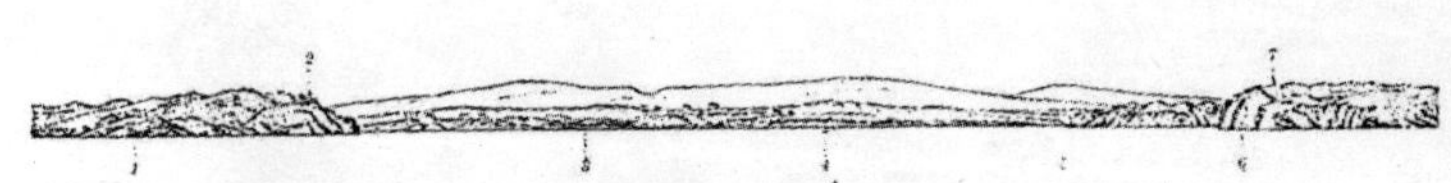

6. Einfahrt von Baltimore Harbour.

1 Wilson Rock; 2 Barrack Point-Leuchtturm rw. 350° (mw. N ½ O. 7 Kblg.; 3 Spanish Island; 4 Low Rock-Turm; [illegible] Point; 6 Bea[illegible] Point [illegible] (7) Turm. — Abschnitt 2.

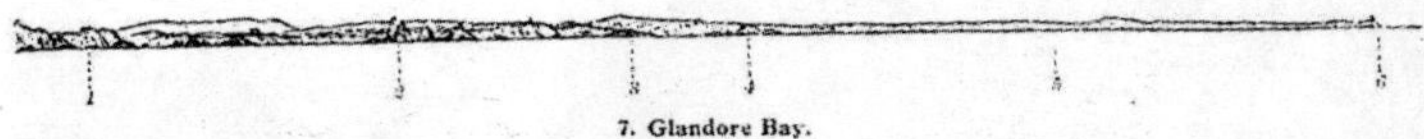

7. Glandore Bay.

1 Toe Head; 2 Stag Rocks rw. 41° (mw. NO/O. 2 Sm; 3 Adam Island; 4 High Island; 5 Rosscarbery Bay; 6 Galley Head rw. 65° (mw. O [illegible] N [illegible] Sm. — Abschnitt 3, Karte A.

5

40

15. Haulbowline Insel (Cork Harbour).
Blick von O über die Insel mit dem Hafenbecken, Stahlwerk, Kasernen und Tanklager. — Abschnitt 7, Karte A.

17. Cork Harbour.
Blick gegen S zur Einfahrt in Cork Harbour. Beiderseits mäßig geböschte Steilküste mit schmalem Strand. — Abschnitt 7, Karte A.

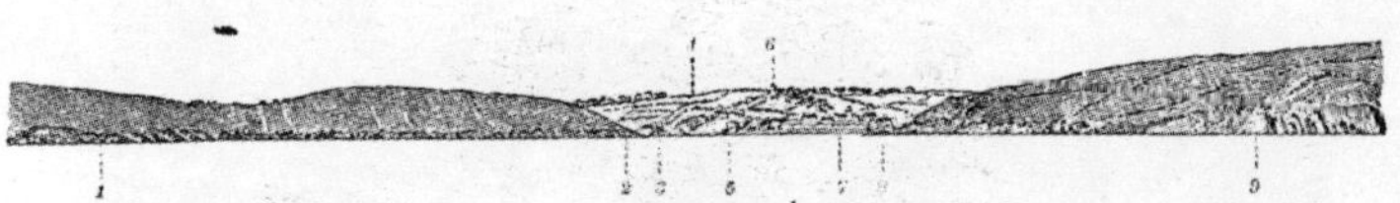

9. Kinsale Harbour.

1 Strockaun Point; 2 Money Point; 3 Ruine; 4 Fairy Field; 5 Fairy Field Bluff; 6 Ardbrack-Kirche; 7 Charles F[illegible] mit Leuchtturm; 8 Preghane Point rw. 0° (mw. NzO ³⁄₄ O) 1 Sm; 9 Hangman Point. — Abschnitt 6.

10. Port of Cork.

1 Templebreedy-Kirche; 2 Lloydsignalstelle; 3 Port of Cork; 4 Leuchtturm; 5 Signalturm in Eins mit Baumgruppe in rw. 17° (mw. NNO ¹⁄₂ O). — Abschnitt 7, Karte A.

59

12. Crosshaven.

Am W-Ufer des Cork Harbour und der Mündung des Owenboy River (am linken Bildrand) zieht sich der Ort an den mäßig gebüschten Hängen hinan. — Abschnitt 7, Karte A.

61

18. Lough Mahon bei Cork.

Mäßig geböschte Steilküste umgibt die seichte Bucht. Von Hecken eingefriedetes Hügelland mit lockeren Waldbeständen. Am S- und O-Ufer laufen Bahnlinien nach Cork. Am unteren Blattrand Teile der Hafenanlagen von Passage-West. Im N auf Little Island Kalksteinbrüche. — Abschnitt 7, Karte A. 67

21. Cork, Hafenanlagen.

0 Blick von O Lee aufwärts auf die Stadt. Im Vordergrund rechts die ausgedehnten Bahnanlagen am North Deep Water Quay und der Hafenbahnhof; links das Marina-Industrie-Gelande (ehem. Ford-Werke). — Abschnitt 7, Karte A.

31. Youghal (5300 Einw.; Grafschaft Cork).

Blick von SW auf den kleinen Hafen an der N-Seite der Youghal-Bucht und der Mündung des River Blackwater (610 m lange Kaianlagen). Im Vordergrund Kliffküste mit vorgelagertem Strand, die in der Ortschaft in mäßig geböschte Steilküste übergeht. — Abschnitt 9, Karte A.

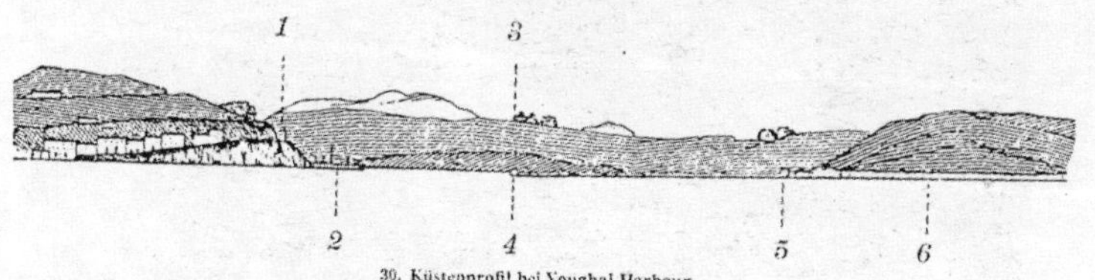

30. Küstenprofil bei Youghal Harbour.

1 Leuchtturm; 2 Küstenwache; 3 Westlicher Baum auf Tinnabinna Hill in Eins mit 4 Ferry House; 5 Monatty House; 6 East Point. — Abschnitt 9, Karte A.

81. Dublin. Kingsbridge.

3 Blick von O Liffey aufwärts auf den großen Kopfbahnhof Kingsbridge-Station. Im Hintergrund rechts der Phoenixpark mit dem Wellington-Denkmal. Im Vordergrund Teile einer großen Branntweinfabrik. — Abschnitt 20, Karte B.

85. Dublin. Royal-Kanal.

2 Blick über den Eingang zum Royal-Kanal vom Liffey River aus. Royal-Canal-Dock (a) und Spencer-Dock (b) mit einer Gesamtlänge von 1524 m dienen hauptsächlich dem Kohlenumschlag. Rechts vom Kanal ein Güterbahnhof (c), links der Schlachtviehhof (d). — Abschnitt 20, Karte B.

45

84. Dublin.

Blick vom Liffey River zum **Grand-Canal-Dock** (1616 m), von wo der 333 km lange Grand Canal seinen Ausgang nimmt. Im Vordergrund am Liffey River liegt das Hauptgaswerk (a), daneben Speicherräume und eine chemische Fabrik (b); auf dem jenseitigen Ufer des Grand Canal liegt mit zwei hohen Schornsteinen das Kraftwerk der Straßenbahn (c); an der Innenkehre des Grand Canal stehen Mühlen (d) mit 5500 t Speichervermögen. Im Hintergrund liegt das Gaswerk Ringsend (e). — Abschnitt 20, Karte B. 131

82. Dublin. Hafen.

Nördlich der Liffey-Mündung das Alexandrabecken (a) mit guten Anlage- und Umschlagmöglichkeiten für Seeschiffe, Trockendocks (b), Werften, Getreidesilos und Öltanks (c). Im N der Vorort Clontarf. Links davon die Great Northern Railway-Linie nach Drogheda und Belfast. — Abschnitt 20, Karte B. 129

46

77. Blick nach SO über Dublin (470 000 Einw.).

Im Hintergrund die Dublin Bay und die Irische See. Dublin (Baile Atha Cliath) an der Liffey-Mündung ist die Hauptstadt des Freistaats Eire; Sitz der Regierung und Universitätsstadt. Bedeutende Dock- und Hafenanlagen; Schwerindustrie, Großmühlen und Brauereien geben dem Wirtschaftsleben der
124 Stadt das Gepräge. Im Vordergrund der Liffey-Fluß mit dem Hauptbahnhof am rechten Ufer nahe der Kings-Bridge. — Abschnitt 20, Karte B.

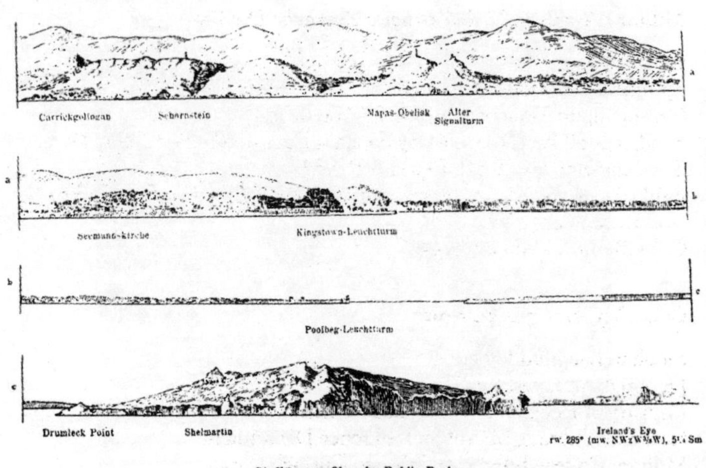

74. Küstenprofil an der Dublin-Bucht.

Ansicht von einem Punkte in der Nähe von Kish-Feuerschiff aus. — Abschnitt 20, Karte B. 121

47

BIBLIOGRAPHY

PRIMARY SOURCES

National Archives, Dublin

Department of An Taoiseach Files (S series)
Department of Defence Files
Department of Foreign Affairs Files

National Library of Ireland

Dr Richard Hayes Papers

Military Archives Cathal Brugha Barracks Dublin

General Papers
Specific Collections Consulted:
Censorship in Time of War, 1925, Costello Papers
Fundamental Factors Affecting Saorstát Defence Problem, May 1936.
The Magazine Fort Raid, December 1939
Findings of the Court of Inquiry into the Magazine Fort Raid, 29 December 1939
COS Memo 23 August 1944

Cork City Archives Institute

Siobhán Langford Papers
National Archives, Kew, London
Ministry of Defence Public Enquiry Office
Cork City Library, Microfilm Reference Department
Military College Library & Schools, Curragh Camp

Private Collections

Papers of Commandant William Egar, Snr (family possession)
Dr Richard Hayes Papers (family possession)

General Dan McKenna, Notes on lecture delivered at the Military College, 12 October 1967 (in author's possession)

Internet Sources

Franklin Delano Roosevelt Library and Museum, one of ten presidential libraries administered by the National Archives and Records Administration, 4079 Albany Post Road, Hyde Park, NY 12538, in collaboration with Marist College and IBM

Official Publications

Dáil Debates
Report of Comptroller and Auditor General, 2000

Periodicals

An Cosantóir
Aubane Historical Society
Capuchin Annual
Diplomacy and Statecraft
Intelligence and National Security
Irish Historical Studies
Irish Sword
Journal of International Affairs
Political Science Quarterly

Newspapers

Irish Independent
Irish Times, The

Interviews

C. F. Breathnach (between 1998 and 2006)
Brigadier General James J. Farrell (between 1980 and 2006)
Commandant R. W. McIntyre, 27 April 1999
R. J. Hayes, 24 August 2006
J. R. Hayes, September 2006
The Honourable Justice Susan Denham, June–July 2008

Other Sources

Television documentary on the formation of 2RN, 'Radio 75 Years On: That Old Hurdy Gurdy', RTÉ 1, 18 September 2001

SECONDARY SOURCES

Andrew, Christopher, *Her Majesty's Secret Service: The Making of the British Intelligence Community* (New York: Penguin, 1987)

Anon, *Rebel Cork's Fighting Story from 1916 to the Truce with Britain* (Tralee: Anvil Books, n.d.)

Anon, *Kerry's Fighting Story, 1916–1921* (Tralee: Anvil Books, n.d.)

Anon, *Dublin's Fighting Story 1913–1921* (Tralee: Anvil Books, n.d.)

Augusteijn, Joost, *From Public Defiance to Guerrilla Warfare: The Experience of Ordinary Volunteers in the Irish War of Independence 1916–1921* (Dublin: Irish Academic Press, 1996)

Barry, Tom, *Guerilla Days in Ireland*, with Introduction by Lieutenant General M. J. Costello (Dublin: Anvil Books, 1962)

Bartlett, Thomas and Jeffrey, Keith, *A Military History of Ireland* (Cambridge: Cambridge University Press, 1996)

Béaslaí, Piaras, *Michael Collins: Soldier and Statesman* (Dublin: Talbot Press, 1937)

Beevor, John G., *SOE: Recollections and Reflections, 1940–1945* (London: Bodley Head, 1981)

Bennett, R, *The Black & Tans* (London: Holton, 1959)

Bonor, H. K., *Investment in Defence 1922/23–1983: Research Paper for Diploma in Administrative Science* (Dublin: Defence Force Printing Press for Institute of Public Administration, 1983)

Bowyer-Bell, J., *The Secret Army: A History of the IRA, 1916–1970* (London: Anthony Blond, 1970)

Breen, Dan, *My Fight for Irish Freedom* (Dublin: Anvil Books, 1989)

Canning, Paul, *British Policy towards Ireland, 1921–1944* (Oxford: Clarendon Press, 1985)

Carroll, Joseph T., *Ireland in the War Years, 1939–1945* (New York: David & Charles, 1975)

Carter, Carole J., *The Shamrock and the Swastika: German Espionage in Ireland in World War II* (Palo Alto, CA: Pacific Books, 1977)

Clifford, Brendan, *Spotlights on Irish History* (Cork: Aubane Historical Society, 1997)

Clifford, Brendan and Lane, Jack, *Elizabeth Bowen: Notes on Éire, Espionage Reports to Winston Churchill, 1940–1942; with a review of Irish Neutrality in WWII* (Cork: Aubane Historical Society, 1999)

Coogan, Tim Pat, *The IRA* (London: Harper Collins, 2000)

Coogan, Tim Pat, *De Valera: Long Fellow, Long Shadow* (London: Hutchinson, 1993)

Coogan, Tim Pat, *Michael Collins: A Biography* (London: Hutchinson, 1990)

Coogan, Tim Pat, *Ireland since the Rising* (London: Greenwood Press, 1977)

Cronin, Seán, *Washington's Irish Policy, 1916–1986* (Dublin: Anvil Press, 1987)

De Valera, Terry, *A Memoir* (Dublin: Currach Press, 2004)

De Vere White, Terence, *Kevin O'Higgins* (London: Methuen, 1966)

Doherty, Gabriel and Keogh, Dermot (eds), *Michael Collins and the Making of the Irish State* (Cork: Mercier Press, 1998)

Duggan, John P., *A History of the Irish Army* (Dublin: Gill & Macmillan, 1991)

Duggan, John P., *Neutral Ireland and the Third Reich* (Dublin: Gill & Macmillan, 1975)

Dwyer, T. Ryle, *Tans, Terror and Troubles: Kerry's Real Fighting Story 1913–23* (Cork: Mercier Press, 2001)

Dwyer, T. Ryle, *De Valera: The Man and the Myths* (Dublin: Poolbeg Press, 1991)

Fanning, Ronan, *Independent Ireland* (Dublin: Helicon, 1983)

Fanning, Ronan, 'Leadership and the Transition from the Politics of Revolution to the Politics of Party: An Example of Ireland 1914–1939', XIV International Congress of Historical Studies, San Francisco, 1975

Fanning, Ronan, *The Irish Department of Finance, 1922–1958* (Dublin: Institute of Public Administration, 1958)

Fanning, Ronan, 'Michael Collins: An Overview', in Doherty and Keogh (eds), *op. cit.*

Fanning, Ronan, Kennedy, Michael, Keogh, Dermot and O'Halpin, Eunan (eds), *Documents on Irish Foreign Policy, Volume I, 1919–22* (Dublin: Royal Irish Academy, 1998)

Farrell, Theo, 'The Model Army: Military Imitation and the Enfeeblement of the Army in Post Revolutionary Ireland 1923–42', *Irish Studies in International Affairs*, vol. 8 (1997)

Fisk, Robert, *In Time of War: Ireland, Ulster and the Price of Neutrality, 1939–45* (Dublin: Gill & Macmillan, 1983)

Foy, Michael T., *Michael Collins's Intelligence War: The Struggle Between the British and the IRA, 1919–1921* (Stroud, Gloucestershire: Sutton Publishing, 2006)

Garvin, Tom, *1922: The Birth of Irish Democracy* (Dublin: Gill & Macmillan, 1996)

Garvin, Tom, *The Evolution of Irish Nationalist Politics* (Dublin: Gill & Macmillan, 1972)

Girvin, Brian, *The Emergency: Neutral Ireland 1939–45* (London: Macmillan, 2006)

Grey, Tony, *The Lost Years: The Emergency in Ireland, 1945* (London: Warner Books, 1997)

Griffith, Kenneth and O'Grady, Timothy, *Curious Journey: An Oral History of Ireland's Unfinished Revolution* (Cork: Mercier Press, 1998)

Guevara, Che, *Guerrilla Warfare* (London: Penguin, 1969)

Harrington, Niall C., *An Episode in the Civil War: Kerry Landing* (Dublin: Anvil Books, 1992)

Hart, Peter, *The IRA at War* (Oxford: Oxford University Press, 2003)

Hart, Peter, *The IRA and its Enemies* (Oxford: Oxford University Press, 1998)

Hart, Peter (ed.), *British Intelligence in Ireland: The Final Reports* (Cork: Cork University Press, 2002)

Hopkinson, Michael, *The Irish War of Independence* (Dublin: Gill & Macmillan, 2002)

Hopkinson, Michael, *Green Against Green: The Irish Civil War* (Dublin: Gill & Macmillan, 1988)

Hopkinson, Michael (ed.), *The Last Days of Dublin Castle: The Diaries of Mark Sturgis* (Dublin: Irish Academic Press, 1999)

Horgan, John, *Seán Lemass: The Enigmatic Patriot* (Dublin: Gill & Macmillan, 1999)

Hull, Mark M., *Irish Secrets: German Espionage in Wartime Ireland, 1939–1945* (Dublin: Irish Academic Press, 2003)

Jackson, William, *Withdrawal from Empire: A Military View* (London: Palgrave Macmillan, 1986)

Jenkins, Roy, *Churchill* (London: Macmillan, 2001)

Keatinge, Patrick, *A Place Among the Nations: Issues of Irish Foreign Policy* (Dublin: Institute of Public Administration, 1978)

Kee, Robert, *Ireland: A History* (London: Abacus, 1995)

Keegan, John, *Intelligence in War, Knowledge of the Enemy from Napoleon to Al-Qaeda* (London: Pimlico, 2004)

Keogh, Dermot, *Jews in Twentieth-Century Ireland: Refugees, Anti-Semitism and the Holocaust* (Cork: Cork University Press, 1998)

Keogh, Dermot, *Ireland and the Vatican: The Policy and Diplomacy of Church–State Relations, 1922–1960* (Cork: Cork University Press, 1995)

Keogh, Dermot, *Twentieth-Century Ireland: Nation and State* (Dublin: Gill & Macmillan, 1994)

Keogh, Dermot, *Ireland and Europe, 1919–1989* (Cork: Hibernian University Press, 1990)

Keogh, Dermot, *Ireland and Europe, 1919–1989: A Diplomatic and Political History* (Cork: Hibernian University Press, 1990)

Keogh, Dermot, *The Vatican, the Bishops and Irish Politics* (Cambridge: Cambridge University Press, 1986)

Keogh, Dermot and McCarthy, Andrew, *Twentieth-Century Ireland: Revolution and State Building* (Dublin: Gill & Macmillan, 2005)

Kennedy, Michael, *Guarding Neutral Ireland: The Coast Watching Service and Military Intelligence 1939–1945* (Dublin: Four Courts Press, 2008)

Langhorne, Richard (ed.), *Diplomacy and Intelligence during the Second World War: Essays in Honour of F. H. Hinsley* (Cambridge: Cambridge University Press, 1985)

Lee, J. J., 'The Challenge of a Collins Biography', in Doherty and Keogh (eds), *op. cit.*

Lee, J. J., *Ireland 1912–1985: Politics and Society* (Cambridge: Cambridge University Press, 1989)

Lee, Joseph and Ó Tuathaigh, Gearóid, *The Age of de Valera* (Dublin: Ward River Press, 1982)

Liddle-Hart, B. H., 'Lessons from Resistance Movements – Guerrilla and Non-Violent', in A. Roberts (ed.), *Civilian Resistance as a National Defence* (London: Penguin, 1969)

Lynch, Pat, 'Organisation of the Fighting Units', in Anon, *Rebel Cork's Fighting Story*

Lyons, F. S. L., 'Beginning of Independence', in Brian Farrell (ed.), *The Irish Parliamentary Tradition* (Dublin: Gill & Macmillan, 1973)

Lytton, Helen, *The World War II Years: The Irish Emergency, an Illustrated History* (Dublin: Wolfhound Press, 2001)

MacArdle, Dorothy, *Tragedies of Kerry* (Dublin: Elo Press, 1998)

MacEoin, Seán, *With the IRA in the Fight for Freeedom: 1919 to the Truce* (Tralee: Kerryman, 1950)

MacEoin, Uinsean, *Harry* (Dublin: Argenta Publications, 1985)

MacEoin, Uinsean, *Survivors* (Dublin: Argenta Publications, 1980)

Machiavelli, Nicolo, *The Prince: The Famed Renaissance Treatise on the Politics of Power* (Ware, Hertfordshire: Wordsworth Editions, 1993)

Macready, Neville, *Annals of an Active Life* (London: Hutchinson & Co., n.d.)

Matanle, Ivor, *History of World War II* (London: Tiger Books International, 1994)

McCarthy, Andrew, 'Reacting to War: Finance and the Economy, 1938–40', in Dermot Keogh and Mervyn O'Driscoll (eds), *Ireland in World War Two: Neutrality and Survival* (Cork: Mercier Press, 2004)

McHugh, Roger (ed.), *Dublin 1916* (London: Arlington Books, 1966)

McMahon, Deirdre, *Republicans and Imperialists: Anglo-Irish Relations in the 1930s* (New Haven, CT: Yale University Press, 1984)

Middlemas, Keith (ed.), *Thomas Jones, Whitehall Diary, Vol. 3: Ireland 1918–1925* (London: Oxford University Press, 1971)

Moynihan, M. (ed.), *Speeches and Statements by E. de Valera 1917–1973* (Dublin: Gill & Macmillan, 1980)

Murphy, Brian P., *The Origins and Organisation of British Propaganda in Ireland* (Cork: Aubane Historical Society, 2006)

Murphy, Brian P., *John Chartres: Mystery Man of the Treaty* (Dublin: Irish Academic Press, 1995)

Murphy, John A., *Ireland in the Twentieth Century* (Dublin: Gill & Macmillan, 1975)

Neeson, Eoin, *Birth of a Republic* (Dublin: Prestige Books, 1998)

Neeson, Eoin, *The Civil War in Ireland, 1921–23* (Cork: Mercier Press, 1966)

Neligan, Dave, *The Spy in the Castle* (Dublin: Prenderville Publications, 1999)

Nowlan, K. B. and Williams, T. D. (eds), *Ireland in the War Years and After, 1939–1951* (Dublin: Gill & Macmillan, 1969)

O'Byrne, John, *O'Machiavelli: Or How to Survive in Irish Politics* (Dublin: Leopold Publishing, 1996)

O'Callaghan, Seán, *Execution* (London: Frederick Muller Limited, 1974)

Ó Dochartaigh, Tomás, *Cathal Brugha: A Shaol is a Thréithe* (Cathair na Mart: FNT, 1969)

O'Donoghue, David, *Hitler's Irish Voices: The Story of German Radio's Wartime Irish Service* (Belfast: Beyond the Pale Publications, 1998)

O'Donoghue, Florence, *No Other Law* (Dublin: Irish Press, 1999)

Ó Drisceoil, Donal, *Censorship in Ireland, 1939–1945: Neutrality, Politics and Society* (Cork: Cork University Press, 1996)

O'Halpin, Eunan, 'Hitler's Irish Hideout: A Case Study of SOE's Black Propaganda Battles', in Mark Seaman (ed.), *Special Operations Executive: A New Instrument of War* (London: Routledge, 2006)

O'Halpin, Eunan, *Defending Ireland: The Irish State and its Enemies since 1922* (Oxford: Oxford University Press, 1999)

O'Halpin, Eunan, *MI5 and Ireland, 1939–1945: The Official History* (Dublin: Irish Academic Press, 2003)

O'Halpin, Eunan, 'Aspects of Intelligence: The Emergency, 1939–1945', *The Irish Sword*, vol. xix (1993–94)

O'Halpin, Eunan, 'Intelligence and Security in Ireland, 1922–1945', *Intelligence and National Security*, vol. 5 (January 1990)

O'Halpin, Eunan, 'Collins and Intelligence 1919–1923: From Brotherhood to Bureaucracy', in Doherty and Keogh (eds), *op. cit.*

O'Higgins O'Malley, Úna, *From Pardon and Protest: Memoirs from the Margins* (Galway: Arlon House, 2001)

O'Malley, Ernie, *The Singing Flame* (Dublin: Anvil Books, 1978)

O'Malley, Ernie, *On Another Man's Wound* (Dublin: Anvil Books, 1936)

O'Neill, T. P. and the Earl of Longford, *De Valera* (Dublin: Gill & Macmillan, 1970)

Packenham, Thomas, *The Boer War* (London: Abacus, 1979).

Quigley, Martin S., *A US Spy in Ireland* (Dublin: Marino Books, 1999)

Rees, R., *Ireland 1905–1925. Volume 1: Text and Historiography* (Newtownards: Colour Point Books, 1998)

Regan, John M., *The Irish Counter-Revolution, 1921–1936* (Dublin: Gill & Macmillan, 2001)

Rumpf, Ernst and Hepburn, A. C., *Nationalism and Socialism in Twentieth-Century Ireland* (Liverpool: Liverpool University Press, 1977)

Ryan, Cornelius, *The Longest Day* (New York: Simon and Schuster, 1959)

Ryan, Meda, *Tom Barry: IRA Freedom Fighter* (Cork: Mercier Press, 2003)

Ryan, Meda, *The Day Michael Collins was Shot* (Dublin: Poolbeg Press, 1989)

Savage, M. B., *Looking Back: The Story of My Life* (Staffordshire Regiment Museum, n.d.)

Share, Bernard, *The Emergency: Neutral Ireland 1939–45* (Dublin: Gill & Macmillan, 1987)

Sheehan, William, *British Voices from the Irish War of Independence 1918–1921* (Cork: The Collins Press, 2005)

Singh, Simon, *The Code Book: The Science of Secrecy from Ancient Egypt to Quantum Cryptography* (London: Fourth Estate, 1999)

Stephan, Enno, *Spies in Ireland* (translated from the German by Arthur Davidson) (London: McDonnell and Co., 1963)

Sun Tzu (translated by Thomas Cleary), *The Art of War* (Boston: Shambhala Publications, 1988)

Sweets, John F., *Choices in Vichy: The French under Nazi Occupation* (Oxford: Oxford University Press, 1987)

Townshend, Charles, *The British Campaign in Ireland, 1919–1921: The Development of Political and Military Policies* (Oxford: Oxford University Press, 1975)

Valiulis, Maryann Gialanella, *Almost a Rebellion: The Irish Army Mutiny of 1924* (Cork: Tower Books, 1985)

Walsh, Maurice, 'The Politics of Irish Defence: From the Civil War to the Congo, 1923–1964', unpublished M.Phil thesis, UCC, 1997

West, Nigel, *The Guy Liddell Diaries. Volume 1: 1939–1942, MI5's Director of Counter-espionage in World War II* (New York: Routledge, 2005)

West, Nigel, *MI6: British Secret Service Operations, 1909–1945* (London: Weidenfeld and Nicholson, 1983)

West, Nigel, *MI5: British Secret Service Operations, 1905–1945* (London: Bodley Head, 1981)

Williams, T. D. (ed.), *The Irish Struggle, 1916–20* (London: Routledge, 1966)

Younger, Carlton, *Ireland's Civil War* (London: Frederick Muller, 1968)

REFERENCES

INTRODUCTION

1 This definition of military intelligence is as taught in the Irish Military College and foreign military colleges attended by Irish officers.
2 *Ibid.*
3 Charles Townshend, *The British Campaign in Ireland 1919–1921: The Development of Political and Military Policies* (Oxford: Oxford University Press, 1975), pp. 123–28. The timeless nature of that assertion rings through in General Sir Gerald Templer's 1952 statement: 'The answer lies not in pouring more soldiers into the jungle, but rests in the hearts and minds of the Malayan people.' Cited in William Jackson, *Withdrawal from Empire* (London: B.T. Batsford, 1986), p. 96.
4 Christopher Andrew, *Her Majesty's Secret Service: The Making of the British Intelligence Community* (New York: Penguin, 1987), pp. 246–58.
5 Townshend, *The British Campaign in Ireland.*
6 Eunan O'Halpin, *Defending Ireland* (Oxford: Oxford University Press, 1999).
7 Eoin Neeson, *Birth of a Republic* (Dublin: Prestige Books, 1998).
8 Joost Augusteijn, *From Public Defiance to Guerrilla Warfare* (Dublin: Irish Academic Press, 1996).
9 Michael T. Foy, *Michael Collins's Intelligence War: The Struggle Between the British and the IRA, 1919–1921* (Stroud, Gloucestershire: Sutton Publishing Limited, 2006).
10 Peter Hart (ed.), *British Intelligence in Ireland, 1920–1921: The Final Reports* (Cork: Cork University Press, 2002).
11 Andrew, *Her Majesty's Secret Service*, p. 251.
12 *Ibid.*, p. 257.
13 Indeed, Andrew cited Harold Wilson and Denis Healy as admitting to a lack of understanding of both MI5 and MI6 and basic mistrust of Foreign Office deliberate misinterpretation of intelligence to suit Foreign Office decisions. The slow trickle of documents released by Irish Military Archives, by permission of the Department of An Taoiseach, is also comparable to that released, or not released, by British government sources to available archival institutes.
14 Ernst Rumpf and A. C. Hepburn, *Nationalism and Socialism in Twentieth Century Ireland* (Liverpool: Liverpool University Press, 1977).
15 Augusteijn, *From Public Defiance to Guerilla Warfare.*

16 *Ibid*. Augusteijn cites Peter Hart, *The I.R.A. and its Enemies* (Oxford: Oxford University Press, 1998).
17 *Ibid*., pp. 20, 21, 22.
18 Maryann Gialanella Valiulis, *Almost a Rebellion: The Irish Army Mutiny of 1924* (Cork: Tower Books, 1985).
19 John M. Regan, *The Irish Counter-Revolution, 1921–1936* (Dublin: Gill & Macmillan, 1999), p. 193.
20 O'Halpin, *Defending Ireland*.
21 *Ibid*.
22 Theo Farrell, 'The model army: military imitation and the enfeeblement of the army in post revolutionary Ireland', *Irish Studies in International Affairs*, vol. 8 (1997).
23 Ronan Fanning, *Irish Department of Finance, 1922–58* (Dublin: Institute of Public Administration, 1978).
24 *Ibid*., pp. 332, 333, and note no. 63, p. 663.
25 Valiulis, *Almost a Rebellion*, p. 113.
26 J. J. Lee, *Ireland 1912–1985: Politics and Society* (Cambridge: Cambridge University Press, 1989), p. 105.
27 The Justice files are held at NAI, JUS 8/series.
28 MA, Costello Papers, File D80; document authors are as stated in text.
29 *Ibid*. It was headed by a note: 'In this Memorandum the word Censorship can be read as denoting publicity.'
30 UCDA, Bryan Papers, Fundamental Factors affecting Saorstát Defence Problem, May 1936, Copy No. 6, P71/8, Ref. No. G.2/0057.
31 Bryan Papers, P71/126. No indication is given by Bryan as to how or when this paper of such strategic importance came into his possession.
32 Military staffs are divided into cells G1, G2, G3, G4, respectively Administration, Intelligence, Operations, Logistics.
33 For an overview of censorship, see Donal Ó Drisceoil, *Censorship in Ireland, 1939–1945: Neutrality, Politics and Society* (Cork: Cork University Press, 1996).
34 O'Halpin, *Defending Ireland*.
35 In general, see Michael Kennedy, *Guarding Neutral Ireland: The Coast Watching Service And Military Intelligence, 1939–1945* (Dublin: Four Courts Press, 2008).
36 See particularly Chapter 2, 'Internments', of John Maguire's study, *IRA Internments and the Irish Government: Subversives and the State, 1939–1962* (Dublin: Irish Academic Press, 2008).
37 This point is borne out in Kennedy, *Guarding Neutral Ireland*, where he outlines successive examples of reports being analysed in London.
38 Garda Archives, AO 6/1942, 8 September 1942 (Order of Commissioner, GS, CM.2252/42, 8 September 1942).
39 Lee, *Ireland 1912–1985*, p. 236.
40 Cranborne's memorandum has been partially reproduced in Ronan Fanning, *Independent Ireland* (Dublin: Helicon Ltd, 1983), pp. 124–5.

41 *Ibid.*
42 Kennedy, *Guarding Neutral Ireland.*
43 Interview with the Honourable Justice Susan Denham, June 2008. Justice Denham confirmed this fact afterwards when I queried the veracity of the first statement.
44 Eunan O'Halpin. 'Aspects of intelligence: The emergency, 1939–1945', *The Irish Sword*, vol. xix (1993–94).
45 O'Halpin, *Defending Ireland*; J. Bowyer-Bell, *The Secret Army: A History of the IRA, 1916–1970* (London: Anthony Blond, 1970).
46 MA, General Dan McKenna, Notes on lecture delivered to the Command and Staff Course, Military College, 12 October 1967 (in author's possession).
47 MA, *Findings of the Court of Inquiry into the Magazine Fort Raid on 29th December 1939*; Tim Pat Coogan, *The IRA* (London: Harper Collins, 2000), pp. 135, 136.
48 *Ibid.*
49 *Ibid.*
50 *Ibid.* See also Seosamh Ó Longaigh, *Emergency Law in Independent Ireland, 1922–1948* (Dublin: Four Courts Press, 2006).
51 Author's interview with Commandant R. McIntyre on 27 April 1999.
52 O'Halpin, *Defending Ireland*; MA, G2/X/0362, Defence memorandum to government, undated, February 1951.
53 MA, COS Memo, 23 August 1944, File No. EDP 65.
54 *Ibid.*
55 *Ibid.*
56 O'Halpin, *Defending Ireland*; Mark M. Hull, *Irish Secrets: German Espionage in Wartime Ireland, 1939–1945* (Dublin: Irish Academic Press, 2003).
57 Dermot Keogh, *Jews in Twentieth-Century Ireland: Refugees, Anti-Semitism and the Holocaust* (Cork: Cork University Press, 1998).
58 NLI, Richard J. Hayes Papers, Manuscript Collection list 108 (courtesy of the National Library of Ireland).
59 Obituary, Colonel Dan Bryan, *The Irish Times*, 17 June 1985.
60 UCDA, Bryan Papers, P71.
61 Andrew, *Her Majesty's Secret Service.*
62 *Ibid.*
63 *Ibid.*, p.3; Ronald Zweig, 'The political uses of military intelligence: Evaluating the threat of a Jewish revolt against Britain', in Richard Langhorne (ed.), *Diplomacy and Intelligence during the Second World War: Essays in Honour of F. H. Hinsley* (Cambridge: Cambridge University Press, 1985), p.125. Zweig gives a clear example of the political manipulations of an intelligence input into the policy-making decision having unintended consequences. Inflated reports sent by the Palestine administration and British authorities in Cairo, to London, exaggerated the Yishuv military threat to British freedom of manoeuvre

in the Middle East. The reports had the opposite effect from that intended. Zweig considered that political manipulation of the intelligence input into the political process had undesirable consequences, such as the British Cabinet's accelerated urgency not to delay a White Paper on the Palestinian question until after the Second World War.

64 Simon Singh, *The Code Book: The Science of Secrecy from Ancient Egypt to Quantum Cryptography* (London: Fourth Estate, 1999), pp. 143–90.

65 NLI, Richard J. Hayes Papers, MS 22984(6) (courtesy of the National Library of Ireland).

66 UCDA, Bryan Papers, 'Fundamental Factors affecting Saorstát Defence Problem', May 1936, Copy No. 6, P71/8, Ref. No. G.2/0057.

67 Nigel West, 'Introduction', in *The Guy Liddell Diaries, Vol. 1: 1939–1942: MI5's Director of Counter-Espionage in World War II* (London: Routledge, 2005), pp. 2, 5, 6.

68 *Ibid.*, pp. 149, 190.

69 Eunan O'Halpin cites Bryan transcripts pp. 38, 48–9 in *Defending Ireland*, pp. 228, 229.

70 John G. Beevor, *SOE: Recollections and Reflections, 1940–1945* (London: Bodley Head, 1981).

71 *Ibid.*

72 *Ibid.*

73 *Ibid.*

74 John F. Sweets, *Choices in Vichy, France: The French under Nazi Occupation* (Oxford: Oxford University Press, 1987).

ONE: The Genesis and Development of the Irish Army Intelligence System

1 Joost Augusteijn, *From Public Defiance to Guerilla Warfare* (Dublin: Irish Academic Press, 1996).

2 Dan Breen, *My Fight for Irish Freedom* (Dublin: Anvil Books, 1989), pp. 33–5.

3 Augusteijn, *op. cit.*, pp. 18, 19.

4 *Ibid.*, pp. 18, 19.

5 Peter Hart, *The Irish Republican Army and its Enemies* (London: Oxford University Press, 1998). Augusteijn states in the bibliography of *From Public Defiance to Guerrilla Warfare* (p. 373) that his references are taken from the page numbers of a draft of Hart's thesis.

6 Ernst Rumpf and A. C. Hepburn, *Nationalism and Socialism in Twentieth-Century Ireland* (Liverpool: Liverpool University Press, 1977), pp. 30–41.

7 F. S. L. Lyons, 'The Meaning of Independence', in Brian Farrell (ed.), *The Irish Parliamentary Tradition* (Dublin: Gill & Macmillan, 1973), pp. 223, 224, 225.

8 Tom Barry, *Guerilla Days in Ireland* (Dublin: Anvil Books, 1962), pp. 105–14; Tim Pat Coogan, *Michael Collins: A Biography* (London: Hutchinson, 1990), pp. 157, 163.
9 Barry, *op. cit.*, p. 9.
10 G. A. Hayes-McCoy, 'The Conduct of the Anglo-Irish War, January 1919 to the Truce in July 1921,' in Desmond Williams (ed.), *The Irish Struggle, 1916–1921* (London: Routledge & Kegan Paul, 1966), p. 66.
11 Eoin Neeson, *Birth of a Republic* (Dublin: Prestige Books, 1998), pp. 228, 229; Barry, *op. cit.*, pp. 205–7.
12 Hayes-McCoy, *op. cit.*, p. 66.
13 *Ibid.*, p. 66.
14 General Sir William Jackson, GBE, KCB, MC, *Withdrawal From Empire: A Military View* (London: B. T. Batsford, 1986), p. 13.
15 Thomas Jones, in Keith Middlemas (ed.), *Thomas Jones, Whitehall Diary, Volume III, Ireland 1918–1925* (London: Oxford University Press, 1971). Jones describes the massacre as follows: 'In April 1919, at Amritsar, General Dyer ordered British troops to fire on an unarmed Indian crowd which threatened riot and 379 people were killed. Dyer was relieved of his command but he received a good deal of support especially in the Lords in the debates which took place in Parliament in July 1919. The diehards of the Conservative Party saw no great difference between suppressing unrest in India and in Ireland.'
16 Thomas Pakenham, *The Boer War* (London: Abacus, 1979, 1998), pp. 493–5, 501–10, 515–18, 548, 553–4, 569, 572, passim.
17 Neeson, *op. cit.*, p. 201.
18 Charles Townshend, *The British Campaign in Ireland, 1919–1921, The Development of Political and Military Policies* (Oxford University Press, 1975), p. 123.
19 Eunan O'Halpin, 'Collins and Intelligence 1919–1923: From Brotherhood to Bureacracy', in Gabriel Doherty and Dermot Keogh (eds.), *Michael Collins and the Making of the Irish Free State* (Cork: Mercier Press, 1998), p. 68.
20 Neeson, *op. cit.*, pp. 208, 209.
21 Seán O'Callaghan, *Execution* (London: Frederick Muller Ltd, 1974), p. 38.
22 *Ibid.*, p. 39.
23 Cited in Neeson, *op. cit.*, p. 209
24 Jackson, *op. cit.*, p. 96.
25 Piaras Béaslaí, *Michael Collins: Soldier and Statesman* (Dublin: Talbot Press, 1937), pp. 59, 60.
26 *Ibid.*, pp. 60–2.
27 Coogan, *op. cit.*, p. 64.
28 Béaslaí, *op. cit.*, p. 76.
29 Coogan, *op. cit.*, pp. 108–9, 234, 238–9, 252, 262–3, 286–7.
30 Brian P. Murphy, *John Chartres: Mystery Man of the Treaty* (Dublin: Irish Academic Press, 1995), pp. 18, 19.

31 *Ibid.*, pp. 18–19.
32 *Ibid.*, pp. 23, 24.
33 Béaslaí, *op. cit.*, p.79.
34 *Ibid.*, p. 82.
35 All intelligence agencies need ready cash to run their own agents and pay spies. The finance office was not running assets for clandestine work, but as part of Collins' role as Minister for Finance from summer 1919. All monies moving through it were audited and set before the Dáil. Brugha suspected funds were diverted to IRB-controlled operations.
36 Coogan, *op. cit.*, p. 116.
37 *Ibid.*, p. 159.
38 John Horgan, *Seán Lemass: The Enigmatic Patriot* (Dublin: Gill & Macmillan, 1999), pp. 17, 18.
39 Béaslaí, *op. cit.*, pp. 206, 207.
40 Breen, *op. cit.*, pp. 31–53.
41 Divisional Commissioner Smith was Colonel Gerald Bryce Ferguson Smith, King's Own Scottish Borderers during the First World War.
42 Anon, *Kerry's Fighting Story, 1916–21* (Tralee: *The Kerryman*, n.d.), pp. 126–9.
43 Cited in Béaslaí, *op. cit.*, pp. 142, 143.
44 Coogan, *op. cit.*, p. 137.
45 Béaslaí, *op. cit.*, pp. 144, 145.
46 *Ibid.*, p. 153.
47 *Ibid.* Spies mentioned are accounted for as follows: Forbes Redmond, pp. 154, 156, 157; Jameson, pp. 154–8; Quinlisk, pp. 146–51; Mulloy, p. 151.
48 *Ibid.*, p. 154.
49 Coogan, *op. cit.*, pp.131, 132.
50 Barry, *op. cit.*, pp. 122–31. Barry's reinforced column of approximately 110 IRA men successfully defeated a British force, committed piecemeal, in a prolonged engagement. The IRA action in Crossbarry must rank as considerably more successful than either of those mentioned.
51 Townshend, *op. cit.*, pp. 90, 91.
52 *Ibid.*, p. 91.
53 *Ibid.*, p. 126.
54 *Ibid.*, p. 126.
55 Peter Hart (ed.), *British Intelligence in Ireland, 1920–21: The Final Reports* (Cork: Cork University Press, 2002), p. 13.
56 Staff histories are normally not published and, as Hart concedes, are usually written by a designated officer or officers. They can, in this author's opinion, be subjective in content and may not, once available for historical research, be considered fully reliable as sources. See Hart, *British Intelligence in Ireland, 1920–21*, p. 6.
57 *Ibid.*, p. 6.

58 *Ibid.*, pp. 1–3, 6, 7, 11, 14.
59 Augusteijn, *op. cit.*, p. 143.
60 Dave Neligan, *The Spy in the Castle* (London: Prendeville Publications Ltd, 1999), p. 183.
61 Augusteijn, *op. cit.*, p. 143.
62 O'Halpin, 'Collins and Intelligence', p. 69.
63 *Ibid.*, p. 71.
64 Florence O'Donoghue, *No Other Law* (Dublin: Anvil Books, 1954), p. 120.
65 *Ibid.*, p. 120.
66 Pat Lynch, *Rebel Cork's Fighting Story: Organisation of the Fighting Units* (Tralee: Anvil, n.d.), pp. 28, 29.
67 *Ibid.*, p. 29.
68 O'Callaghan, *op. cit.*, pp. 52, 53.
69 O'Donoghue, *op. cit.*, p. 120.
70 O'Callaghan, *op. cit.*, pp. 59–62.
71 *Ibid.*, pp. 63–4.
72 Hart, *The IRA and Its Enemies*. Hart emphasises the severity of the terror, as shown by the scores of Protestant men and women who suffered mental breakdowns, even to the point of insanity and suicide. He describes Tilson's death as a most sensational suicide, p. 314. Vide footnote 140.
73 Roy Jenkins, *Churchill* (London: Pan Macmillan, 2001), p. 362.
74 *Ibid.*, p. 363.
75 O'Halpin , 'Collins and Intelligence', p. 69.
76 *Ibid.*, p. 71.
77 Neeson, *op. cit.*, p. 231.
78 Augusteijn, *op. cit.*, pp. 246, 247.
79 Author's interview with Lieutenant Colonel Seán Hennessy, son of Company Captain Mike Hennessy, of the relevant flying column battalion.
80 Hart, *The IRA and Its Enemies*, pp. 88, 99, 296.
81 My mother, Áine de Barra, was a serving Cumann na mBan member at the time of the Ballycannon incident and knew all the IRA men who were massacred. She lived in the area which was called Barryoge, which bounded both Ballycannon and the northern part of Blarney Road. For many years afterwards, when my elder brothers were growing up, she could still openly grieve at the tortuous death these men suffered. Such was the depth of mourning and grieving among the general populace of the area after the butchery, that the legacy of those who saw the bodies of those who were tortured and maltreated to death is a residual republican ethos throughout much of the northern part of Cork city.
82 Extract from Siobhán Langford Papers. She acted as intelligence agent for General Liam Lynch throughout the War of Independence (Cork Archives Institute, Christchurch).

83 *Cork Examiner* microfilm copies in Cork City Reference Library, commencing 24 March 1921.
84 Townshend, *op. cit.*, p. 31.
85 *Ibid.*, p. 31.
86 *Ibid.*, p. 57.
87 *Ibid.*, p. 50.
88 *Ibid.*, pp. 50, 51.
89 *Ibid.*, p. 58.
90 *Ibid.*, p. 58.
91 *Ibid.*, p. 62. See footnote 173 on p. 62; B. H. Liddle-Hart, 'Lessons from Resistance Movements – Guerrilla and Non-Violent,' in A. Roberts (ed.), *Civilian Resistance as a National Defence* (London: Penguin, 1969), p. 235.
92 Coogan, *op. cit.*, p. 188.
93 Townshend, *op. cit.* Forty-eight courthouses and sixteen occupied barracks were destroyed and twenty-nine damaged in the first six months of 1920. Some 424 abandoned barracks were destroyed, 298 of them in a well coordinated operation, to mark the anniversary of Easter Week, pp. 64, 65.
94 Hart, *The IRA and Its Enemies*, p. 296.
95 *Ibid.*, pp. 306–7.
96 *Ibid.*, pp. 314–15.
97 Augusteijn, *op. cit.*, p. 339.
98 Neeson, *op. cit.*, p. 275.
99 Kenneth Griffith and Timothy O'Grady, *Curious Journey: An Oral History of Ireland's Unfinished Revolution* (Cork: Mercier Press, 1998), pp. 335–37. Barry came into contact with the Israeli revolutionary army, the Irgun Zvai Leumi, who sought his advice against the British. It also became one of the standard texts in the American Westpoint Military Academy and even, to the delight of its author, at Sandhurst, the British Military Academy. He bore no ill will against erstwhile opponents, though remaining a committed republican throughout his life.
100 Hopkinson, *Green Against Green: The Irish Civil War* (Dublin: Gill & Macmillan, 1988), pp. 136–37.
101 *Ibid.*, p. 209.
102 Hopkinson, *op. cit.*, p. 209.
103 Townshend, *op. cit.*, p. 53.
104 Hopkinson, *op. cit.*, p. 10.
105 *Ibid.*, pp. 10, 11.
106 *Ibid.*, p. 145.
107 Hopkinson, *op. cit.*, excerpts as related, p. 145.
108 Richard Sinott, *Irish Voters Decide: Voting Behaviour in Elections and Referendums since 1918* (Manchester: Manchester University Press, 1995), pp. 96–8.

109 J. J. Lee, *Ireland, 1912–1985, Politics and Society* (Cambridge: Cambridge University Press, 1989), pp. 94–5.
110 Neeson, *op. cit.*, p. 309.
111 Eunan O'Halpin, *Defending Ireland, The Irish State and its Enemies since 1922* (Oxford: Oxford University Press, 1999), p. 19: Bryan interview, 1983; C. S. Andrews, *Dublin Made Me* (Cork: Mercier Press, 1979), p. 237.
112 O'Halpin, *Defending Ireland*, pp. 29, 30. The Public Safety Act, October 1922, conferred judicial and punitive powers on military courts.
113 *Ibid.*, p. 36.
114 *Ibid.*, pp. 36, 37. Peter Hart, *The Protestant Experience of Revolution in Southern Ireland* (New York: Oxford University Press, 2005); R. English and G. Walker (eds), *Unionism in Modern Ireland: New Perspectives on Politics and Culture* (Basingstoke: Macmillan, 1996), pp. 81–98. Brian Murphy's debunking of Hart's credibility as a reliable scholar infers Hart's selective use of archival material. One should beware of his revisionist mindset before accepting his interpretion of his reading of 'evidence'. See Brian Murphy critique, 21 June 2005, of Peter Hart's, 'The Issue of Sources', *Irish Political Review*, 20, 7 (2005).
115 O'Halpin, *Defending Ireland*, p. 38.
116 *Ibid.*, pp. 24, 25.
117 Eoin Neeson, *The Civil War in Ireland, 1921–23* (Cork: Mercier Press, 1966), p. 92.
118 *Ibid.*, p. 92. See footnote 8, pp. 94, 95.
119 *Ibid.*, p. 92.
120 *Ibid.*, p. 193.
121 *Ibid.*, p. 201.
122 *Ibid.*, pp. 230, 231, 320, 321.
123 Hopkinson, *op. cit.* Chapters 15, 16, pp. 115–26 give a comprehensive description of the chaotic conduct of the early fighting in Dublin which began the Civil War, and the attendant pressures on leaders of both factions.
124 Tomás Ó Dochartaigh, *Cathal Brugha: A Shaol agus a Shaothar* (Cathair na Mart: FNT, 1969), Paragraphs 14, 15, 21. This author translated the excerpts from the pre-standardised Irish in which it was printed.
125 *Ibid.*, pp. 125, 126.
126 Ronan Fanning, 'Michael Collins: An Overview', in Doherty and Keogh (eds), *op. cit.*, pp. 202–10.
127 *Ibid.*, p. 208.
128 Hopkinson, *op. cit.*, pp. 12, 13.
129 *Ibid.*, p. 14.
130 *Ibid.*, p. 14.
131 *Ibid.*, pp. 16, 17.

132 *Ibid.*, p. 17.
133 Cited by Neeson, *The Civil War in Ireland*, pp. 192, 193.
134 Neeson, *Birth of a Republic*, pp. 192, 193; Seán MacEoin, *With the IRA in the Fight for Freeedom: 1919 to the Truce* (Tralee: *Kerryman*, 1950), p. 15.
135 Seán Ó Muirthile memoir, undated (c.1929), University College Dublin Archives (hereafter UCDA), Mulcahy Papers, P7a/209, 1–2.
136 John Regan, *The Irish Counter-Revolution, 1921–1936* (Dublin: Gill & Macmillan, 2001), p. 8.
137 *Ibid.*, p. 9.
138 Neeson, *op. cit.*, p. 320 (see Connor Cruise O'Brien's article in *The Irish Times*, 4 December 1981).
139 Jenkins, *op. cit.*, p. 366.
140 Hopkinson, *op. cit.*, p. 145.
141 Cited in Griffith and O'Grady, *op. cit.*, p. 276.
142 Hopkinson, *op. cit.*, pp. 9, 138.
143 *Ibid.*, pp. 137, 138.
144 *Ibid.*, p. 138.
145 Griffith and O'Grady, *op. cit.*, pp. 274, 275.
146 Collection of papers of Commandant William Egar, War of Independence veteran. A copy of the affidavit is in this author's possession, courtesy of Commandant A. T. Egar.
147 Major General Joe Sweeney commanded the pro-Treaty troops in Donegal during the Civil War. He was General Officer Commanding Western Command 1925–27 and 1939–40.
148 Coogan, *op. cit.*, pp. 334–85.
149 Augusteijn, *op. cit.*, pp. 348, 303, 256, 158, 56.
150 Charles Haughey was minister for finance from 1966 to 1970. No indication is given in the affidavit or in the late Commandant Egar's papers that the allusion to Charles Haughey is other than a casual comment. Neither the affidavit nor Commandant Egar's papers contain a reason for how or why the affidavit was made at the particular time.

TWO: Post-Civil War Strategic Military Planning, 1924–36

1 Regan, *op. cit.*, p. 193.
2 *Ibid.*, pp. 186, 187, 192, 193–5.
3 Eunan O'Halpin, 'Intelligence and Security in Ireland, 1922–45', *Intelligence and National Security*, vol. 5 (January 1990).
4 Maryann Gialanella Valiulis, *Almost a Rebellion: The Irish Army Mutiny of 1924* (Cork: Tower Books, 1985).
5 O'Halpin, 'Intelligence and Security in Ireland', p. 54.

6 *Ibid.*, p. 55. Colonel Dan Bryan Papers, P71/81.
7 O'Halpin, 'Intelligence and Security in Ireland, Note No 33, Minutes of Executive Council, 13 January 1923, CI/29, p. 55.
8 *Ibid.*, p. 55.
9 *Ibid.*, p. 195.
10 Regan, *op. cit.*, pp. 173, 174, 196.
11 *Ibid.*, pp. 196, 197.
12 Terence De Vere White, *Kevin O'Higgins* (London: Methuen, 1948).
13 *Ibid.*, pp. 1, 128, 131.
14 *Ibid.*, p. 132.
15 Úna O'Higgins O'Malley, *From Pardon and Protest: Memoirs from the Margins* (Galway: Arlen House, 2001), pp. 18–19.
16 Uinseann MacEoin, *Harry* (Dublin: Argenta Publications, 1985).
17 *Ibid.*, pp. 94, 104–6, 109, 119, 122, 132–3, 138, 145.
18 *Ibid.*, p. 94.
19 *Ibid.*, pp. 104, 105.
20 Queries to various retired Board of Works senior management personnel, on behalf of the author, were met with impervious negativity. It is logical to assume that the name of Archie Doyle was deliberately expunged from both family and Board of Works mental recall.
21 MacEoin, *Harry*, p. 106.
22 *Ibid.*, p. 106.
23 Lee, *op. cit.*, p. 154.
24 Griffith and O'Grady, *op. cit.*, p.284.
25 *Ibid.*, p. 330.
26 Hopkinson, *op. cit.*, p. 240.
27 Regan, *op. cit.*, pp. 266, 291, 331.
28 Griffith and O'Grady, *op. cit.*, p. 329.
29 *Ibid.*, pp. 291–5.
30 Griffith and O'Grady, *op. cit.*, pp. 329, 330.
31 Maurice Manning, *The Blueshirts* (Dublin: Gill & Macmillan, 1970), pp. 207, 208; Mike Cronin, *The Blueshirts and Irish Politics* (Dublin: Four Courts Press, 1997), pp. 24–25.
32 Griffith and O'Grady, *op. cit.*, p. 330.
33 Military Archives, Cathal Brugha Barracks, Dublin (hereafter MA), 'Request for Direction on Defence Policy, Defence Coucil of Executive, 22 July 1925', File No. A/14786.
34 *Ibid.*, p. 10.
35 *Ibid.*, p. 11.
36 MA, File No. A/14748, S. 4541.
37 O'Halpin, *Defending Ireland*, p. 81.
38 Theo Farrell, 'The Model Army: Military Imitation and the Enfeeblement of the Army in Post-Revolutionary Ireland, 1922–42', *Irish Studies in International Affairs*, vol. 8 (1997), p. 111.
39 *Ibid.*, p. 111.

40 J. J. Lee, Television documentary on the formation of 2RN, 'Radio 75 Years On: That Old Hurdy Gurdy', RTÉ 1, Tuesday 18 September 2001.

41 Ronan Fanning, *The Irish Department of Finance, 1922–1958* (Dublin: Institute of Public Administration, 1958); Farrell, *op. cit.*, p. 216.

42 Valiulis, *op. cit.*, p. 113.

43 O'Halpin, *Defending Ireland*, p. 51.

44 The chief of staff, although holding responsibility for certain military branches and literally coordinating the work of the general staff, does not hold an overall command portfolio within the defence force structure.

45 Valiulis, *op. cit.*, p. 123.

46 Lee, *Ireland 1912–1985*, pp. 104, 105.

47 MA, 'Request for Direction on Defence Policy, Defence Council of Executive, 22 July 1925', File No. A/14786.

48 Farrell, *op. cit.*, p. 112.

49 'Memorandum as to the Financial Procedure for Circulation to Ministers, May 10 1922', National Archives of Ireland (hereafter NAI), DT, S1223.

50 Farrell, *op. cit.*, p. 114.

51 Interviews with C. F. Bhreathnach, deputy director, Office of the Comptroller and Auditor General, Irish representative at the Collége des Commissaires aux Comptes, OECD 1989–1992 inclusive. See Chapter XV, 'Financial Control, Memorandum on General Financial Procedure as furnished by the Department of Finance, 7 May 1924', referring to the Central Fund by the Adaption of Enactments Act, 1922. See Comptroller and Auditor General, pp. 38, 42–6, 47, 58, 75, 136, 138–42, 152, 159, 212–21 of Memorandum.

52 Eunan O'Halpin, 'Aspects of Intelligence', *Irish Sword* (1993/1994), pp. 57, 58.

53 *Ibid.*, p. 58.

54 MA, Costello Papers, File D80. Document authors are as stated in text.

55 *Ibid.* Costello obviously was not aware of de Valera's intention to appoint Frank Aiken minister for co-ordination of military affairs, literally the minister for censorship, during the Second World War.

56 *Ibid.*

57 *Ibid.*

58 *Ibid.*

59 *Ibid.*

60 *Ibid.*

61 *Ibid.*

62 O'Halpin, *Defending Ireland*, p. 97.

63 *Ibid.*, pp. 101, 102.

64 MA, 'General Staff Estimate of the Situation that Would Arise in the Eventuality of a War between Ireland and Great Britain', No. 1, October 1934, File DP/00020.

65 Farrell, *op. cit.*, p.119.
66 UCDA, Bryan Papers, 'Fundamental Factors Affecting Saorstát Defence Problem', Copy No. 6, P71/8, Ref. No. G2/0057.
67 Lee, *Ireland 1912–1985*, p. 234.
68 UCDA, Bryan Papers, 'Fundamental Factors'.
69 *Ibid*.
70 *Ibid*.
71 *Ibid*.
72 Farrell, *op. cit.*, p. 112.
73 Report by Director of Intelligence, 8 January 1924. P7/B/140.
74 MA, File on Intelligence Branch: Co-operation with the Civic Guards; Notes from GOCs' meeting on 15 December 1923, MP, PB/B/179; Excerpt from Director of Intelligence monthly reports, 9 Jan., 5 Feb., 1924, MP, P7/B/138; Reports from Waterford CIO, 14 Jan. 1924.
75 O'Halpin, *Defending Ireland*, p. 47. Footnote 14 refers to notes of meetings, 25 June and 7 July 1923; Director of Intelligence Report, 6 November 1923, P7/B/140.
76 Cited in O'Halpin, *Defending Ireland*, p. 48.
77 *Ibid*., p. 53. DT, S. 12134A.
78 *Ibid*., p. 53.
79 *Ibid*., pp. 53–5.
80 *Ibid*., pp. 53, 54.
81 *Ibid*., p. 56.
82 *Ibid*., p.57.
83 O'Halpin, 'Security and Intelligence in Ireland', pp. 55–8.
84 O'Halpin, *Defending Ireland*, pp. 57, 58. See footnote 34 on p. 58. MA, Memorandum by Director of Intelligence, 14 September 1925, file on 'Co-operation with the Civic Guards', undated minute by Cosgrave, 1924, DT, S. 8047.
85 Cited by O'Halpin in *Defending Ireland*, pp. 60, 61.
86 *Ibid*.
87 *Ibid*., pp. 60, 61, 62.
88 UCDA, Bryan Papers, P71/126. No indication is offered by Colonel Bryan as to how or when this paper of such strategic importance came into his possession.
89 Kingstown and Queenstown had been renamed Dún Laoghaire and Cobh respectively by the Irish authorities, but perhaps the chiefs of staff found it difficult to accept such change, even by 1936.
90 UCDA, Bryan Papers, P71/126(2).
91 *Ibid*., P71/126 (1–4).
92 Robert Fisk, *In Time of War: Ireland, Ulster and the Price of Neutrality, 1939–45* (Dublin: Gill & Macmillan, 1983), pp. 2, 9, 10, 25–7, 29–32, 35–44, 49, 54.
93 John P. Duggan, *Neutral Ireland and the Third Reich* (Dublin: Lilliput Press, 1989), p. 205.

94 UCDA, Bryan Papers, 'Fundamental Factors'.
95 *Ibid.*
96 UCDA, Bryan Papers, P71/8, Ref. G2 Branch, Army Headquarters, Parkgate, Dublin. A copy of the paper also exists in Military Archives, Dublin, G2/0057.
97 *Ibid.*
98 O'Halpin, *Defending Ireland*, p. 137.
99 Joseph Lee and Gearóid Ó Tuathaigh, *The Age of de Valera* (Dublin: Ward River Press, 1982), pp. 34, 80.
100 Lee, *Ireland, 1912–1985*, p. 236.
101 *Ibid.*, pp. 250, 251.
102 *Ibid.*, p. 251.
103 Cited in *ibid.*, p. 243.
104 MA, G2/0057: UCDA, Bryan Papers, 'Fundamental Factors'.
105 Fisk, *op. cit.*, pp. 38, 39.
106 *Ibid.*, p. 39.
107 Seosamh Ó Longaigh, *Emergency Law in Independent Ireland, 1922–1948* (Dublin: Four Courts Press, 2006), pp. 185, 186.
108 Fisk, *op. cit.*, p. 78.
109 John P. Duggan, *A History of the Irish Army* (Dublin: Gill & Macmillan, 1992), pp. 179, 180, 181.
110 For comprehensive coverage of this development, see Deirdre McMahon, *Republicans and Imperialists* (New Haven, CT: Yale University Press, 1984).
111 Andrew McCarthy, 'Reacting to War: Finance and the Economy, 1938–40', in Dermot Keogh and Mervyn O'Driscoll (eds), *Ireland in World War Two: Neutrality and Survival* (Cork: Mercier Press, 2004), p. 48.
112 Bernard Share, *The Emergency: Neutral Ireland 1939–45* (Dublin: Gill & Macmillan, 1978), p. 95.
113 *Ibid.*, pp. 94, 95.
114 Neeson, *op. cit.*, p. 161.
115 Share, *op. cit.*, p. 95. See also Fisk, *op. cit.*, p. 245.
116 Fisk, *op. cit.*, p. 248.
117 UCDA, Bryan Papers, 'Fundamental Factors'.
118 *Ibid.*
119 *Ibid.*
120 UCDA, Bryan Papers, 'Fundamental Factors'; MA G2/0057, Copy 31.
121 Hardback, dust cover review, unnamed reviewer. Share, *op. cit.*
122 Article 6 provided for the defence of Britain and Ireland by sea by the Royal Navy. Article 7 provided harbour defence of the ports and anchorages of Bear Island, Cobh, Lough Swilly, together with moorings at Cobh, oil storage at Lough Swilly and Cobh, civil and military seaplane facilities, submarine, cable and wireless communication. See Ronan Fanning, Michael Kennedy, Dermot Keogh and Eunan

O'Halpin (eds), *Documents on Irish Foreign Policy, Volume I, 1919–22* (Dublin: Royal Irish Academy, 1998), p. 357.

123 UCDA, Bryan Papers, 'Fundamental Factors'.
124 *Ibid.*
125 Maurice Walsh, 'The Politics of Irish Defence: From the Civil War to the Congo, 1923–1964', unpublished MPhil thesis, 1997, p. 36.
126 Lee, *Ireland 1912–1985*, p. 243.
127 UCDA, Bryan Papers, 'Fundamental Factors'.
128 MA, File No. A/14786.
129 O'Halpin, 'Aspects of Intelligence', p. 59.
130 Keogh, *Twentieth-Century Ireland: Nation and State* (Dublin: Gill & Macmillan, 1994), p. 109.
131 Ivor Matanle, *History of World War II* (London: Tiger Books, 1994), p. 24.
132 Cornelius Ryan, *The Longest Day* (New York: Touchstone, 1994), pp. 228–32.
133 Keogh, *Twentieth-Century Ireland*, p. 110.
134 *Ibid.*, p. 111.
135 O'Halpin, 'Aspects of Intelligence', p. 57.
136 Duggan, *A History of the Irish Army*, p. 104.
137 Fisk, *op. cit.*, p. 440.
138 *Ibid.*, pp. 252–4.

THREE: The Army: From Nadir to Proficiency, 1936–9

1 MA, General Dan McKenna, Notes on lecture delivered at Military College, 12 October 1967. Copy of notes in author's possession. McKenna Papers have not been released by his family to an archival source to date.
2 MA. The raid was carried out on 23 December 1939, as outlined in the 'Findings of the Court of Inquiry into Magazine Fort Raid on 29 December 1939', a copy of which is in the author's possession. To date, file reference of findings has not been made available to author.
3 *Ibid.*
4 MA, General Dan McKenna, Notes on lecture delivered at the Military College, 12 October 1967.
5 MA, 'Findings of the Court of Inquiry into the Magazine Fort Raid on 29 December 1939'.
6 *Ibid.*
7 MA, Statement of 53rd witness, Major General Brennan, p. 85.
8 MA, 'Findings of the Court of Inquiry into the Magazine Fort Raid on 29 December 1939', pp. 84–7.
9 *Ibid.*
10 *Ibid.*

11 *Ibid.*, p. 87.
12 *Ibid.*
13 Keogh, *Twentieth-Century Ireland*, p. 111.
14 *Ibid.*
15 The captain was known to this author and contemporaries during the early years of our army service.
16 *Dáil Debates*, vol 79, col. 2001 (30 April 1940).
17 *Ibid.*, vol. 79, cols 2008–9 (30 April 1940).
18 *Ibid.*, Emergency Powers (Amendment) Bill, vol. 78, col. 1415 (3 January 1940).
19 *Ibid.*, Emergency Powers (Amendment) Bill, vol. 78, col. 1416 (3 January 1940).
20 *Ibid.*, Supplementary Estimate for the Army, vol. 79, col. 68 (5 March 1940).
21 MA, General Dan McKenna, Notes on lecture delivered at the Military College, 12 October 1967.
22 H. K. Bonar, 'Investment in Defence, 1922/23 to 1983', Research Paper for the Diploma in Administrative Science, Institute of Public Administration, 1983.
23 Lee, *Ireland 1912–1985*, pp. 234, 235, 236.
24 *Ibid.*, p. 242.
25 J. Bowyer-Bell, *The Secret Army: A History of the IRA, 1916–1970* (London: Anthony Blond Ltd, 1970), p. 174.
26 *Ibid.*, p. 173
27 Robert Kee, *Ireland: A History* (London: Abacus, 1995), p. 145.
28 Bowyer-Bell, *op. cit.*, p. 175.
29 *Ibid.*, p. 174.
30 *Ibid.*, p. 174.
31 *Ibid.*, p. 174.
32 Ó Longaigh, *op. cit.*, pp. 188–250, passim.
33 O'Halpin, *Defending Ireland*, p. 248.
34 *Ibid.*, pp. 247, 248.
35 Cited in *ibid.*, p. 248.
36 Cited in *ibid.*, p. 249.
37 UCDA, Transcript of Bryan Tapes, pp. 1, 7.
38 Donal Ó Drisceoil, *Censorship in Ireland 1939–1945: Neutrality, Politics and Society* (Cork: Cork University Press, 1996), p. 1.
39 MA, File G2/X/0042, Correspondence from Thomas J. Coyne to Private Secretary to the Minister for Co-ordination for Military Measures, 15 September 1940.
40 *Ibid.*
41 Ó Drisceoil, *op. cit.*, p. 20.
42 NAI, Department of An Taoiseach, S11586A, Aiken memo to Government, 'Neutrality, Censorship and Democracy', 23 January 1940.
43 *Ibid.*, p. 8.

44 Appendix to Aiken memo, 23 January, 1940, furnished by Dr Rynne, Department of External Affairs.
45 Cited in Keogh, *Twentieth-Century Ireland*, p. 124.
46 Cited in *ibid.*, p. 119.
47 *Ibid.*, p. 124.
48 Cited in Ó Drisceoil, *op. cit.*, p. 20.
49 Joseph T. Carroll, *Ireland in the War Years, 1939–1945* (Newton Abbot: David and Charles, 1975), pp. 21, 22.
50 *Ibid.*, p. 22.
51 *Ibid.*, p. 35.
52 *Ibid.*, p. 35.
53 *Ibid.*, pp. 35, 36.
54 *Ibid.*, p. 36.
55 *Ibid.*, p. 22.
56 Better known as Lord Longford, Pakenham served as a junior minister in the Labour government of 1945–51 and in Cabinet 1964–8.
57 *Ibid.*, pp. 22, 23.
58 See Bunreacht na hÉireann, Article 40, 1–6, Article 41, 1–3, Article 42, 1–5, Article 43, 1–2, Article 44, 1–6.
59 Irish ambassador to Germany, 1933–39. Following his sacking by de Valera in 1939, Bewley became an intelligence agent for the Germans during the Second World War.
60 Irish ambassador to Spain, 1935–46.
61 Keogh, *Twentieth-Century Ireland*, pp. 127, 128.
62 Fisk, *op. cit.*, pp. 98, 99.
63 *Dáil Debates*, vol. 74, col. 719 (16 February 1939).
64 *Ibid.*
65 Fisk, *op. cit.*, p. 99.
66 *Ibid.*, p. 255.
67 *Ibid.*, p. 255, asterisk footnote 149.
68 *Ibid.*, p. 248.
69 See M. J. Costello's 'Introduction', in Barry, *Guerrilla Days in Ireland.*
70 *Ibid.*, p. 248.
71 O'Halpin, *Defending Ireland*, p. 127.

FOUR: The Irish Army Intelligence System: Role, Methodology and Strategic Planning during the Emergency

1 MA, File Ref. EDP/19/1, EDP/19/2, Table 104W.
2 MA, File Ref. EDP/19/1, EDP/19/2.
3 A separate officer staff, tasked to feed in information to commanders and report on commanders and unit reaction.
4 MA, File Ref. EDP/19/1.
5 MA, Confidential Report on Army Exercises 1942, Copy No. 30.

6 *Ibid*.
7 *Ibid*.
8 *Ibid*., pp. 50, 51.
9 NLI, Richard J. Hayes Papers, Manuscript Collection 108, Foreword.
10 Author's conversation with Dr Hayes' son, Mr J. R. Hayes, September 2005.
11 NLI, Richard J. Hayes Papers, MS 22984 (6), p. 2 (courtesy of the National Library of Ireland).
12 *Ibid*., p. 6.
13 *Ibid*., pp. 7, 8.
14 Mark M. Hull, *Irish Secrets: German Espionage in Wartime Ireland* (Dublin: Irish Academic Press, 2003), pp. 18, 118, 160, 195, 198, 244, 247, 262–3, 292, 358, 361, 364.
15 O'Halpin, *Defending Ireland*, pp. 257–8, 269.
16 NLI, Hayes Papers, MS 22984 (6), p. 1 (courtesy of the National Library of Ireland).
17 Irene Young, *Enigma Variations: Love, War and Bletchley Park* (Oxford: Mainstream Publishing, 1990).
18 Cited by Young, *ibid*., p. 87.
19 Michael Smith, *Station X: The Codebreakers of Bletchley Park* (London: Macmillan, 1998), p. 15.
20 *Ibid*., 'Acknowledgment'.
21 *Ibid*., Figure cited for 1939, front jacket; Young, *op. cit*., figures cited for 1942–43, p. 93.
22 NLI, Hayes Papers, MS 22984 (6), List 108, p. 1 (courtesy of the National Library of Ireland).
23 UCDA, Bryan Papers, P71/30.
24 NLI, Hayes Papers, MS 22984, p. 2 (courtesy of the National Library of Ireland).
25 UCDA, Bryan Papers, P71/30.
26 NLI, Hayes Papers, MS 22984 (6), List 108, pp. 2, 3 (courtesy of the National Library of Ireland).
27 O'Halpin, *Defending Ireland*, p. 241 (MA, G2/4174). Hull, *op. cit*., pp. 218–26.
28 O'Halpin cites an unspecified Hayes report which states that O'Neill arrived (in Ireland) at the end of 1942, but enters the caveat that there is no reference to this in O'Neill's file, MA, G2/4174.
29 Hull, *op. cit*., pp. 226, 227. This author does not doubt the veracity of Hayes' report in respect of the cipher.
30 MA, File No. G2/4174.
31 NLI, Hayes Papers, MS 22984 (6), p. 3 (courtesy of the National Library of Ireland).
32 O'Halpin, *Defending Ireland*, p. 241.
33 NLI, Hayes Papers, MS 22984, pp. 3, 4 (courtesy of the National Library of Ireland).

34 Matanle, *op. cit.*, pp. 203–7.
35 NLI, Hayes Papers, MS 22984 (6), p. 4; MS 22982 (7), Goertz file, three unnumbered pages (courtesy of the National Library of Ireland).
36 *Ibid.*, MS 22984 (7), List 108.
37 Helen Lytton, *The World War II Years: The Irish Emergency, An Illustrated History* (Dublin: Wolfhound Press, 2001), p. 32.
38 NLI, Hayes Papers, MS 22982 (5), Note on cipher used by Irish army, two unnumbered pages (courtesy of the National Library of Ireland).
39 NLI, Hayes Papers, MS 22984 (6), p. 5 (courtesy of the National Library of Ireland).
40 James Hayes, grandson of Dr Richard Hayes, allowed author access to unpublished document in Hayes family possession.
41 Hull, *op. cit.*, pp. 18, 118, 160, 195, 198, 244, 247, 262–3, 292, 358, 361, 364.
42 *Ibid.*, pp. 196, 197.
43 *Ibid.*, pp. 197–9.
44 James Hayes allowed author access to unpublished document as outlined in thesis.
45 Unpublished document to which author was allowed access by James Hayes.
46 *Ibid.*
47 *Ibid.*
48 *Ibid.*
49 NLI, Hayes Papers, MS 22984 (7), Goertz chronology (courtesy of the National Library of Ireland).
50 NLI, Hayes Papers, MS 22982 (7) (courtesy of the National Library of Ireland).
51 Christopher Andrew, Foreward to Eunan O'Halpin, *MI5 and Ireland, 1939–1945* (Dublin: Irish Academic Press, 2003), p. xii.
52 O'Halpin, *MI5 and Ireland*, pp. 5–7.
53 O'Halpin, 'Security and Intelligence in Ireland', pp. 82, 83.
54 *Ibid.*, pp. 63, 64.
55 *Ibid.*, p. 64.
56 Ó Drisceoil, *op. cit.*, pp. 12, 68.
57 O'Halpin, 'Security and Intelligence in Ireland', p. 65. See also transcript of tapes, p. 5.
58 Duggan, *Neutral Ireland and the Third Reich*, pp. 229, 230.
59 Bryan, in my view, may even have pre-empted President Lyndon Johnson's caveat in respect of appointing personnel to his government!
60 Duggan, *Neutral Ireland and the Third Reich*, pp. 228–31.
61 *Ibid.*, p. 230.
62 UCDA, Transcript of Bryan tapes, cited by O'Halpin, p. 8.
63 Walsh, 'The Politics of Irish Defence', p. 30.
64 MA, COS Memo, 23 August 1944, File No. EDP 65.
65 Cited in COS Memo.

66 Fall Gruen is a detailed military document giving precise information of tides, coast, rivers, roads, nature and suitability of terrain for military operations, field aerodromes, artillery positions, beaten zones, obstacles and geographical features and geological data (see Appendix VI). The Germans had maps specially prepared on the metric scale and overprinted with military grids in the following editions: 1:50,000; 1:100,000; 1:250,000; 1:500,000 air edition and 1:1,000,000 international edition. Two of these editions were to be read in conjunction with the military handbook.
67 MA, COS Memo, 23 August 1944, File No. EDP 65.
68 *Ibid.*
69 *Ibid.*
70 *Ibid.*
71 MA, File Ref. 2/64212.

FIVE: Case Studies of Individuals Involved in Pro- and Anti-Irish State Security and Maintenance of Neutrality, 1939–45

1 Sanitised personal file, Tom Barry. The file has been sent to MA by author. Except where otherwise stated, all references in this chapter concerning Tom Barry are transcripts from his sanitised personal file.
2 My father, Maurice Walsh, was a veteran of both the War of Independence and anti-Treaty forces during the Civil War. He remained loyal to Barry and was one of those who resigned from the IRA in 1938 and served throughout the Emergency in the LDF.
3 The detailed record of the commissioning of the personnel mentioned is filed in the Military College Library.
4 Meda Ryan, *Tom Barry: IRA Freedom Fighter* (Cork: Mercier Press, 2003), p. 231.
5 Barry, *op. cit.*
6 Author's interview with Commandant R. McIntyre on 27 April 1999.
7 *Ibid.*
8 *Ibid.*
9 Ryan, *Tom Barry*, pp. 230–3.
10 Barry, *op. cit.*, p. ix.
11 *Ibid.*, pp. ix, x, xi.
12 Officers Records Section, Defence Forces Headquarters.
13 Author's interview with Commandant R. J. McIntyre, 20 August 2002.
14 Barry, *op. cit.*, p. 158.
15 Bureau of Military History, Document No. 554, Witness Statement by Major Florence O'Donoghue (undated) on the projected purchase of arms in Italy, 1920–1921. National Archives, File No. S. 1825.
16 *Ibid.*

17 John Borgonovo, *Florence and Josephine O'Donoghue's War of Independence: A Destiny That Shapes Our Ends* (Dublin: Irish Academic Press, 2006).
18 *Ibid.*, p. ix.
19 *Ibid.*, pp. 1–5.
20 Cited by O'Halpin, *Defending Ireland*, p.165, footnote 41; Defence memorandum to government, undated, February 1951, MA, G2/X/0362. See also MA, G2/X/863, MA, G2/X/363.
21 The author served in the Cavalry Corps and is conversant with corps terminology.
22 K104 was a code number of an SIS leader in the area.
23 O'Halpin, *Defending Ireland*, p. 205.
24 O'Halpin is quoting directly from the transcript of the Bryan tapes, pp. 32, 49–50, and an interview with Colonel Bryan dated July 1983.
25 O'Halpin, 'Security and Intelligence in Ireland', p. 166.
26 Tim Pat Coogan, *The IRA* (London: Harper Collins, 2000), p. 155.
27 Bowyer-Bell, *The Secret Army*, pp. 192, 193.
28 UCDA, transcript of Bryan tapes, p. 3.
29 MA, G2/X/S482, G2/X/1160, Award of Emergency Service Medal to members of SIS.
30 MA, G2/0363.
31 MA, G2/0363. See also CM 2220/620, 13 July 1940, General Murphy's instruction to Garda Superintendents.
32 O'Halpin, *Defending Ireland*, pp. 203, 204, 208.
33 Fall Gruen. Translated for the author by Ms Deirdre O'Conner as follows: Military-geographical report about Ireland, South and Eastward (from Mizen Head to Malin Head), Text and Pictures with Map Layout, Taken on 31 May 1941, General Staff of the Army, Department for war maps and land surveying office, Berlin 1941.
34 Lytton, *op. cit*; see illustrated map enclosed between pp. 112–14.
35 UCDA, Bryan Papers, P71/30.
36 *Ibid.*, P71/30 (20).
37 Parachute, radio transmitter, documents in clear and in cipher, quantity of usable currency.
38 Hull, *op. cit.*, p. 46.
39 NLI, Hayes Papers, MS 22982 (7), List 108. MS 22981 (8, 9) (courtesy of the National Library of Ireland).
40 UCDA, Bryan Papers, P/71/125. Raymond to Bryan, 7 November 1979.
41 UCDA, Mulcahy Papers, de Valera–Richard Mulcahy, 12 February 1941, P7/11/113.
42 Enno Stephan, *Spies in Ireland* (London: Macdonald & Co., 1963), pp. 135–44, 209, 254, 256, 268, 269, 295; Hull, *op. cit.*, pp. 57, 108–13, 241, 242, 254, 322, 35.
43 *Ibid.*, pp. 203, 204, 209.

44 Hull, *op. cit.*, pp. 229, 230, 235, 237, 251, 259–60, 294, 334–36, 357, 358, 362.
45 UCDA, Bryan Papers, P71/30.
46 Hull, *op. cit.*, pp. 106, 107.
47 Stephan, *op. cit.*, pp. 204, 268, 294; Hull, *op. cit.*, pp. 26, 110, 153, 162–69, 260, 293–94, 337–38.
48 O'Halpin, *Defending Ireland*, pp. 215, 216.
49 Hull, *op. cit.*, p. 165.
50 Schutz, cited by Bryan. UCDA, Bryan Papers, P71/30, Unland file.
51 Ó Drisceoil, *op. cit.*, pp. 4–6.
52 UCDA, Bryan Papers, P71/30 (24).
53 Hull, *op. cit.*, pp. 111–12.
54 *Ibid.*, pp. 113–17, 242, 254–5, 323–4; Stephan, *op. cit.*, p. 143.
55 UCDA, Bryan Papers, P71/30 (25).
56 Hull, *op. cit.*, p. 113.
57 UCDA, Bryan Papers, P71/31 (3).
58 *Ibid.*
59 O'Halpin, 'Aspects of Intelligence'; Hull, *op. cit.*, p. 275.
60 O'Halpin, *Defending Ireland*, pp. 147–9; Hull, *op. cit.*, pp. 55–7.
61 Hull, *op. cit.*, p. 56.
62 UCDA, Bryan Papers, P71/31 (2).
63 O'Halpin, *Defending Ireland*, p. 252; Stephan, *op. cit.*, pp. 27–38; Hull, *op. cit.*, pp. 56–64.
64 UCDA, Bryan Papers, P71/31 (3).
65 O'Halpin, *Defending Ireland*, p. 167. Note that Duggan, Hull and Ó Drisceoil do not reflect such concern by G2.
66 This practice was discontinued in 1991.
67 *Ibid.*, p. 167. See also footnote 44.
68 *Ibid.*, p. 167. Refer also to footnotes 44, 45. Later, Irish army commitment to UN service in the Middle East may have reflected a practice where Jewish candidates for recruitment might be considered 'suspect'.
69 *Ibid.*, p. 167.
70 Keogh, *Jews in Twentieth-Century Ireland* (Cork: University College Cork Press, 1998), pp. 106, 107; Duggan, *Neutral Ireland and the Third Reich*, pp. 22, 24, 63, 64, 145, 167; David O'Donoghue, *Hitler's Irish Voices* (Belfast: Beyond the Pale Publications, 1998), pp. 21, 25, 68, 170, 171, 177.
71 Keogh, *Jews in Twentieth-Century Ireland*, p. 106.
72 *Ibid.*, p. 107.
73 *Ibid.*, p. 106. See footnotes 119 and 120 on p. 270.
74 Duggan, *Neutral Ireland and the Third Reich*, p. 63.
75 Keogh, *Jews in Twentieth-Century Ireland*, p. 151.
76 *Ibid.*, p. 194.
77 O'Halpin, *Defending Ireland*, p. 236.

78 Keogh, *Jews in Twertieth-Century Ireland*, pp. 159, 160; O'Halpin, *Defending Ireland*, p. 236.
79 Duggan, *Neutral Ireland and the Third Reich*, pp. 165, 166.
80 O'Halpin, *Defending Ireland*, p. 243. See footnote 98.
81 Author's parentheses.
82 Duggan, *Neutral Ireland and the Third Reich*, pp. 161–78.
83 *Ibid*., pp. 177, 178.
84 *Ibid*., p. 10.
85 *Ibid*., p. 173.
86 *Ibid*., p. 173.
87 O'Halpin, *Defending Ireland*, pp. 252, 253.
88 *Ibid*., pp. 252, 253.
89 Certificate of the Comptroller and Auditor General on the Account for the Secret Service. Audited Appropriation Account of the Public Service, 2005.
90 O'Halpin, *Defending Ireland*, pp. 252, 253.
91 Duggan, *Neutral Ireland and the Third Reich*, p. 205.
92 MA, unspecified file, Intelligence Note No. 81, produced by G2 Branch, Army Headquarters, January 1942.
93 Duggan, *A History of the Irish Army*, pp. 206–9. O'Halpin, *Defending Ireland*, pp. 174, 175.
94 A copy of Fall Gruen has been given by this author to Irish Military Archives.
95 UCDA, Bryan Papers, P/71.
96 Nigel West, *MI5: British Security Operations, 1909–1945* (London: Bodley Head, 1981).
97 *Ibid*., pp. 323, 327.
98 *Ibid*., pp. 327, 328.
99 Duggan, *Neutral Ireland and the Third Reich*, p. 196.
100 West, *op. cit*., p. 328.
101 *Ibid*., pp. 208, 209.
102 Bryan's review of Nigel West's books, *The Irish Times*, 19 November 1983.
103 Marlin, *The Irish Times*, 26 June 1985.
104 West, *op. cit*., p. 325.
105 Marlin, *The Irish Times*, 26 June 1985.
106 O'Halpin, *Defending Ireland*, p. 239.
107 Marlin, *The Irish Times*, 26 June 1985; O'Halpin, *Defending Ireland*, pp. 230, 231.
108 Duggan, *Neutral Ireland and the Third Reich*, p. 196, footnote 12, explanatory note on p. 268.
109 Franklin Delano Roosevelt Library and Museum. Developed in collaboration with Marist College and IBM.
110 Obituary, Colonel Dan Bryan, *The Irish Times*, 17 June 1985.
111 Romer: A square cardboard grid with which a definitive six-figure map reference can be determined.

112 UCDA, Bryan Papers, P 71/28 (1).
113 *Ibid.*, P71/28 (2).
114 Author is convinced, after forty years' experience in military appointments at home and abroad, that such appointments are well worthwhile, in the interests of both the state and the defence forces.
115 UCDA, Bryan Papers, P71/32 (1).
116 *Ibid.*
117 *Ibid.*, P71/29 (1).
118 Lee, *Ireland 1912–1985*, p. 236.
119 UCDA, Bryan Papers, P71/33 (3).
120 Ref. No. G2/X/0314; UCDA, Bryan Papers, P71/36 (1–3).
121 *Ibid.*, P71/36 (1).
122 *Ibid.*, P71/36 (1–3).
123 *Ibid.*, P71/37.
124 *Ibid.*, P71/37. All Archer's intelligence notes bore the same file reference: G2/X/0314.
125 UCDA, Bryan Papers, P71/38–41.
126 *Ibid.*, P71/145 (9).
127 *Ibid.*, P71/145 (1–9).
128 Joe Carroll, 'Behind a Secret Web of Spies', *The Irish Times*, 20 January 2004.
129 UCDA, Bryan Papers, P71/145 (1–9).
130 *Ibid.*, P71/145 (4); Fisk, *op. cit.*, pp. 28, 342. Stephan, *op. cit.*, p. 157.
131 O'Halpin, *Defending Ireland*, pp. 186–90.
132 O'Donoghue, *Hitler's Irish Voices*, pp. 50, 51, 146, 151, 153–55, 211–12; Duggan, *Neutral Ireland and the Third Reich*, pp. xv, xviii, 6, 79, 80, 120, 121, 234; Hull, *op. cit.*, pp. 131– 40, 173, 186–90, 195, 197–98, 328.
133 T. Ryle Dwyer, *De Valera: The Man and the Myths* (Dublin: Poolbeg Press, 1991), p. 249.
134 MA, General Dan McKenna, Notes on lecture delivered at Military College, 12 October 1967, unreferenced.
135 Author's conversation with Commandant Victor Laing, Officer in Charge of Military Archives, 5 December 2006.
136 Coogan, *The IRA*, pp. 50, 57, 61, 62, 64, 71, 72, 83, 89–91, 114, 127, 148; O'Halpin, *Defending Ireland*, pp. 79, 117, 120, 121, 125, 202, 248, 253, 297, 300.
137 Excerpt from Bryan's tribute to General McKenna, *An Cosantóir* (July 1975).
138 Brigadier General James Farrell, as a young instructer in the Military College, attended General McKenna's lecture on 12 October 1967 and revealed McKenna's remark to author.
139 De Valera's Dáil tribute as recorded in *Dáil Debates*, vol. 120, col. 722 (19 April 1950).

140 *Ibid.*, vol. 114, col. 1951 (30 March 1949).
141 *Ibid.*, col. 1967.
142 *Ibid.*, col. 2006.

CONCLUSION

1 Hopkinson, *op. cit.*, p.145.
2 UCDA, Bryan Papers, P71/126. No indication is offered by Colonel Bryan as to how or when this paper of such strategic importance came into his possession.
3 John Keegan, *Intelligence in War: Knowledge of the Enemy from Napoleon to Al-Qaeda*, p. 398.
4 *Ibid.*, p. 398.
5 *Ibid.*, p. 399.
6 The whole tiny island was one densely fortified position, but was taken because the American marines, at a cost of thousands of their own lives, inched their way forward from bunker to bunker.
7 *Ibid.*, pp. 369–72.
8 Sun Tzu (translated by Thomas Cleary), *The Art of War* (Boston: Shambhala Publications, 1988), p. vii.
9 Lee, *Ireland 1912–1985*, p. 236.
10 O'Halpin, *Defending Ireland*, p. 187.

INDEX